A Complete Life of
General George A. Custer

VOLUME 2: FROM APPOMATTOX TO THE
LITTLE BIG HORN

G. A. Custer.

A Complete Life of
General George A. Custer

VOLUME 2: FROM APPOMATTOX TO THE
LITTLE BIG HORN

BY

Frederick Whittaker,

BREVET CAPTAIN SIXTH NEW YORK VETERAN CAVALRY.

Introduction by Robert M. Utley

University of Nebraska Press
Lincoln and London

Introduction copyright © 1993 by the University of Nebraska
Press
Manufactured in the United States of America

First Bison Book printing: 1993
Most recent printing indicated by the last digit below:
10   9   8   7   6   5   4   3   2   1

Library of Congress Cataloging-in-Publication Data
Whittaker, Frederick, 1838–1889.
A complete life of general George A. Custer / by Frederick
Whittaker; introduction by Gregory J.W. Urwin.
p.   cm.
Originally published: New York: Sheldon, 1876.
"Bison."
Includes bibliographical references (p.   ) and index.
Contents: v. 1. Through the Civil War—v. 2. From Appomattox to
the Little Big Horn.
ISBN 0-8032-4766-4 (cloth: v. 1).—ISBN 0-8032-9742-4 (pbk.: v. 1).—
ISBN 0-8032-4767-2 (cloth: v. 2).—ISBN 0-8032-9743-2 (pkb.: v. 2).—
ISBN 0-8032-9744-0 (set)
1. Custer, George Armstrong, 1839–1876. 2. Generals—United
States—Biography. 3. United States. Army—Biography. I. Title.
E467.1.C99W6   1993   v. 2
973.8'2'092—dc20
[B]
92-37701   CIP

Reprinted from the original 1876 edition published by Sheldon &
Company, New York. This Bison Book edition has been divided
into two volumes. Volume 1, which was subtitled *Through the
Civil War,* covered the first six books. Volume 2 begins with the
Seventh Book, "On the Plains." It carries an index for both Volumes 1 and 2.

♾

CONTENTS.

SEVENTH BOOK.—ON THE PLAINS.

EIGHTH BOOK.—THE LAST CAMPAIGN.

NINTH BOOK.—SOLDIER AND MAN.

CHAPTER I.

CUSTER, THE SOLDIER.

CHAPTER II.

CUSTER, THE INDIAN-FIGHTER.

CHAPTER III.

CUSTER, THE MAN.

TENTH BOOK.—PERSONAL RECOLLECTIONS.

LIST OF ILLUSTRATIONS.

Volume 2

INTRODUCTION
by Robert M. Utley

Early in 1942, at the impressionable age of twelve, I thrilled to Errol Flynn's portrayal of General Custer in *They Died with Their Boots On*. That prompted a visit to the public library of Lafayette, Indiana, and my introduction to Frederick Whittaker's *Life of Custer*. This massive tome, which must have challenged the reading skills of a seventh-grader, reinforced the movie version, and George Armstrong Custer became my boyhood hero—a soldier, as Whittaker phrased it poetically, with "no spot on his armor," a man with "no taint on his honor."

No serious student of General Custer can ignore Whittaker's book. It is significant both as a contribution to legend and as a contribution (although some of it is bad) to history.

The contribution to legend is the more important. In the lavish hyperbole of the dime novels and penny dreadfuls in which he specialized, Whittaker created a demigod. Custer was the best general of horse in all American history, the nation's preeminent Indian fighter and plainsman, and a paragon of virtue in whom "truth and sincerity, honor and bravery, tenderness and sympathy, unassuming piety and temperance, were the mainspring of Custer, the man."

Reviewers were quick to point out flaws in the portrait and errors of fact and interpretation in the history. But the swashbuckling image, redolent of cavalier heroics and magnified by the drama and tragedy of the Little Bighorn, found high favor with a Victorian America that prized uncomplicated idols.

Rushed into print within six months after the Battle of the Little Bighorn, Whittaker's *Life* embedded Whittaker's Custer in the public consciousness. Despite the scorn of critics, it furnished almost the only source to which other writers could turn. Throughout the 1880s and 1890s, book after book appeared that relied heavily on Whittaker's interpretations. In many he was the sole authority consulted. In some he was flagrantly plagiarized. Thus did the embodiment of perfection that he fashioned loom ever larger in the popular conception, and thus did Whittaker surpass all other writers in his influence on the legend of George Armstrong Custer.

Whittaker's Custer, reinforced by the widely read books of Elizabeth Custer, dominated popular perceptions well into the twentieth century. Not until Frederick F. Van de Water published *Glory Hunter* in 1934 did the clay feet shaped by Whittaker begin to crumble. A star of the debunking school fashionable in the 1930s, Van de Water forged a bizarre Custer in every way the opposite of Whittaker's. For his and subsequent generations, Van de Water contributed to the Custer legend nearly as influentially and fully as unhistorically as Whittaker.

Despite the rhetorical gilding, Whittaker's *Life* contains scraps of historically important material. For the frontier years, 1866–76, these relate almost entirely to the Battle of the Little Bighorn. The earlier years Whittaker handled largely by extensively quoting from Custer's book, *My Life on the Plains,* published in 1874. This and other sources of quotation, such as official reports and the magazine article in which Custer described his fight with Sioux on the Yellowstone, are readily available in their original form or in anthologies.

For the Little Bighorn, however, Whittaker had access to at least two participants. One was Captain Thomas B. Weir, a Custer partisan who provided Whittaker with his own perceptions before an untimely death in December 1876. The other, who fought in the valley conflict under Major Marcus A. Reno, cannot be certainly identified but must have been either Captain Myles Moylan or Captain

Thomas H. French. The observations of these officers afford valuable insights into some of the issues destined to fuel endless debate.

Two other contributors enhance the historical merit of the book. One was Lawrence Barrett, an eminent Shakespearian tragedian who was one of Custer's dearest friends. His memoir, written specially for the book, is a genuine testament of friendship and appreciation and deserves consideration as an original source document. The other was Elizabeth Custer herself, who furnished Whittaker with numerous anecdotes and appraisals and whose influence must be accounted of historical significance.

As Whittaker's contribution to legend lay largely in a ripple effect over several decades, so his contribution to history lay more in consequence than content. His studies, especially his association with Captain Weir, persuaded Whittaker that Custer suffered disaster at the Little Bighorn because of the failings of Major Reno. In the concluding paragraph of the chapter on "The Last Battle," therefore, Whittaker called on the army to organize an official court of inquiry, empowered to take the testimony of participants and judge whether or not his conclusions were valid. "The nation demands such a court," he declared, "to vindicate the name of a dead hero from the pitiless malignity, which first slew him and then pursued him beyond the grave."

Charging Reno with "gross cowardice" in failing to push his attack on the Sioux village, Whittaker urged the U.S. Congress to mandate a court of inquiry. Legislation to accomplish that purpose failed in the House of Representatives, but it created enough of a stir to move Reno himself to request such a court, "that the many rumors started by camp gossip may be set at rest and the truth made fully known."

Thus to Frederick Whittaker and his book, more than any other influence, may be credited the Reno Court of Inquiry. It met for a full month in Chicago's Palmer House in January and February 1879. For history, the court's innocuous finding exonerating Reno was less important than the mass of first-hand source material bequeathed to posterity. Officers, enlisted men, and civilian participants testified and were cross-examined. With a few exceptions, they closed ranks and, while hardly praising Reno, resisted condemning him. In sum, however, the transcript of their testimony constitutes the single most important body of evidence for reconstructing the Battle of the Little Bighorn.

"Major Reno's prosecutor," newspapers had labeled Whittaker. That he was, first in leveling charges in the *Life of Custer* and then in agitating for a court of inquiry. He tried to influence the court, but failed; he had nothing but his own opinion to offer. Even so, historians owe a large debt of gratitude to the gadfly dime novelist who wrote Custer's first biography.

As if locked together by a perverse destiny, Whittaker and Reno met equally ill-fated ends within two months of each other. Dismissed from the army for a variety of offenses originating in the bottle, Reno had fallen almost to the level of a derelict when he died in Washington, D.C., on March 1, 1889. Whittaker, embracing spiritualism with irrational fervor, behaved with increasing eccentricity and irascibility. Carrying a pistol for defense against imagined enemies, on May 13, 1889, he caught his cane in a stair railing and fell. The pistol discharged and sent a bullet fatally into his head.

Frederick Whittaker's dime novels have long since turned to dust. Had he written nothing else, only a few specialists in this genre would recognize his name. But his *Life of Custer* lives on, faults and all, an essential volume on any bookshelf devoted to George Armstrong Custer and the Battle of the Little Bighorn.

SEVENTH BOOK.—ON THE PLAINS.

CHAPTER I.

THE HANCOCK EXPEDITION.

THE Seventh Cavalry was first mounted, armed, and sent to the plains in the spring of 1867, and as this was the opening of a fresh experience for Custer, it is peculiarly fortunate that we are able to present his impressions in his own words. It was the first time in his life, it must be remembered, that he officiated as the commander of a single regiment, and against Indians, and all his former experience was at fault. He had to learn everything anew, and the record of his first experiences is so fresh and interesting that we shall extract freely therefrom.

Of the many important expeditions, says he, organized to operate in the Indian country, none, perhaps, of late years has excited more general and unfriendly comment, considering the slight loss of life inflicted upon the Indians, than the expedition organized and led in person by Major-General Hancock, in the spring of 1867. The clique generally known as the " Indian Ring " were particularly malevolent and bitter in their denunciations of General Hancock for precipitating, as they expressed it, an Indian war. This expedition was quite formidable in appearance, being made up of eight troops of cavalry, seven companies of infantry, and one battery of light artillery, numbering altogether about 1,400 men. As General Hancock at the time and since has been so often accused of causelessly bringing on an Indian war, a word in explanation may not be amiss.

Being in command of the cavalry connected with the expedition, I had ample and frequent opportunities for learning the true purposes and objects of the march into the heart of the Indian country.

It may be asked, What had the Indians done to make this incursion necessary? They had been guilty of numerous thefts and murders during the preceding summer and fall, for none of which had they been called to account. They had attacked the stations of the overland mail route, killed the employees, burned the stations, and captured the stock. Citizens had been murdered in their homes on the frontier of Kansas; murders had been committed on the Arkansas route. The principal perpetrators of these acts were the Cheyennes and Sioux. The agent of the former, if not a party to the murder on the Arkansas, knew who the guilty persons were, yet took no steps to bring the murderers to punishment. Such a course would have interfered with his trade and profits. It was not to punish for these sins of the past that the expedition was set on foot, but rather by its imposing appearance and its early presence in the Indian country to check or intimidate the Indians from a repetition of their late conduct. This was deemed particularly necessary from the fact that the various tribes from which we had greatest cause to anticipate trouble had during the winter, through their leading chiefs and warriors, threatened that as soon as the grass was up in spring a combined outbreak would take place along our entire frontier, and especially against the main routes of travel. To assemble the tribes for the desired council, word was sent early in March to the agents of those tribes whom it was desirable to meet. The agents sent runners to the villages, inviting them to meet us at some point near the Arkansas River.

General Hancock, with the artillery and six companies of infantry, reached Fort Riley, Kansas, from Fort Leavenworth, by rail, the last week in March; here he was joined by four companies of the Seventh Cavalry and an additional company of the Thirty-seventh Infantry. It was at this point that I joined the expedition.

From Fort Riley we marched to Fort Harker, a distance of ninety miles, where our force was strengthened by the addition of two more troops of cavalry. Halting only long enough to replenish our supplies, we next directed our march toward Fort Larned, near the Arkansas, about seventy miles to the southeast. A march from the 3d to the 7th of April brought us to Fort Larned. The agent for the Comanches and Kiowas accompanied us. At Fort Larned we found the agent of the Cheyennes, Arapahoes, and Apaches; from the latter we learned that he had, as requested, sent runners to the chiefs of his agency inviting them to the council, and that they had agreed to assemble near Fort Larned on the 10th of the month, requesting that the expedition would remain there until that date. To this request General Hancock acceded.

On the 9th of April, while encamped awaiting the council, which was to be held the following day, a terrible snow-storm occurred, lasting all day until late in the evening. It was our good fortune to be in camp rather than on the march; had it been otherwise, we could not well have escaped without loss of life from the severe cold and blinding snow. The cavalry horses suffered seriously, and were only preserved by doubling their ration of oats, while to prevent their being frozen during the intensely cold night which followed, the guards were instructed to keep passing along the picket lines with a whip, and to keep the horses moving constantly. The snow was eight inches in depth. The council, which was to take place the next day, had to be postponed until the return of good weather. Now began the display of a kind of diplomacy for which the Indian is peculiar. The Cheyennes and a band of the Sioux were encamped on Pawnee Fork, about thirty miles above Fort Larned. They neither desired to move nearer to us nor have us approach nearer to them. On the morning of the 11th, they sent us word that they had started to visit us, but discovering a large herd of buffalo near their camp, they had stopped to procure a supply of meat. This message was not received with much confidence, nor was a buffalo hunt deemed of sufficient importance to justify the Indians in breaking their engagement. General Hancock decided, however, to delay another day, when if the Indians still failed to come in, he would move his command to the vicinity of their village and hold the conference there.

Orders were issued on the evening of the 12th for the march to be resumed on the following day.

Rightly concluding that the Indians did not intend to come to our camp, as they had at first agreed to, it was decided to move nearer to their village. Our entire force therefore marched from Fort Larned up Pawnee Fork in the direction of the main village, encamping the first night about twenty-one miles from the fort. Several parties of Indians were seen in our advance during the day, evidently watching our movements; while a heavy smoke, seen to rise in the direction of the Indian village, indicated that something more than usual was going on. This smoke we afterward learned arose from the burning grass. * The Indians, thinking to prevent us from encamping in their vicinity, had set fire to and burned all the grass for miles in the direction from which they expected us. Before we arrived at our camping-ground we were met by several chiefs and warriors belonging to the Cheyennes and Sioux. Among the chiefs were Pawnee Killer of the Sioux, and White Horse of the Cheyennes. It was arranged that these chiefs should accept our hospitality and remain with us during the night, and in the morning all the chiefs of the two tribes then in the village were to come to General Hancock's headquarters and hold a council. On the

---

* This was the dried grass of the previous year, always peculiarly easy to fire. The battles of Hooker's and Grant's troops in the Wilderness of Virginia, in the early spring, were almost always noted by similar fires, the dead grass catching first from the artillery flashes.

morning of the 14th, Pawnee Killer left our camp at an early hour, for the purpose, as he said, of going to the village to bring in the other chiefs to the council. Nine o'clock had been agreed upon as the hour at which the council should assemble. The hour came, but the chiefs did not. Now an Indian council is not only often an important but always an interesting occasion. And, somewhat like a famous recipe for making a certain dish, the first thing necessary in holding an Indian council is to get the Indian. Half-past nine o'clock came, and still we were lacking this one important part of the council. At this juncture Bull Bear, an influential chief among the Cheyennes, came in and reported that the chiefs were on their way to our camp, but would not be able to reach it for some time. This was a mere artifice to secure delay. General Hancock informed Bull Bear that as the chiefs could not arrive for some time, he would move his forces up the stream nearer to the village, and the council could be held at our camp that night. To this proposition Bull Bear gave his assent.

At 11 A. M. we resumed the march, and had proceeded but a few miles when we witnessed one of the finest and most imposing military displays, prepared according to the Indian art of war, which it has ever been my lot to behold. It was nothing more nor less than an Indian line of battle drawn directly across our line of march ; as if to say, thus far and no further. Most of the Indians were mounted ; all were bedecked in their brightest colors, their heads crowned with the brilliant war-bonnet, their lances bearing the crimson pennant, bows strung, and quivers full of barbed arrows. In addition to these weapons, which with the hunting-knife and tomahawk are considered as forming the armament of the warrior, each one was supplied with either a breech-loading rifle or revolver, sometimes with both—the latter obtained through the wise forethought and strong love of fair play which prevails in the Indian Department, which, seeing that its wards are determined to fight, is

23

equally determined that there shall be no advantage taken, but that the two sides shall be armed alike; proving, too, in this manner the wonderful liberality of our government, which not only is able to furnish its soldiers with the latest improved style of breech-loaders to defend it and themselves, but is equally able and willing to give the same pattern of arms to their common foe. The only difference is, that the soldier, if he loses his weapon, is charged double price for it; while to avoid making any charge against the Indian, his weapons are given him without conditions attached. In the line of battle before us there were several hundred Indians, while further to the rear and at different distances were other organized bodies acting apparently as reserves. Still further were small detachments who seemed to perform the duty of couriers, and were held in readiness to convey messages to the village. The ground beyond was favorable for an extended view, allowing the eye to sweep the plain for several miles. As far as the eye could reach, small groups or individuals could be seen in the direction of the village; these were evidently parties of observation, whose sole object was to learn the result of our meeting with the main body and hasten with the news to the village.

For a few moments appearances seemed to foreshadow anything but a peaceful issue. The infantry was in the advance, followed closely by the artillery, while my command, the cavalry, was marching on the flank. General Hancock, who was riding with his staff at the head of the column, coming suddenly in view of the wild fantastic battle array, which extended far to our right and left and not more than half a mile in our front, hastily sent orders to the infantry, artillery, and cavalry to form line of battle, evidently determined that if war was intended we should be prepared. The cavalry, being the last to form on the right, came into line on a gallop, and, without waiting to align the ranks carefully, the command was given to "draw sabre." As the bright blades flashed from their scabbards into the morning sunlight, and the infantry brought their mus-

kets to a carry, a most beautiful and wonderfully interesting
sight was spread out before and around us, presenting a contrast
which, to a military eye, could but be striking. Here in battle
array, facing each other, were the representatives of civilized
and barbarous warfare. The one, with but few modifications,
stood clothed in the same rude style of dress, bearing the same
patterned shield and weapon that his ancestors had borne cen-
turies before; the other confronted him in the dress and supplied with the implements of war which the most advanced stage
of civilization had pronounced the most perfect. Was the com-
parative superiority of these two classes to be subjected to the
rude test of war here? Such seemed the prevailing impression
on both sides. All was eager anxiety and expectation. Neither
side seemed to comprehend the object or intentions of the other;
each was waiting for the other to deliver the first blow. A
more beautiful battle-ground could not have been chosen. Not
a bush or even the slightest irregularity of ground intervened
between the two lines which now stood frowning and facing
each other. Chiefs could be seen riding along the line as if
directing and exhorting their braves to deeds of heroism.

After a few moments of painful suspense, General Hancock, accompanied by General A. J. Smith and other officers,
rode forward, and through an interpreter invited the chiefs to
meet us midway, for the purpose of an interview. In response
to this invitation Roman Nose, bearing a white flag, accompanied by Bull Bear, White Horse, Gray Beard, and Medicine
Wolf, on the part of the Cheyennes, and Pawnee Killer, Bad
Wound, Tall Bear that Walks under the Ground, Left Hand,
Little Bear, and Little Bull on the part of the Sioux, rode forward to the middle of the open space between the two lines.
Here we shook hands with all of the chiefs, most of them exhibiting unmistakable signs of gratification at this apparently
peaceful termination of our encounter. General Hancock very
naturally inquired the object of the hostile attitude displayed
before us, saying to the chiefs that if war was their object we

were ready then and there to participate. Their immediate answer was that they did not desire war, but were peacefully disposed. They were then told that we would continue our march toward the village and encamp near it, but would establish such regulations that none of the soldiers would be permitted to approach or disturb them. An arrangement was then effected by which the chiefs were to assemble at General Hancock's headquarters as soon as our camp was pitched. The interview then terminated, and the Indians moved off in the direction of the village, we following leisurely in rear.

Custer then proceeds to tell at some length how the Indians managed to deceive them, and the whole affair is very characteristic of the difference between savage and civilized warfare. The preliminary councils, the threatening demonstrations, were all part of a scheme to gain time, and when the troops were safely encamped close to the village, it was found that all the women and children of the Indians had left the lodges and fled, in anticipation of a massacre. The chiefs themselves announced this, at the same time that two of them volunteered to follow after the fugitives and bring them back, if General Hancock would lend them two Government horses to ride on. This was done, and they set off at seven in the evening. It was the last seen of them or the horses. Two hours later, one of Hancock's scouts, who had been into the Indian camp, reported that the chiefs themselves were saddling up to leave. This scout was a half-breed Cheyenne, and the result showed that he was in all probability playing a double game.

Custer was at once directed to mount his cavalry, to surround the Indian village and prevent the departure of its inhabitants. This was done, and the village was found all peaceful and quiet, as if every one was asleep. When it was entered, however, it was found that the birds had flown, that the camp was empty. The Indians had left all their goods and fled in the night. The suddenness of their departure, and their abandonment of so much property gives color to their own plea, that they feared a repetition of the " Chivington Massacre," that had taken place only a year previous.

The next thing was to pursue the Indians. The scout who reported their approaching departure, had in all probability seen them go before he came, and the long operation of stealthily surrounding the camp had consumed much valuable time. Custer's description of the affair and of his own cautious approach, reminds one strongly of his first scout after Confederates, under Kearny. The cavalry was now ordered to follow the Indians; and the time occupied in getting ready was another illustration of how perfectly green every one then was in Indian warfare. It must be remembered that the Indians were off and marching, and that speed was absolutely needed to catch them. This was the sort of speed of which the Seventh Cavalry in those early days was capable.

Mess kits were overhauled, says Custer, and fresh supplies of coffee, sugar, flour, and the other articles which go to supply the soldier's larder, were laid in. Blankets were carefully rolled so as to occupy as little space as possible; every useless pound of luggage was discarded, for in making a rapid pursuit after Indians much of the success depends upon the lightness of the order of march. Saratoga trunks and their accompaniments are at a discount. Never was the old saying that in Rome one must do as Romans do more aptly illustrated than on an Indian campaign. The Indian, knowing that his safety either on offensive or defensive movements depends in a great measure upon the speed and endurance of his horse, takes advantage of every circumstance which will favor either the one or the other. To this end he divests himself of all superfluous dress and ornament when preparing for rapid movements. The white man, if he hopes for success, must adopt the same rule of action, and encumber his horse as little as possible. Something besides well-filled mess chests and carefully rolled blankets is necessary in preparing for an Indian campaign. Arms must be re-examined, cartridge-boxes refilled, so that each man should carry about one hundred rounds of ammunition "on his person," while each troop commander must see that in the company wagon there are placed a few boxes of reserve ammunition. Then, when the equipment of the soldier has been attended to, his horse, without whose assistance he is helpless, must be looked after; loose shoes are tightened, by the driving of an additional nail, and to accomplish this one may see the company black-smith, a soldier, with the few simple tools of his kit on the ground beside him, hurriedly fastening the last shoe by the un-certain light of a candle held in the hands of the rider of the horse, their mutual labor being varied at times by queries as to "How long shall we be gone?" "I wonder if we will catch Mr. Lo?" "If we do, we'll make it lively for him." So energetic had everybody been that before daylight everything was in readiness for the start.

Before daylight, however, according to Custer's own account, all chance was over. The cavalry followed the trail, preceded by their company of plainsmen and friendly Indians, but they failed to catch the Indians. The cavalry pressed the latter so close that they compelled them to disperse into small parties to lose the trail, but finally the trackers were obliged to give it up as a bad job.

It was while on this march and before the Indians had dis-persed, that Custer had his first buffalo adventure. He says that he felt satisfied that the Indians must be many miles ahead, and that the country was full of game. Therefore he called his dogs around him, and galloped off after some antelope in the distance. He says:

Although an ardent sportsman, I had never hunted the buffalo up to this time, consequently was exceedingly desirous of tasting of its excitement. I had several fine English grey-hounds, whose speed I was anxious to test with that of the ante-lope, said to be—which I believe—the fleetest of animals. I was mounted on a fine large thoroughbred horse. Taking with me but one man, the chief bugler, and calling my dogs around me, I galloped ahead of the column as soon as it was daylight. A stirring gallop of a few minutes brought me near enough to the antelope, of which there were a dozen or more, to enable the dogs to catch sight of them. Then the chase began, the antelope running in a direction which took us away from the command. By availing myself of the turns in the course, I was able to keep well in view of the exciting chase, until it was evident that the antelope were in no danger of being caught by the dogs, which latter had become blown from want of proper exercise. I succeeded in calling them off, and was about to set out on my return to the column. The horse of the chief bugler, being a common-bred animal, failed early in the race, and his rider wisely concluded to regain the command, so that I was alone. How far I had travelled from the troops I was trying to determine, when I discovered a large, dark looking animal grazing nearly a mile distant. As yet I had never seen a wild buffalo, but I at once recognized this as not only a buffalo, but a very large one. Here was my opportunity. A ravine near by would enable me to approach unseen until almost within pistol range of my game. Calling my dogs to follow me, I slowly pursued the course of the ravine, giving my horse opportunity to gather himself for the second run. When I emerged from the ravine I was still several hundred yards from the buffalo, which almost instantly discovered me, and set off as fast as his legs could carry him. Had my horse been fresh the race would have been a short one, but the preceding long run had not been without effect. How long or how fast we flew in pursuit, the intense excitement of the chase prevented me from knowing. I only knew that even the greyhounds were left behind, until finally my good steed placed himself and me close alongside the game. It may be because this was the first I had seen, but surely of the hundreds of thousands of buffaloes which I have since seen, none have corresponded with him in size and lofty grandeur. My horse was above the average size, yet the buffalo towered even above him. I had carried my revolver in my hand from the moment the race began. Repeatedly could I have placed the muzzle against the shaggy body of the huge beast, by whose side I fairly yelled with wild excitement and delight, yet each time would I withdraw the weapon, as if to prolong the enjoyment of the race. It was a race for life or death, yet how different the award from what could be imagined. Still we sped over the springy turf, the high breeding and mettle of my horse being plainly visible over that of the huge beast that struggled by his side. Mile after mile was traversed in this way, until the rate and distance began to tell perceptibly on the bison, whose protruding tongue and labored breathing plainly betrayed his distress. Determined to end the chase and bring down my game, I again placed the muzzle of the revolver close to the body of the buffalo, when as if divining my intention, and feeling his inability to escape by flight, he suddenly determined to fight, and at once wheeled, as only a buffalo can, to gore my horse. So sudden was this movement, and so sudden was the corresponding veering of my horse to avoid the attack, that to retain my control over him I hastily brought up my pistol hand to the assistance of the other. Unfortunately as I did so my finger, in the excitement of the occasion, pressed the trigger, discharged the pistol, and sent the fatal ball into the very brain of the noble animal I rode. Running at full speed he fell dead in the course of his leap. Quick as thought I disengaged myself from the stirrups and found myself whirling through the air over and beyond the head of my horse. My only thought, as I was describing this trajectory, and my first thought on reaching *terra firma*, was, " what will the buffalo do with me ? " Although at first inclined to rush upon me, my strange procedure seemed to astonish him. Either that, or pity for the utter helplessness of my condition, inclined him to alter his course and leave me alone to my own bitter reflections.

Such was the close of Custer's first buffalo hunt. He remained by his dead horse a little while, decidedly crestfallen, and then started for his command, attended by his dogs only. Luckily, the course of his last chase unwittingly took him ahead of his own column, and he was found by them.

The pursuit having failed to catch the village, it was judged best that the column should push on for the Smoky Hill River stage route, to warn the stations that the Indians were up and would soon be on the war-path. This was done, but too late for useful purposes. The Indians were already out, and war had begun. General Hancock had lost his opportunity when he first had the Indian village in his power and allowed it to escape. Henceforth, the Indians were more than his match. It was Custer's first introduction to Indian warfare, and the lesson he then received sunk deep into his heart. He made no more mistakes.

To be sure he was not responsible for the blunders of the campaign, not holding chief command. Being a young officer, naturally modest, he did not pretend to be competent to advise measures in Indian warfare, in which he had as yet no experience. Hancock was an old soldier, his experience dating back to 1844, and had served on the plains long before the rebellion. It was not for Custer to presume to offer an opinion that the Indians were fooling his commander, although such was the fact. All the remedy left to Hancock was to do what he actually did, burn up the abandoned village of the Cheyennes and Sioux. He did so, and war was formally opened, a war in which the Indians had decidedly the best of it.

Having burned the village, the next thing in order was a council. Hancock called one of all the Indian chiefs, and it was held at Fort Dodge, Kansas. The result of this council is thus adverted to by Custer:

" The most prominent chiefs in council were Satanta, Lone Wolf, and Kicking-Bird of the Kiowas, and Little Raven and Yellow Bear of the Arapahoes. During the council extravagant promises of future good conduct were made by these chiefs. So effective and convincing was the oratorical effort of Satanta, that at the termination of his address the department commander and staff presented him with the uniform coat, sash, and hat of a major-general. In return for this compliment Satanta, within a few weeks after, attacked the post at which the council was held, arrayed in his new uniform."

Custer, with the cavalry, had in the meantime marched down the stage route, and finally camped at Fort Hays, where he was joined by Hancock with the rest of the expedition, at the termination of the council. Hancock then left for Fort Leavenworth, and, as it soon appeared that the war was fairly opened, Custer started on the 1st of June, from Fort Hays, the spring grass being fairly started at last. His column consisted of three hundred and fifty men of the Seventh Cavalry, and twenty wagons, and his course was towards Fort McPherson on the Platte River, two hundred and twenty-five miles off.

It was his first Indian scout.

CHAPTER II.

THE FIRST SCOUT.

GENERAL CUSTER gives the object of his journey in the following words: It had been decided that my command should thoroughly scout the country from Fort Hays near the Smoky Hill river, to Fort McPherson, on the Platte; thence describe a semicircle to the southward, touching the head waters of the Republican, and again reach the Platte at or near Fort Sedgwick, at which post we would replenish our supplies; then move directly south to Fort Wallace, on the Smoky Hill, and from there march down the overland route to our starting-point at Fort Hays. This would involve a ride of upwards of one thousand miles.

In telling the story of this, his first Indian expedition, we shall, in all cases, adopt Custer's own words, where they are practicable. The column saw but one war party of Indians on the way to Fort McPherson, and they were off before they could be caught. The scouts learned from the trail that the Indians were mounted on stage-horses, showing that they must have swept the stage routes clean by this time.

"At Fort McPherson," says Custer, "we refilled our wagons with supplies and forage. At the same time, in accordance with my instructions, I reported by telegraph my arrival to General Sherman, who was then further west on the line of the Union Pacific road. He did not materially change my instructions, further than to direct me to remain near Fort McPherson until his arrival, which would be in the course of a few days."

The interval was diversified by another "council," this time with Pawnee Killer, a Sioux chief. Like all the other councils it amounted to nothing. Pawnee Killer came in to fool the white man, to find what he was doing and where he was going. The chief promised to bring in his band to encamp by the fort, and received from Custer presents of coffee and sugar and such finery as gratified his Indian fancy. Of course he lied, but Custer was in his first season, and learning Indian tactics. Pawnee Killer left the fort, and soon after General Sherman arrived.

The common sense of Sherman realized that Custer, like Hancock, had been duped, and he at first proposed to send after Pawnee Killer and his band, and to retain some of them as hostages. It was too late, so that Custer only learned a valuable lesson from the transaction. This was, never to trust to the professions of an Indian in time of war, when it is his interest to deceive.

Failing in catching Pawnee Killer, Custer was ordered to move to the forks of the Republican river, a country full of Indians at all times, and there to try and find Pawnee Killer's village, and make that chief do as he had promised. In the coming war, it was important to discriminate between friends and enemies, not so much for the sake of the Indians as on account of the Indian agents and Congress, and still more for fear of the newspapers at home. Custer was also to look after the Cheyennes and Sioux whom Hancock had let slip. He thus describes his departure :

" Owing to the rough and broken character of the bluffs which bound the valley of the Platte on the south side, it was determined to march up the men about fifteen miles from the fort and strike south through an opening in the bluffs known as Jack Morrow's canon. General Sherman rode with us as far as this point, where, after commending the Cheyennes and Sioux to us in his expressive manner, he bade us good-bye, and crossed the river to the railroad station on the north side. Thus far we had had no real Indian warfare. We were soon to experience it, attended by all its frightful barbarities."

Nothing particular happened for the first few days ; on the fourth, the column reached the forks of the river in the heart of the Indian country, and as the adventures of the next few days were affected by Custer's determination on reaching that spot, it is well to resume in his own words. It must be remembered that his force consisted of the Seventh Cavalry, (350 strong and 20 wagons), exclusive of scouts and guides. He thus proceeds :

When I parted from General Sherman the understanding was, that after beating up the country thoroughly about the forks of the Republican river, I should march my command to Fort Sedgwick, and there I would either see General Sherman again or receive further instructions from him. Circumstances seemed to favor a modification of this plan, at least as to marching the entire command to Fort Sedgwick. It was therefore decided to send a trusty officer with a sufficient escort to Fort Sedgwick with my despatch, and to receive the despatches which might be intended for me. My proposed change of programme contemplated a continuous march, which might be prolonged twenty days or more. To this end additional supplies were necessary. The guides all agreed in the statement that we were then about equidistant from Fort Wallace on the south and Fort Sedgwick on the north, at either of which the required supplies could be obtained ; but that while the country between our camp and the former was generally level and unbroken—favorable to the movement of our wagon-train—that between us and Fort Sedgwick was almost impassable for heavily-laden wagons. The train then was to go to Fort Wallace under sufficient escort, be loaded with fresh supplies, and rejoin us in camp. At the same time the officer selected for that mission could proceed to Fort Sedgwick, obtain his despatch, and return.

Major Joel A. Elliot, a young officer of great courage and enterprise, was selected as bearer of despatches to Fort Sedgwick. As the errand was one involving considerable danger, requiring for the round trip a ride of almost two hundred miles, through a country which was not only almost unknown but infested by large numbers of hostile Indians, the Major was authorized to arrange the details in accordance with his own judgment.

Knowing that small detachments can move more rapidly than large ones, and that he was to depend upon celerity of movement rather than strength of numbers to evade the numerous war parties prowling in that vicinity, the Major limited the size of his escort to ten picked men and one of the guides, all mounted on fleet horses. To elude the watchful eyes of any parties that might be noting our movements, it was deemed advisable to set out from camp as soon as it was dark, and making a rapid night ride get beyond the circle of danger. In this way the little party took its departure on the night of the 23d of June.

On the same day our train of wagons set out for Fort Wallace to obtain supplies. Colonel West * with one full squadron of cavalry was ordered to escort the train to Beaver Creek, about midway, and there halt with one of his companies, while the train, under escort of one company commanded by Lieutenant Robbins, should proceed to the front and return—Colonel West to employ the interval in scouting up and down Beaver Creek. The train was under special management of Colonel Cook, who on this occasion was acting in the capacity of a staff officer.

After the departure of the two detachments, which left us in almost opposite directions, our camp settled down to the dull and unexciting monotony of waiting patiently for the time when we should welcome our comrades back again, and listen to such items of news as they might bring to us.

It will be remembered that Custer set out to find Pawnee Killer's village. He thus relates how Pawnee Killer found him next morning:

* The rank of the officers of the Seventh Cavalry, owing to the strange system of brevets and titles of courtesy in use in our army at the close of the war, is often very puzzling. It is the etiquette of the army to call a man by the highest title he has borne, brevet or volunteer, except on duty. West was really only a captain, Cook, subsequently mentioned, a lieutenant.

It was just that uncertain period between darkness and day-light on the following morning, and I was lying in my tent deep in the enjoyment of that perfect repose which only camp life offers, when the sharp, clear crack of a carbine near by brought me to my feet. I knew in an instant that the shot came from the picket posted not far from the rear of my camp. At the same moment my brother, Colonel Custer, who on that occasion was officer of the day and whose duties required him to be particularly on the alert, rushed past my tent, halting only long enough to show his face through the opening and shout " They are here ! "

Now I did not inquire who were referred to, or how many were included in the word " they," nor did my informant seem to think it necessary to explain. " They," referred to Indians, I knew full well. Had I doubted, the brisk fusillade which opened the next moment, and the wild war-whoop, were convincing evidences that in truth " they were here ! "

My orderly, as was his custom, on my retiring had securely tied all the fastenings to my tent, and it was usually the work of several minutes to undo this unnecessary labor. I had no time to throw away in this manner. Leaping from my bed, I grasped my trusty Spencer, which was always at my side whether waking or sleeping, and with a single dash burst open the tent, and, hatless as well as shoeless, ran to the point where the attack seemed to be concentrated.

It was sufficiently light to see our enemies and be seen. The first shot had brought every man of my command from his tent, armed and equipped for battle. The Indians, numbering hundreds, were all around the camp, evidently intending to surround us, while a party of about fifty of their best mounted warriors had, by taking advantage of a ravine, contrived to approach quite close before being discovered. It was the intention of this party to dash through our camp, stampede all our horses, which were to be caught up by the parties surrounding us, and then finish us at their leisure.

The picket, however, discovered the approach of this party, and by firing gave timely warning, thus frustrating the plan of the Indians, who almost invariably base their hopes of success upon effecting a surprise.

My men opened on them such a brisk fire from their carbines that they were glad to withdraw beyond range. The picket who gave the alarm was shot down at his post by the Indians, the entire party galloping over his body, and being prevented from scalping him only by the fire from his comrades who dashed out and recovered him. He was found to be badly though not mortally wounded by a rifle ball through the body.

The Indians, seeing that their attempt to surprise us and to stampede our horses had failed, then withdrew to a point but little over a mile from us, where they congregated, and seemed to hold a conference with each other. We did not fear any further attack at this time. They were satisfied with this attempt, and would wait another opportunity.

It was desirable, however, that we should learn if possible to what tribe our enemies belonged. I directed one of our interpreters to advance midway between our camp and the Indians, and make the signal for holding a parley, and in this way ascertain who were the principal chiefs.

The ordinary manner of opening communication with parties known or supposed to be hostile, is to ride toward them in a zigzag manner or to ride in a circle. The interpreter gave the proper signal, and was soon answered by a small party advancing from the main body of the Indians to within hailing distance. It was then agreed that I, with six of the officers, should come to the bank of the river, which was about equidistant from my camp and from the point where the Indians had congregated, and there be met by an equal number of the leading chiefs. To guard against treachery, I placed most of my command under arms, and arranged with the officer left in command that a blast from the bugle should bring assistance to me if required.

Custer then tells how they arrived at the bank of the river, and were met by their old friend Pawnee Killer and his chiefs, taking matters very coolly. His presence was one more lesson for Custer on Indian treachery, and he soon had another. On the pretext of coming over to say " How," several other Indians waded the river, and finally it appeared as if an attempt at murder was to take place, could the white man's suspicions be allayed. Custer then broke off the conference, which had served no purpose except to inform them who their enemy had been. The close of the conference was characteristic; Pawnee Killer, who seems to have imbibed a great contempt for the youth and inexperience of Custer, had the impudence to beg for coffee, sugar and ammunition. It is needless to say that he did not get them. Custer returned to his regiment, and pursued the Sioux for some hours, but was unable to catch the fleet Indian ponies with the coarse heavy troop horses of his command. He finally returned to camp.

Soon after returning, more Indians, a very small party, were seen in the opposite direction, and Captain Hamilton's troop was sent after them. The Indians divided their party, lured Hamilton on for several miles, and finally turned on him, as soon as he had divided his own party to pursue them. They fought Hamilton two to one for about an hour, but he kept them off and returned to camp unharmed, having shot two Indians dead, and wounded two others. The Indians fought in the peculiar manner known as " circling," which will be fully described in the next chapter.

Hamilton's affair occurred in the direction of Fort Sedgwick, whereas Pawnee Killer had retired toward Fort Wallace. It became clear therefore, that the country was full of Indians, and it became a matter of doubt where they were thickest on the route taken by Major Elliot, or that pursued by Robbins and Cook with the wagon train. The party that attacked Hamilton numbered forty-three, whereas Pawnee Killer had several hundred, but the greatest anxiety was felt for Major

24

Elliot's little band of eleven, which had gone in the other direction.   Many or few, there were clearly enough Indians on the trail to overwhelm him.   Major Elliot, however, proved to be a careful and skillful officer.   In five days after, he rode into camp, having trusted to his guide, an old hunter.   The party had hidden in ravines all day, and only travelled by night.

The fate of the wagon train falls naturally into another chapter.

THE ATTACK UPON THE TRAIN.

CHAPTER III.

THE WAGON TRAIN.

THE story of the attack on the train and its results in connection with the expedition is thus told by Custer:

Now that the Major and his party had returned to us, our anxiety became centred in the fate of the larger party which had proceeded with the train to Fort Wallace for supplies. The fact that Major Elliot had made his trip unmolested by Indians, proved that the latter were most likely assembled south of us, that is, between us and Fort Wallace. Wherever they were, their numbers were known to be large. It would be impossible for a considerable force, let alone a wagon train, to pass from our camp to Fort Wallace and not be seen by the Indian scouting parties. They had probably observed the departure of the train and escort at the time, and, divining the object which occasioned the sending of the wagons, would permit them to go to the fort unmolested, but would waylay them on their return in hope of obtaining the supplies they contained. Under this supposition the Indians had probably watched the train and escort during every mile of their progress; if so, they would not fail to discover that the larger portion of the escort halted at Beaver Creek, while the wagons proceeded to the fort guarded by only forty-eight men; in which case the Indians would combine their forces and attack the train at some point between Fort Wallace and Beaver Creek.

Looking at these probable events, I not only felt impelled to act promptly to secure the safety of the train and its escort, but a deeper and stronger motive stirred me to leave nothing undone to circumvent the Indians. My wife, who, in answer to my letter, I believed was then at Fort Wallace, would place herself under the protection of the escort of the train and attempt to rejoin me in camp. The mere thought of the danger to which she might be exposed spurred me to decisive action. One full squadron, well mounted and armed, under the command of Lieutenant-Colonel Myers, an officer of great experience in Indian affairs, left our camp at dark on the evening of the day that Captain Hamilton had had his engagement with the Indians, and set out in the direction of Fort Wallace. His orders were to press forward as rapidly as practicable, following the trail made by the train. Written orders were sent in his care to Colonel West, who was in command of that portion of the escort which had halted at Beaver Creek, to join Colonel Myers's command with his own, and then to continue the march toward Fort Wallace until he should meet the returning train and escort. The Indians, however, were not to be deprived of this opportunity to secure scalps and plunder.

From our camp to Beaver Creek was nearly fifty miles. Colonel Myers marched his command without halting until he joined Colonel West at Beaver Creek. Here the two commands united, and under the direction of Colonel West, the senior officer of the party, proceeded toward Fort Wallace, following the trail left by the wagon-train and escort. If the escort and Colonel West's forces could be united, they might confidently hope to repel any attack made upon them by Indians. Colonel West was an old Indian fighter, and too thoroughly accustomed to Indian tactics to permit his command to be surprised or defeated in any manner other than by a fair contest.

Let us leave them for a time and join the wagon-train and its escort—the latter numbering, all told, as before stated, forty-eight men under the immediate command of Lieutenant Robbins. Colonel Cook, whose special duty connected him with the train and its supplies, could also be relied upon for material assistance with the troops, in case of actual conflict with the enemy. Comstock, the favorite scout, a host in himself, was sent to guide the party to and from Fort Wallace. In addition to these were the teamsters, who could not be expected to do more than control their teams should the train be attacked.

The march from camp to Beaver Creek was made without incident. Here the combined forces of Colonel West and Lieutenant Robbins encamped together during the night. Next morning at early dawn Lieutenant Robbins's party, having the train in charge, continued the march toward Fort Wallace, while Colonel West sent out scouting parties up and down the stream to search for Indians.

As yet none of their party were aware of the hostile attitude assumed by the Indians within the past few hours, and Colonel West's instructions contemplated a very friendly meeting between his forces and the Indians, should the latter be discovered. The march of the train and escort was made to Fort Wallace without interruption. The only incident worthy of remark was an observation of Comstock's, which proved how thoroughly he was familiar with the Indian and his customs.

The escort was moving over a beautifully level plateau. Not a mound or hillock disturbed the evenness of the surface for miles in either direction. To an unpracticed eye there seemed no recess or obstruction in or behind which an enemy might be concealed, but everything appeared open to the view for miles and miles, look in what direction one might. Yet such was not the case. Ravines of greater or less extent, though not perceptible at a glance, might have been discovered if searched for, extending almost to the trail over which the party was moving. These ravines, if followed, would be found to grow deeper and deeper, until after running their course for an indefinite extent, they would terminate in the valley of some running stream. These were the natural hiding-places of Indian war parties, waiting their opportunities to dash upon unsuspecting victims. These ravines serve the same purpose to the Indians of the timberless plains that the ambush did to those Indians of the Eastern States accustomed to fighting in the forests and everglades. Comstock's keen eyes took in all at a glance, and he remarked to Colonel Cook and Lieutenant Robbins, as the three rode together at the head of the column, that "If the Injuns strike us at all, it will be just about the time we are comin' along back over this very spot. Now mind what I tell ye all." We shall see how correct Comstock's prophecy was.

Arriving at the fort, no time was lost in loading up the wagons with fresh supplies, obtaining the mail intended for the command, and preparing to set out on the return to camp the following day.

On the following morning Colonel Cook and Lieutenant Robbins began their return march. They had advanced one half the distance which separated them from Colonel West's camp without the slightest occurrence to disturb the monotony of their march, and had reached the point where, on passing before, Comstock had indulged in his prognostication regarding Indians; yet nothing had been seen to excite suspicion or alarm.

Comstock, always on the alert and with eyes as quick as those of an Indian, had been scanning the horizon in all directions. Suddenly he perceived, or thought he perceived, strange figures, resembling human heads, peering over the crest of a hill far away to the right. Hastily leveling his field-glass, he pronounced the strange figures, which were scarcely perceptible, to be neither more nor less than Indians. The officers brought into requisition their glasses, and were soon convinced of the correctness of Comstock's report. It was some time before the Indians perceived that they were discovered. Concealment then being no longer possible, they boldly rode to the crest and exposed themselves to full view. At first but twenty or thirty made their appearance; gradually their number became augmented, until about a hundred warriors could be seen.

It may readily be imagined that the appearance of so considerable a body of Indians produced no little excitement and speculation in the minds of the people with the train. The speculation was as to the intentions of the Indians, whether hostile or friendly. Upon this subject all doubts were soon dispelled. The Indians continued to receive accessions to their numbers, the reinforcements coming from beyond the crest of the hill on which their presence was first discovered. Finally, seeming confident in their superior numbers, the warriors, all of whom were mounted, advanced leisurely down the slope leading in the direction of the train and its escort. By the aid of field-glasses, Comstock and the two officers were able to determine fully the character of the party now approaching them. The last doubt was thus removed. It was clearly to be seen that the Indians were arrayed in full war costume, their heads adorned by the brilliantly colored war bonnets, their faces, arms, and bodies painted in various colors, rendering their naturally repulsive appearance even more hideous. As they approached nearer they assumed a certain order in the manner of their advance. Some were to be seen carrying the long glistening lance with its pennant of bright colors; while upon the left arm hung the round shield, almost bullet-proof, and ornamented with paint and feathers according to the taste of the wearer. Nearly all were armed with carbines and one or two revolvers, while many in addition to these weapons carried the bow and arrow.

When the entire band had defiled down the inclined slope, Comstock and the officers were able to estimate roughly the full strength of the party. They were astonished to perceive that between six and seven hundred warriors were bearing down upon them, and in a few minutes would undoubtedly commence the attack. Against such odds, and upon ground so favorable for the Indian mode of warfare, it seemed unreasonable to hope for a favorable result. Yet the entire escort, officers and men, entered upon their defence with a determination to sell their lives as dearly as possible.

As the coming engagement, so far as the cavalry was concerned, was to be purely a defensive one, Lieutenant Robbins at once set about preparing to receive his unwelcome visitors. Colonel Cook formed the train in two parallel columns, leaving ample space between for the horses of the cavalry. Lieutenant Robbins then dismounted his men and prepared to fight on foot. The led horses, under charge of the fourth trooper, were placed between the two columns of wagons, and were thus in a measure protected from the assaults which the officers had every reason to believe would be made for their capture. The dismounted cavalrymen were thus formed in a regular circle enclosing the train and horses. Colonel Cook took command of one flank, Lieutenant Robbins of the other, while Comstock, who, as well as the two officers, remained mounted, galloped from point to point wherever his presence was most valuable. These dispositions being perfected, the march was resumed in this order, and the attack of the savages calmly awaited.

The Indians, who were interested spectators of these preparations for their reception, continued to approach, but seemed willing to delay their attack until the plain became a little more favorable for their operations. Finally, the desired moment seemed to have arrived. The Indians had approached to within easy range, yet not a shot had been fired, the cavalrymen having been instructed by their officers to reserve their fire for close quarters. Suddenly, with a wild ringing war-whoop, the entire band of warriors bore down upon the train and its little party of defenders.

On came the savages, filling the air with their terrible yells. Their first object, evidently, was to stampede the horses and draught animals of the train ; then, in the excitement and consternation which would follow, to massacre the escort and drivers. The wagon-master in immediate charge of the train had been ordered to keep his two columns of wagons constantly moving forward and well closed up. This last injunction was hardly necessary, as the frightened teamsters, glancing at the approaching warriors and hearing their savage shouts, were sufficiently anxious to keep well closed upon their leaders.

The first onslaught of the Indians was made on the flank which was superintended by Colonel Cook. They rode boldly forward as if to dash over the mere handful of cavalrymen, who stood in skirmishing order in a circle about the train. Not a soldier faltered as the enemy came thundering upon them, but waiting until the Indians were within short rifle range of the train, the cavalrymen dropped upon their knees, and taking deliberate aim poured a volley from their Spencer carbines into the ranks of the savages, which seemed to put a sudden check upon the ardor of their movements and forced them to wheel off to the right. Several of the warriors were seen to reel in their saddles, while the ponies of others were brought down or wounded by the effectual fire of the cavalrymen.

Those of the savages who were shot from their saddles were scarcely permitted to fall to the ground before a score or more of their comrades dashed to their rescue and bore their bodies beyond the possible reach of our men. This is in accordance with the Indian custom in battle. They will risk the lives of a dozen of their best warriors to prevent the body of any one of their number from falling into the white man's possession. The reason for this is the belief, which generally prevails among all the tribes that if a warrior loses his scalp he forfeits his hope of ever reaching the happy hunting-ground.

As the Indians were being driven back by the well-directed volley of the cavalrymen, the latter, overjoyed at their first success, became reassured, and sent up a cheer of exultation, while Comstock, who had not been idle in the fight, called out to the retreating Indians in their native tongue, taunting them with their unsuccessful assault.

The Indians withdrew to a point beyond the range of our carbines, and there seemed to engage in a parley. Comstock, who had closely watched every movement, remarked that "There's no sich good look for us as to think them Injuns mean to give it up so. Six hundred red devils ain't agoin' to let fifty men stop them from getting at the coffee and sugar that is in these wagons. And they ain't agoin' to be satisfied until they get some of our scalps to pay for the bucks we popped out of their saddles a bit ago."

It was probable that the Indians were satisfied that they could not dash through the train and stampede the animals. Their recent attempt had convinced them that some other method of attack must be resorted to. Nothing but their great superiority in numbers had induced them to risk so much in a charge.

The officers passed along the line of skirmishers—for this in reality was all their line consisted of—and cautioned the men against wasting their ammunition. It was yet early in the afternoon, and should the conflict be prolonged until night, there was great danger of exhausting the supply of ammunition. The Indians seemed to have thought of this, and the change in their method of attack encouraged such a result.

But little time was spent at the parley. Again the entire band of warriors, except those already disabled, prepared to renew the attack, and advanced as before—this time, however, with greater caution, evidently desiring to avoid a reception similar to the first. When sufficiently near to the troops the Indians developed their new plan of attack. It was not to advance *en masse*, as before, but fight as individuals, each warrior selecting his own time and method of attack. This is the habitual manner of fighting among all the Indians of the Plains, and is termed " circling." First the chiefs led off, followed at regular intervals by the warriors, until the entire six or seven hundred were to be seen riding in single file as rapidly as their fleet-footed ponies could carry them. Preserving this order, and keeping up their savage chorus of yells, war-whoops, and taunting epithets, this long line of mounted barbarians was guided in such manner as to envelope the train and escort, and make the latter appear like a small circle within a larger one.

The Indians gradually contracted their circle, although maintaining the full speed of their ponies, until sufficiently close

to open fire upon the soldiers. At first the shots were scattering and wide of their mark; but, emboldened by the silence of
their few but determined opponents, they rode nearer and
fought with greater impetuosity. Forced now to defend themselves to the uttermost, the cavalrymen opened fire from their
carbines, with most gratifying results. The Indians, however,
moving at such a rapid gait and in single file, presented a most
uncertain target. To add to this uncertainty, the savages
availed themselves of their superior—almost marvellous—powers
of horsemanship. Throwing themselves upon the sides of their
well-trained ponies, they left no part of their persons exposed to
the aim of the troopers except the head and one foot, and in
this posture they were able to aim the weapons either over or
under the necks of their ponies, thus using the bodies of the
latter as an effective shield against the bullets of their adversaries.

At no time were the Indians able to force the train and its
escort to come to a halt. The march was continued at an un-
interrupted gait. This successful defence against the Indians
was in a great measure due to the presence of the wagons, which,
arranged in the order described, formed a complete barrier to
the charges and assaults of the savages; and, as a last resort,
the wagons could have been halted and used as a breastwork,
behind which the cavalry, dismounted, would have been almost
invincible against their more numerous enemies. There is
nothing an Indian dislikes more in warfare than to attack a foe,
however weak, behind breastworks of any kind. Any con-
trivance which is an obstacle to his pony is a most serious obstacle to the warrior.

The attack of the Indians, aggravated by their losses in
warriors and ponies, as many of the latter had been shot down,
was continued without cessation for three hours. The supply
of ammunition of the cavalry was running low. The "fourth
troopers," who had remained in charge of the led horses between the four columns of wagons, were now replaced from the

skirmishers, and the former were added to the list of active combatants. If the Indians should maintain the fight much longer, there was serious ground for apprehension regarding the limited supply of ammunition.

If only night or reinforcements would come! was the prayerful hope of those who contended so gallantly against such heavy odds. Night was still too far off to promise much encouragement; while as to reinforcements, their coming would be purely accidental—at least so argued those most interested in their arrival. Yet reinforcements were at that moment striving to reach them. Comrades were in the saddle and spurring forward to their relief. The Indians, although apparently turning all their attention to the little band inside, had omitted no precaution to guard against interference from outside parties. In this instance, perhaps, they were more than ordinarily watchful, and had posted some of their keen-eyed warriors on the high line of bluffs which ran almost parallel to the trail over which the combatants moved. From these bluffs not only a good view of the fight could be obtained, but the country for miles in either direction was spread out beneath them, and enabled the scouts to discern the approach of any hostile party which might be advancing. Fortunate for the savages that this precaution had not been neglected, or the contest in which they were engaged might have become one of more equal numbers. To the careless eye nothing could have been seen to excite suspicion. But the warriors on the lookout were not long in discovering something which occasioned them no little anxiety. Dismounting from their ponies and concealing the latter in a ravine, they prepared to investigate more fully the cause of their alarm.

That which they saw was as yet but a faint dark line on the surface of the plain, almost against the horizon. So faint was it that no one but an Indian or practiced frontiersman would have observed it. It was fully ten miles from them and directly in their line of march. The ordinary observer would have pronounced it a break or irregularity in the ground, or perhaps the shadow of a cloud, and its apparent permanency of location would have dispelled any fear as to its dangerous character. But was it stationary? Apparently, yes. The Indians discovered otherwise. By close watching, the long faint line could be seen moving along, as if creeping stealthily upon an unconscious foe. Slowly it assumed a more definite shape, until what appeared to be a mere stationary dark line drawn upon the green surface of the plain, developed itself to the searching eyes of the red man into a column of cavalry moving at a rapid gait toward the very point they were then occupying.

Convinced of this fact, one of the scouts leaped upon his pony and flew with almost the speed of the wind to impart this knowledge to the chiefs in command on the plain below. True, the approaching cavalry, being still several miles distant, could not arrive for nearly two hours; but the question to be considered by the Indians was, whether it would be prudent for them to continue their attack on the train—their ponies already becoming exhausted by the three hours' hard riding given them—until the arrival of the fresh detachment of the enemy, whose horses might be in condition favorable to a rapid pursuit, and thereby enable them to overtake those of the Indians whose ponies were exhausted. Unwilling to incur this new risk, and seeing no prospect of overcoming their present adversaries by a sudden or combined dash, the chiefs decided to withdraw from the attack, and make their escape while the advantage was yet in their favor.

The surprise of the cavalrymen may be imagined at seeing the Indians, after pouring a shower of bullets and arrows into the train, withdraw to the bluffs, and immediately after continue their retreat until lost to view.

This victory for the troopers, although so unexpected, was none the less welcome. The Indians contrived to carry away with them their killed and wounded. Five of their bravest warriors were known to have been sent to the happy hunting-ground, while the list of their wounded was much larger.

After the Indians had withdrawn and left the cavalrymen masters of the field, our wounded, of whom there were comparatively few, received every possible care and attention. Those of the detachment who had escaped unharmed were busily engaged in exchanging congratulations and relating incidents of the fight.

In this manner nearly an hour had been whiled away, when far in the distance, in their immediate front, fresh cause for anxiety was discovered. At first the general opinion was that it was the Indians again, determined to contest their progress. Field-glasses were again called into requisition, and revealed, not Indians, but the familiar blue blouses of the cavalry. Never was the sight more welcome. The next moment Colonel Cook, with Comstock and a few troopers, applied spurs to their horses and were soon dashing forward to meet their comrades.

The approaching party was none other than Colonel West's detachment, hastening to the relief of the train and its gallant little escort. A few words explained all, and told the heroes of the recent fight how it happened that reinforcements were sent to their assistance ; and then was explained why the Indians had so suddenly concluded to abandon their attack and seek safety in quietly withdrawing from the field.

THE KIDDER MASSACRE.

CHAPTER IV.

THE KIDDER MASSACRE.

SO far Custer's first Indian campaign had progressed, on the whole, favorably. He had been duped by the Indians in common with General Hancock, but he had suffered no disaster, and all his parties, large or small, had succeeded in beating off the Indians. At that time, the American army in regard to the Indians was much in the attitude of the Romans towards the Gauls, as depicted by Sallust in the closing sentences of his "War against Jugurtha." Sallust says: "The Romans had always been strongly of opinion, and now no less so, that all other nations must yield to them in bravery; but that when they fought with the Gauls they were to aim only at the preservation of their state, and not at glory." Much the same opinion prevailed among army officers in America, to judge from the cautious proceedings, till Custer came. In this campaign, as a beginner, he was feeling his way, and learning pretty rapidly. The first disaster that was to befall any of his troops, befell an officer sent on a similar errand to that of Major Elliot, before mentioned, but in the other direction.

"On the morning of the 28th," continues Custer, "the train returned to the camp on the Republican. All were proud of the conduct of those detachments of the command which had been brought into actual conflict with the Indians. The heroes of the late fights were congratulated heartily upon their good luck, while their comrades who had unavoidably remained in camp, consoled themselves with the hope that the next opportunity might be theirs.

" The despatches brought by Major Elliot from General Sherman directed me to continue my march, as had been suggested, up the North Republican, then strike northward and reach the Platte again at some point west of Fort Sedgwick, near Riverside Station. This programme was carried out. Leaving our camp on the Republican, we marched up the north fork of that river about sixty miles, then turned nearly due north, and marched for the valley of the Platte."

At the Platte the column arrived, after a march of sixty-five miles without water, and found itself near Riverside Telegraph Station, fifty miles west of Fort Sedgwick. They learned that the Indians had attacked the nearest stage station the night before they arrived, and had killed three men. This information was obtained by a detachment which reached the station. Custer then relates the incident of the Kidder Massacre as follows :

Believing that General Sherman must have sent later instructions for me to Fort Sedgwick, than those last received from him, I sent a telegram to the officer in command at the fort, making inquiry to that effect. To my surprise I received a despatch saying that, the day after the departure of Major Elliot and his detachment from Fort Sedgwick with despatches, of which mention has been previously made, a second detachment of equal strength, viz., ten troopers of the Second United States Cavalry, under command of Lieutenant Kidder, and guided by a famous Sioux chief Red Bead, had left Fort Sedgwick with important despatches for me from General Sherman, and that Lieutenant Kidder had been directed to proceed to my camp near the forks of the Republican, and failing to find me there, he was to follow immediately on my trail until he should overtake my command. I immediately telegraphed to Fort Sedgwick that nothing had been seen or heard of Lieutenant Kidder's detachment, and requested a copy of the despatches borne by him to be sent me by telegraph. This was done; the instructions of General Sherman were for me to march my command, as was at first contemplated, across the country from the Platte to the Smoky Hill River, striking the latter at Fort Wallace. Owing to the low state of my supplies, I determined to set out for Fort Wallace at daylight next morning.

Great anxiety prevailed throughout the command concerning Lieutenant Kidder and his party. True, he had precisely the same number of men that composed Major Elliot's detachment when the latter went upon a like mission, but the circumstances which would govern in the one case had changed when applied to the other. Major Elliot, an officer of experience and good judgment, had fixed the strength of his escort, and performed the journey before it was positively known that the Indians in that section had entered upon the war path. Had the attack on the commands of Hamilton, Robbins, and Cook been made prior to Elliot's departure, the latter would have taken not less than fifty troopers as escort. After an informal interchange of opinions between the officers of my command regarding the whereabouts of Lieutenant Kidder and party, we endeavored to satisfy ourselves with the following explanation. Using the capital letter Y for illustration, let us locate Fort Sedgwick, from which post Lieutenant Kidder was sent with despatches, at the right upper point of the letter. The camp of my command at the forks of the Republican would be at the junction of the three branches of the letter. Fort Wallace relatively would be at the lower termination, and the point on the Platte at which my command was located the morning referred to, would be at the upper termination of the left branch of the letter. Robbins and Cook, in going with the train to Wallace for supplies, had passed and returned over the lower branches. After their return and that of Major Elliot and his party, my entire command resumed the march for the Platte. We moved for two or three miles out on the heavy wagon trail of Robbins and Cook, then suddenly changed our direction to the right. It was supposed that Kidder and his party arrived at our deserted camp at the forks of the Republi-

25

can about nightfall, but finding us gone had determined to avail themselves of the moonlight night and overtake us before we should break camp next morning. Riding rapidly in the dim light of evening, they had failed to observe the point at which we had diverged from the plainer trail of Robbins and Cook, and instead of following our trail had continued on the former in the direction of Fort Wallace. Such seemed to be a plausible if not the only solution capable of being given.

Anxiety for the fate of Kidder and his party was one of the reasons impelling me to set out promptly on my return. From our camp at the forks of the Republican to Fort Wallace was about eighty miles—but eighty miles of the most dangerous country infested by Indians. Remembering the terrible contest in which the command of Robbins and Cook had been engaged on this very route within a few days, and knowing that the Indians would in all probability maintain a strict watch over the trail to surprise any small party which might venture over it, I felt in the highest degree solicitous for the safety of Lieutenant Kidder and party. Even if he succeeded in reaching Fort Wallace unmolested, there was reason to apprehend that, impressed with the importance of delivering his despatches promptly, he would set out on his return at once and endeavor to find my command.

The third night after leaving the Platte my command encamped in the vicinity of our former camp near the forks of the Republican. So far, nothing had been learned which would enable us to form any conclusion regarding the route taken by Kidder. Comstock, the guide, was frequently appealed to for an opinion, which, from his great experience on the plains, might give us some encouragement regarding Kidder's safety. But he was too cautious and careful a man, both in word and deed, to excite hopes which his reasoning could not justify. When thus appealed to he would usually give an ominous shake of the head and avoid a direct answer.

On the evening just referred to the officers and Comstock

were grouped near headquarters discussing the subject which was then uppermost in the mind of every one in camp. Comstock had been quietly listening to the various theories and surmises advanced by different members of the group, but was finally pressed to state his ideas as to Kidder's chances of escaping harm.

" Well, gentle*men*," emphasizing the last syllable as was his manner, " before a man kin form any ijee as to how this thing is likely to end, thar are several things he ort to be acquainted with. For instance, now, no man need tell me any p'ints about Injuns. Ef I know anything, it's Injuns. I know jest how they'll do anything and when they'll take to do it; but that don't settle the question, and I'll tell you why. Ef I knowed this young lootenint—I mean Lootenint Kidder—ef I knowed what for sort of a man he is, I could tell you mighty near to a sartainty all you want to know; for you see Injun huntin' and Injun fightin' is a trade all by itself, and like any other bizness a man has to know what he's about, or ef he don't he can't make a livin' at it. I have lots uv confi*dence* in the fightin' sense of Red Bead the Sioux chief, who is guidin' the lootenint and his men, and ef that Injun kin have his own way thar is a fair show for his guidin' 'em through all right; but as I sed before, there lays the difficulty. Is this lootenint the kind of a man who is willin' to take advice, even ef it does cum from an Injun? My experience with you army folks has allus bin that the youngsters among ye think they know the most, and this is particularly true ef they hev just cum from West P'int. Ef some of them young fellers knowed half as much as they b'lieve they do, you couldn't tell them nothin'. As to rale book-larnin', why I s'pose they've got it all; but the fact uv the matter is, they couldn't tell the difference twixt the trail of a war party and one made by a huntin' party to save their necks. Half uv 'em when they first cum here can't tell a squaw from a buck, just because both ride straddle; but they soon larn. But that's neither here nor thar. I'm told that the lootenint we're talkin' about is a new-comer, and that this is his first scout. Ef that be the case, it puts a mighty onsartain look on the whole thing, and twixt you and me, gentle*men*, he'll be mighty lucky ef he gits through all right. To-morrow we'll strike the Wallace trail, and I kin mighty soon tell ef he has gone that way."

But little comfort was to be derived from these expressions. The morrow would undoubtedly enable us, as Comstock had predicted, to determine whether or not the lieutenant and his party had missed our trail and taken that leading to Fort Wallace.

At daylight our column could have been seen stretching out in the direction of the Wallace trail. A march of a few miles brought us to the point of intersection. Comstock and the Delawares had galloped in advance, and were about concluding a thorough examination of the various tracks to be seen in the trail, when the head of the column overtook them. " Well, what do you find, Comstock ? " was my first inquiry. " They've gone toward Fort Wallace, sure," was the reply; and in support of this opinion he added, " The trail shows that twelve American horses, shod all round, have passed at a walk, goin' in the direction of the fort; and when they went by this p'int they were all right, because their horses were movin' along easy, and there are no pony tracks behind 'em, as wouldn't be the case ef the Injuns had got an eye on 'em." He then remarked, as if in parenthesis, " It would be astonishin' ef that lootenint and his lay-outs gits into the fort without a scrimmage. He may; but ef he does, it will be a scratch ef ever there was one, and I'll lose my confidence in Injuns."

The opinion expressed by Comstock as to the chances of Lieutenant Kidder and party making their way to the fort across eighty miles of danger unmolested, was the concurrent opinion of all the officers. And now that we had discovered their trail, our interest and anxiety became immeasurably increased as to their fate. The latter could not remain in doubt much longer, as two days' marching would take us to the fort. Alas ! we were to solve the mystery without waiting so long.

Pursuing our way along the plain, heavy trail made by Robbins and Cook, and directing Comstock and the Delawares to watch closely that we did not lose that of Kidder and his party, we patiently but hopefully awaited further developments. How many miles we had thus passed over without incident worthy of mention, I do not now recall. The sun was high in the heavens, showing that our day's march was about half completed, when those of us who were riding at the head of the column discovered a strange looking object lying directly in our path, and more than a mile distant. It was too large for a human being, yet in color and appearance, at that distance, resembled no animal frequenting the plains with which any of us were familiar. Eager to determine its character, a dozen or more of our party, including Comstock and the Delawares, galloped in front.

Before riding the full distance the question was determined. The object seen was the body of a white horse. A closer examination showed that it had been shot within the past few days, while the brand, U. S., proved that it was a government animal. Major Elliot then remembered that while at Fort Sedgwick he had seen one company of cavalry mounted upon white horses. These and other circumstances went far to convince us that this was one of the horses belonging to Lieutenant Kidder's party. In fact there was no room to doubt that this was the case.

Almost the unanimous opinion of the command was that there had been a contest with Indians, and this only the first evidence we should have proving it. When the column reached the point where the slain horse lay, a halt was ordered, to enable Comstock and the Indian scouts to thoroughly examine the surrounding ground to discover, if possible, any additional evidence, such as empty cartridge shells, arrows, or articles of Indian equipment, showing that a fight had taken place. All the horse equipments, saddle, bridle, etc., had been carried away, but whether by friend or foe could not then be determined. While the preponderance of circumstances favored the belief that the horse had been killed by the Indians, there was still room to hope that he had been killed by Kidder's party and the equipments taken away by them; for it frequently happens on a march that a horse will be suddenly taken ill and be unable for the time being to proceed further. In such a case, rather than abandon him alive, with a prospect of his recovering and falling into the hands of the Indians to be employed against us, orders are given to kill him, and this might be the true way of accounting for the one referred to.

The scouts being unable to throw any additional light upon the question, we continued our march, closely observing the ground as we passed along. Comstock noticed that instead of the trail showing that Kidder's party was moving in regular order, as when at first discovered, there were but two or three tracks to be seen in the beaten trail, the rest being found on the grass on either side.

We had marched two miles perhaps from the point where the body of the slain horse had been discovered, when we came upon a second, this one, like the first, having been killed by a bullet, and all of his equipments taken away. Comstock's quick eyes were not long in detecting pony tracks in the vicinity, and we had no longer any but the one frightful solution to offer: Kidder and his party had been discovered by the Indians, probably the same powerful and bloodthirsty band which had been resisted so gallantly by the men under Robbins and Cook; and against such overwhelming odds the issue could not be doubtful.

We were then moving over a high and level plateau, unbroken either by ravines or divides, and just such a locality as would be usually chosen by the Indians for attacking a party of the strength of Kidder's. The Indians could here ride unobstructed and encircle their victims with a continuous line of armed and painted warriors, while the beleaguered party, from the even character of the surface of the plain, would be unable to find any break or depression from behind which they might make a successful defence. It was probably this relative condition of affairs which had induced Kidder and his doomed comrades to endeavor to push on in the hope of finding ground favorable to their making a stand against their barbarous foes.

The main trail no longer showed the footprints of Kidder's party, but instead Comstock discovered the tracks of shod horses on the grass, with here and there numerous tracks of ponies, all by their appearance proving that both horses and ponies had been moving at full speed. Kidder's party must have trusted their lives temporarily to the speed of their horses—a dangerous venture when contending with Indians. However, this fearful race for life must have been most gallantly contested, because we continued our march several miles further without discovering any evidence of the savages having gained any advantage.

How painfully, almost despairingly exciting must have been this ride for life! A mere handful of brave men struggling to escape the bloody clutches of the hundreds of red-visaged demons who, mounted on their well-trained war ponies, were straining every nerve and muscle to steep their hands in the life-blood of their victims. It was not death alone that threatened this little band. They were not riding simply to preserve life. They rode, and doubtless prayed as they rode, that they might escape the savage tortures, the worse than death which threatened them. Would that their prayer had been granted!

We began leaving the high plateau and to descend into a valley, through which, at the distance of nearly two miles, meandered a small prairie stream known as Beaver Creek. The valley near the banks of this stream was covered with a dense growth of tall wild grass intermingled with clumps of osiers. At the point where the trail crossed the stream, we hoped to obtain more definite information regarding Kidder's party and their pursuers, but we were not required to wait so long. When within a mile of the stream I observed several large buzzards floating lazily in circles through the air, and but a short distance to the left of our trail. This, of itself, might not have attracted my attention seriously, but for the rank stench which pervaded the atmosphere, reminding one of the horrible sensations experienced upon a battle-field when passing among the decaying bodies of the dead.

As if impelled by one thought, Comstock, the Delawares, and half a dozen officers, detached themselves from the column, and separating into squads of one or two, instituted a search for the cause of our horrible suspicions. After riding in all directions through the rushes and willows, when about to relinquish the search as fruitless, one of the Delawares uttered a shout which attracted the attention of the entire command ; at the same time he was seen to leap from his horse and assume a stooping posture, as if critically examining some object of interest. Hastening, in common with many others of the party, to his side, a sight met our gaze which even at this remote day makes my very blood curdle. Lying in irregular order, and within a very limited circle, were the mangled bodies of poor Kidder and his party, yet so brutally hacked and disfigured as to be beyond recognition save as human beings.

Every individual of the party had been scalped, and his skull broken—the latter done by some weapon, probably a tomahawk—except the Sioux chief Red Bead, whose scalp had simply been removed from his head and then thrown down by his side. This, Comstock informed us, was in accordance with a custom which prohibits an Indian from bearing off the scalp of one of his own tribe. This circumstance, then, told us who the perpetrators of the deed were. They could be none other than the Sioux, led in all probability by Pawnee Killer.

Red Bead being less disfigured and mutilated than the others, was the only individual capable of being recognized. Even the clothes of all the party had been carried away ; some of the bodies were lying in beds of ashes, with partly burned fragments of wood near them, showing that the savage had put some of them to death by the terrible tortures of fire. The sinews of the arms and legs had been cut away, the nose of every man hacked off, and the features otherwise defaced so that it would have been scarcely possible for even a relative to recognize a single one of the unfortunate victims. We could not even distinguish the officer from his men. Each body was pierced by from twenty to fifty arrows, and the arrows were found as the savage demons had left them, bristling in the bodies. While the details of that fearful struggle will probably never be known, telling how long and gallantly this ill-fated little band contended for their lives, yet the surrounding circumstances of ground, empty cartridge shells, and distance from where the attack began, satisfied us that Kidder and his men fought as only brave men fight when the watchword is victory or death.

As the officer, his men, and his no less faithful Indian guide, had shared their final dangers together and met the same dreadful fate at the hands of the same merciless foe, it was but fitting that their remains should be consigned to one common grave. This was accordingly done. A single trench was dug near the spot where they had rendered up their lives upon the altar of duty. Silently, mournfully, their comrades of a brother regiment consigned their mangled remains to mother earth, there to rest undisturbed, as we supposed, until the great day of final review. But this was not to be so: while the closest scrutiny on our part had been insufficient to enable us to detect the slightest evidence which would aid us or others in identifying the body of Lieutenant Kidder or any of his men, it will be seen hereafter how the marks of a mother's thoughtful affection were to be the means of finding the remains of her murdered son, even though months had elapsed after his untimely death.

This sequel to the story mentioned by Custer is told by him in narrating subsequent events. It seems that Mr. Kidder, father of the lieutenant, came west in search of the body of his son, and learned that only a single mark remained, by which to identify any of the bodies except that of Red Bead. The incident occurred at Fort Leavenworth in the winter of 1867. Custer thus describes the interview.

Mr. Kidder, after introducing himself, announced the object of his visit; it was to ascertain the spot where the remains of his son lay buried, and, after procuring suitable military escort to proceed to the grave and disinter his son's remains preparatory to transferring them to a resting place in Dakota, of which territory he was at that time one of the judiciary. It was a painful task I had to perform when I communicated to the father the details of the killing of his son and followers. And equally harassing to the feelings was it to have to inform him that there was no possible chance for his being able to recognize his son's remains. "Was there not the faintest mark or fragment of his uniform by which he might be known?" inquired the anxious parent. "Not one," was the reluctant reply. "And yet, since I now recall the appearance of the mangled and disfigured remains, there was a mere trifle which attracted my attention, but it could not have been your son who wore it." "What was it?" eagerly inquired the father. "It was simply the collar-band of one of those ordinary check overshirts so commonly worn on the plains, the color being black and white; the remainder of the garment, as well as all other articles of dress, having been torn or burned from the body." Mr. Kidder then requested me to repeat the description of the collar and material of which it was made; happily I had some cloth of very similar appearance, and upon exhibiting this to Mr. Kidder, to show the kind I meant, he declared that the body I referred to could be no other than that of his murdered son. He went on to tell how his son had received his appointment in the army but a few weeks before his lamentable death, he only having reported for duty with his company a few days before being sent on the scout which terminated his life; and how, before leaving his home to engage in the military service, his mother, with that thoughtful care and tenderness which only a mother can feel, prepared some articles of wearing apparel,

among others a few shirts made from the checked material
already described. Mr. Kidder had been to Fort Sedgwick,
on the Platte, from which post his son had last departed, and
there learned that on leaving the post he wore one of the
checked shirts and put an extra one in his saddle pockets.
Upon this trifling link of evidence Mr. Kidder proceeded four
hundred miles west to Fort Wallace, and there being furnished
with military escort, visited the grave containing the bodies of
the twelve massacred men. Upon disinterring the remains a
body was found as I had described it, bearing the simple checked
collar-band ; the father recognized the remains of his son, and
thus, as was previously stated, was the evidence of a mother's
love made the means by which her son's body was recognized
and reclaimed, when all other had failed.

In closing this episode, which gives a realizing idea of the
terrible nature of Indian warfare, it may interest the reader to
know that the engraving which illustrates it was executed under
the personal supervision of General Custer himself, during his
life, as well as that representing the attack on the train. They
give a truthful idea of two representative scenes, one the Indian
method of battle, the other the appearance of Indian victims.
It will be noticed that the slain have their throats cut. This is
one of the marks by which the scouts knew that the Sioux had
done it. The Arapahoes mark their victims by slitting the
right arm, others in other manners.

It has often excited enquiry as well as horror in white men,
to know the reason that the present Indians of the plains per-
petrate these mutilations on the bodies of their slain ; and the
records seem to point to great exasperation of feeling for the
principal cause. In the battles of the last century, between
the wood-Indians and the whites, as well as those in the early
part of the present cycle, between the prairie-Indians and the
hardy hunters of the Fur Companies, it is very rare to hear of
these refinements of mutilation. The slain were scalped, and
living prisoners were generally taken to the villages for tortures

which, however cruel, possessed a certain nobility of cruelty, and lacked those peculiarly debasing and disgusting features which mark the modern Indian of the plains. Catlin, Bonne-ville, Kendall, Lewis and Clark, and all those early voyagers who crossed the plains, down to the days of Fremont, record no such atrocities in their few contests with Indians, and leave, on the whole, a decidedly favorable impression of the savage character. At the present day, there is no doubt that such things are common, and the real reason is not far to seek, judging from the circumstances surrounding both periods. I am very strongly inclined to ascribe these mutilations to a mixture of *hatred* and *contempt*, produced by the different nature of the present contests from those waged up to the year 1850. In the past century in the woods, and up to 1850 on the plains, the Indians were principally fought by frontiersmen and veteran regulars, men of physical strength generally superior to the Indians, better shots, nearly as good riders, and their superiors in hand to hand fights. Above all things, savages respect physical prowess and courage, and there are strong indications that they were so proud to take the scalp of a brave white man, in the days when they respected him, that they scorned to otherwise mutilate his body when dead.

Now the case is reversed. They know that, man to man, almost all the green recruits in the regular army *fear them*, and the frontiersmen they meet and mutilate are no longer brave *hunters*, but, in their eyes, despicable *tillers of the ground*. Hating and despising these men as cowards and plodders, yet finding themselves, slowly but surely, yielding to these loathed creatures, they take the same satisfaction in hacking them to pieces that many white men and boys do in beating a snake. This view comes out plainly in the Kidder massacre. The warriors mutilated his party, because it ran in the first place, and allowed them to conquer it in the second. The only man partially respected was the chief Red Bead, probably because he was the bravest there.]

CHAPTER V.

THE COURT MARTIAL.

CUSTER, who had come from the east with much experience and more previous success as a cavalry general, had speedily discovered, while on the plains, the difference between fighting civilized foes and Indians. No doubt he had frequently been reminded of this difference, and of the experience of older officers, in his intercourse with his official superiors. He was now to experience the further difference between getting along with a regiment in time of war, formal and declared, and the same body in time of nominal and legal peace, but of actual hostilities. The occasion of his trouble was during the search for Lieutenant Kidder's remains, and is thus described by himself:

In a previous chapter reference has been made to the state of dissatisfaction which had made its appearance among the enlisted men. This state of feeling had been principally superinduced by inferior and insufficient rations, a fault for which no one connected with the troops in the field was responsible, but which was chargeable to persons far removed from the theatre of our movements, persons connected with the supply departments of the army. Added to this internal source of disquiet, we were then on the main line of overland travel to some of our most valuable and lately discovered mining regions. The opportunity to obtain marvelous wages as miners and the prospect of amassing sudden wealth proved a temptation sufficiently strong to make many of the men forget their sworn obligations to their government and their duty as soldiers. Forgetting for a moment that the command to which they belonged was actually engaged in war, and was in a country infested with armed bodies of the enemy, and that the legal penalty of desertion under such circumstances was death, many of the men formed a combination to desert their colors and escape to the mines.

The first intimation received by any person in authority of the existence of this plot, was on the morning fixed for our departure from the Platte. Orders had been issued the previous evening for the command to march at daylight. Upwards of forty men were reported as having deserted during the night. There was no time to send parties in pursuit, or the capture and return of a portion of them might have been effected.

The command marched southward at daylight. At noon, having marched fifteen miles, we halted to rest and graze the horses for one hour. The men believed that the halt was made for the remainder of the day, and here a plan was perfected among the disaffected by which upwards of one-third of the effective strength of the command was to seize their horses and arms during the night and escape to the mountains. Had the conspirators succeeded in putting this plan into execution, it would have been difficult to say how serious the consequence might be, or whether enough true men would remain to render the march to Fort Wallace practicable. Fortunately it was decided to continue the march some fifteen miles further before night. The necessary orders were given and everything was being repacked for the march, when attention was called to thirteen soldiers who were then to be seen rapidly leaving camp in the direction from which we had marched. Seven of these were mounted and were moving off at a rapid gallop; the remaining six were dismounted, not having been so fortunate as their fellows in procuring horses. The entire party were still within sound of the bugle, but no orders by bugle note or otherwise served to check or diminish their flight. The boldness of this attempt at desertion took every one by surprise. Such an occurrence as enlisted men deserting in broad daylight and under the immediate eyes of their officers had never been heard of. With the exception of the horses of the guard and a few belonging to the officers, all others were still grazing and unsaddled. The officer of the guard was directed to mount his command promptly, and if possible overtake the deserters. At the same time those of the officers whose horses were in readiness were also directed to join the pursuit and leave no effort untried to prevent the escape of a single malcontent. In giving each party sent in pursuit instructions, there was no limit fixed to the measures which they were authorized to adopt in executing their orders. This, unfortunately, was an emergency, which involved the safety of the entire command, and required treatment of the most summary character.

It was found impossible to overtake that portion of the party which was mounted, as it was afterward learned that they had selected seven of the fleetest horses in the command. Those on foot, when discovering themselves pursued, increased their speed, but a chase of a couple of miles brought the pursuers within hailing distance.

Major Elliot, the senior officer participating in the pursuit, called out to the deserters to halt and surrender. This command was several times repeated, but without effect. Finally, seeing the hopelessness of further flight, the deserters came to bay, and to Major Elliot's renewed demand to throw down their arms and surrender, the ringleader drew up his carbine to fire upon his pursuers. This was the signal for the latter to open fire, which they did successfully, bringing down three of the deserters, although two of them were worse frightened than hurt.

Rejoining the command with their six captive deserters, the pursuing party reported their inability to overtake those who had deserted on horseback. The march was resumed and continued until near nightfall, by which time we had placed thirty miles between us and our last camp on the Platte. While on the march during the day, a trusty sergeant, one who had served as a soldier long and faithfully, imparted the first information which could be relied upon as to the plot which had been formed by the malcontents to desert in a body. The following night had been selected as the time for making the attempt. The best horses and arms in the command were to be seized and taken away. I believed that the summary action adopted during the day would intimidate any who might still be contemplating desertion, and was confident that another day's march would place us so far in a hostile and dangerous country, that the risk of encountering war parties of Indians would of itself serve to deter any but large numbers from attempting to make their way back to the settlements. To bridge the following night in safety was the next problem. While there was undoubtedly a large proportion of the men who could be fully relied upon to remain true to their obligations and to render any support to their officers which might be demanded, yet the great difficulty at this time, owing to the sudden development of the plot, was to determine who could be trusted.

The difficulty was solved by placing every officer in the command on guard during the night. The men were assembled as usual for roll-call at tattoo, and then notified that every man must be in his tent at the signal " taps," which would be sounded half an hour later; that their company officers, fully armed, would walk the company streets during the entire night, and any man appearing outside the limits of his tent between the hours of " taps " and reveille would do so at the risk of being fired upon after being once hailed.

The night passed without disturbance, and daylight found us in the saddle and pursuing our line of march toward Fort Wallace.

The lesson given by Custer as thus told by him was sufficient. No further attempt was made at desertion. After the finding of the bodies of Lieutenant Kidder's party, the column proceeded on its way. It will be remembered that the telegraphic orders of General Sherman from Fort Sedgwick had directed Custer to go to Fort Wallace.

His proceedings after reaching that point we note, because, in connection with the shooting of the deserters, they constituted the ground of his second court martial. The humorous commencement and ending of the first, on Custer's graduation from West Point, will be remembered. Thoughtless violation of military rule got him into trouble then. A very different course of conduct took him into similar trouble now. He tells his own story as frankly as ever.

On the evening, says he, of the day following that upon which we had consigned the remains of Lieutenant Kidder's party to their humble resting-place, the command reached Fort Wallace on the Smoky Hill route. From the occupants of the fort we learned much that was interesting regarding events which had transpired during our isolation from all points of communication. The Indians had attacked the fort twice within the past few days, in both of which engagements men were killed on each side. The fighting on our side was principally under the command of Colonel Barnitz, whose forces were composed of detachments of the Seventh Cavalry.

Our arrival at Fort Wallace was most welcome as well as opportune. The Indians had become so active and numerous that all travel over the Smoky Hill route had ceased; stages had been taken off the route, and many of the stage stations had been abandoned by the employees, the latter fearing a repetition of the Lookout Station massacre. No despatches or mail had been received at the fort for a considerable period, so that the occupants might well have been considered as undergoing a state of siege. Added to these embarrassments, which were partly unavoidable, an additional, and, under the circumstances, a more frightful danger, stared the troops in the face. We were over two hundred miles from the terminus of the railroad over which our supplies were drawn, and a still greater distance from the main dépots of supplies. It was found that the reserve of

26

stores at the post was well-nigh exhausted, and the commanding officer reported that he knew of no fresh supplies being on the way.

I decided to select upward of a hundred of the best mounted men in my command, and with this force open a way through to Fort Harker, a distance of two hundred miles, where I expected to obtain abundant supplies ; from which point the latter could be conducted, well protected against Indians by my detachment, back to Fort Wallace. Owing to the severe marching of the past few weeks, the horses of the command were generally in an unfit condition for further service without rest. So that after selecting upward of a hundred of the best, the remainder might for the time be regarded as unserviceable ; such they were in fact. There was no idea or probability that the portion of the command to remain in camp near Fort Wallace would be called upon to do anything but rest and recuperate from their late marches. It was certainly not expected that they would be molested or called out by Indians; nor were they. Regarding the duties to be performed by the picked detachment as being by far the most important, I chose to accompany it.

The immediate command of the detachment was given to Captain Hamilton, of whom mention has been previously made. He was assisted by two other officers. My intention was to push through from Fort Wallace to Fort Hays, a distance of about one hundred and fifty miles, as rapidly as was practicable ; then, being beyond the most dangerous portion of the route, to make the remainder of the march to Fort Harker with half a dozen troopers, while Captain Hamilton with his command should follow leisurely. Under this arrangement I hoped to have a train loaded with supplies at Harker, and in readiness to start for Fort Wallace, by the time Captain Hamilton should arrive.

Leaving Fort Wallace about sunset on the evening of the 15th of July, we began our ride eastward, following the line of the overland stage route. At that date the Kansas Pacific

Railway was only completed as far westward as Fort Harker. Between Forts Wallace and Harker we expected to find the stations of the overland stage company, at intervals of from ten to fifteen miles. In time of peace these stations are generally occupied by half a dozen employees of the route, embracing the stablemen and relays of drivers. They were well supplied with firearms and ammunition, and every facility for defending themselves against Indians. The stables were also the quarters for the men. They were usually built of stone, and one would naturally think that against Indians no better defensive work would be required. Yet such was not the case. The hay and other combustible material usually contained in them enabled the savages, by shooting prepared arrows, to easily set them on fire, and thus drive the occupants out to the open plain, where their fate would soon be settled. To guard against such an emergency, each station was ordinarily provided with what on the plains is termed a " dug-out." The name implies the character and description of the work. The " dug-out " was commonly located but a few yards from one of the corners of the stable, and was prepared by excavating the earth so as to form an opening not unlike a cellar, which was usually about four feet in depth, and sufficiently roomy to accommodate at close quarters half a dozen persons. This opening was then covered with logs, and loopholed on all sides at a height of a few inches above the original level of the ground. The earth was thrown on top until the " dug-out " resembled an ordinary mound of earth, some four of five feet in height. To the outside observer, no means apparently were provided for egress or ingress ; yet such was not the case. If the entrance had been made above ground, rendering it necessary for the defenders to pass from the stable unprotected to their citadel, the Indians would have posted themselves accordingly, and picked them off one by one as they should emerge from the stable. To provide against this danger, an underground passage was constructed in each case, leading from the " dug-out " to the interior of the stable. With these arrangements for defence a few determined men could withstand the attacks of an entire tribe of savages. The recent depredations of the Indians had so demoralized the men at the various stations, that many of the latter were found deserted, their former occupants having joined their forces with those of other stations. The Indians generally burned the deserted stations.

Almost at every station we received intelligence of Indians having been seen in the vicinity within a few days of our arrival. We felt satisfied they were watching our movements, although we saw no fresh signs of Indians until we arrived near Downer's station. Here, while stopping to rest our horses for a few minutes, a small party of our men, who had without authority halted some distance behind, came dashing into our midst, and reported that twenty-five or thirty Indians had attacked them some five or six miles in rear, and had killed two of their number. As there was a detachment of infantry guarding the station, and as time was important, we pushed on toward our destination. The two men reported killed were left to be buried by the troops on duty at the station. Frequent halts and brief rests were made along our line of march ; occasionally we would halt long enough to indulge in a few hours' sleep. About three o'clock on the morning of the 18th, we reached Fort Hays, having marched about one hundred and fifty miles in fifty-five hours, including all halts. Some may regard this as a rapid rate of marching ; in fact, a few officers of the army who themselves have made many and long marches (principally in ambulances and railroad cars) are of the same opinion. It was far above the usual rate of a leisurely made march, but during the same season with a larger command I marched sixty miles in fifteen hours. This was officially reported, but occasioned no remark. During the war, and at the time the enemy's cavalry under General J. E. B. Stuart made its famous raid around the Army of the Potomac in Maryland, a portion of our cavalry, accompanied by horse artillery, in attempting to overtake them, marched over ninety miles in twenty-four hours. A year subsequent to the events narrated in this chapter, I marched a small detachment eighty miles in seventeen hours, every horse accompanying the detachment completing the march in as fresh condition apparently as when the march began.

Leaving Hamilton and his command to rest one day at Hays and then to follow on leisurely to Fort Harker, I continued my ride to the latter post, accompanied by Colonels Cook and Custer and two troopers. We reached Fort Harker at two o'clock that night, having made the ride of sixty miles without change of animals in less than twelve hours. As this was the first telegraph station, I immediately sent telegrams to headquarters and to Fort Sedgwick, announcing the fate of Kidder and his party. General A. J. Smith, who was in command of this military district, had his headquarters at Harker. I at once reported to him in person, and acquainted him with every incident worthy of mention which had occurred in connection with my command, since leaving him, weeks before. Arrangements were made for the arrival of Hamilton's party and for a train containing supplies to be sent back under their escort. Having made my report to General Smith as my next superior officer, and there being no occasion for my presence until the train and escort should be in readiness to return, *I applied for and received authority to visit Fort Riley, about ninety miles east of Harker by rail, where my family was then located.*

So ends Custer's story. The civilian reader, who has perused the account, will think nothing very wicked was done. Yet, for the events narrated in this chapter, Custer was actually court-martialed, tried, and sentenced to be suspended from rank and pay for a whole year. In the very last sentence of the above frank account, the part quoted in italics, the officers at the time set over him found the whole wickedness.

Charges were brought against him on two counts: first, for leaving Fort Wallace without permission, marching his men excessively, allowing two of them to be killed, and losing several United States horses—all *in a journey on private business:* second, for excessive cruelty and illegal conduct in putting down mutiny in the Seventh, by shooting the deserters.

The second charge was not, however, seriously pressed: it was the first on which his enemies relied, and on which they obtained the conviction and sentence. The one inexcusable sin which Custer had committed, in the estimation of the military authorities, was going to Fort Riley to see his wife, and the preparation of the charges was due to the ingenuity of one of his personal enemies, an officer who was soon after obliged to leave the service for drunkenness.

The court-martial now under notice, indeed, brings us to that part of Custer's life when he was first surrounded with those enemies who followed him ever after, and the course of his trial will well illustrate those future crosses, which were to develop him into one of the noblest characters of modern time. Hitherto, Custer had enjoyed a life of constant success. His labors had been altogether external, and had included no misfortunes nor serious set-backs. In the great Union Volunteer Army, where there were so many prizes, those which he gained had not excited that actively malignant envy which he afterwards experienced. Now, for the first time, he found the atmosphere changed, and also found the great and fundamental difference between the war service of a great army and the nominal peace service of a small one.

In the present regular army of the United States, the great trouble is found in the fact that its rewards are so few, its officers so numerous. The consequence is that this little army is the constant abiding place, to an extent of which civilians have little or no idea, of the most intense jealousy and envy from the majority towards every one who possesses any great military merit and has attained early distinction. The one fact, and the only one which commands respect in the regular army is *seniority*, and officers are forever computing their place on the list of their rank and calculating how soon they will "gain a step." Before and since the war, merit has no place in the promotions of the regular army, the rigid rule of seniority being inflexibly adhered to, no services, however brilliant, being allowed to confer a single step on the officer rendering them. The war changed all this for the time, and promoted, for merit alone, a few talented officers, of whom the most conspicuous at that time were Sherman, Sheridan and Custer. As a matter of course, all three of these officers were then, and are to-day, hated most cordially by most other officers, especially by those who graduated from West Point before them and found them-selves at the close of the war junior to them. The system was to blame for this as much as the men, and inevitably tended to breed the feeling. The tendency of the seniority rule is and always has been to enervate and destroy military spirit. It offers a premium to all the lazy ones, the skulkers, the cowards, to keep out of danger themselves, to do anything that promises to keep themselves alive and to kill off every senior in their rank, so that they may "gain steps." Not an Indian fight comes off, not an attack of yellow fever visits a post, but every officer in the army falls to calculating how many "steps" he will gain by so many deaths. Towards the regular "seniority seniors" as they may be called—men who have gained their present rank by living long enough, keeping up respectability the while—no animosity seems to exist among the juniors. The expectants are always looking for another death to give them "a step." It is the men of brilliant talent, the real born soldiers, the successful ones of the war, that they hate, and how bitterly they hate them soon appears when a group of juniors get to drinking freely. Then the spite, envy, and jealousy, restrained at other times by official reticence and *esprit de corps*, break out ; and it is rare, very rare, almost unknown, to hear from army officers a single word of frank generous praise of their seniors. They can talk as much ill-natured gossip as fashionable women at a society ball, and for the same reason, each and all, *jealousy.*

The close of the Indian campaign of 1867 was the first experience which came to Custer of the effects of this feeling, and from henceforth it dogged him all his life. In the present instance, the charges were presented by an officer of his own regiment whom he had been compelled to place in arrest for repeated drunkenness on duty, and who afterwards had to leave the service for similar offences. They were carefully and ingeniously drawn, and the acts of Custer himself gave them a color of reason. He *had* left Fort Wallace without direct orders, but governed by military necessity; he *had* made a tremendous march; and some of his men *were* killed; and all the main facts were as alleged. The only doubt was as to the intention. Custer in his defence showed that he was acting under the last orders he had received—those from General Sherman—which were to *move towards Fort Wallace to meet General Hancock, who would give him further orders.* He showed that when he reached Fort Wallace Hancock had already passed through, and that he thought it his duty to follow him personally, to obtain his orders for the future prosecution of the campaign. He showed that while his main command was temporarily quite unfit for active work, the picked detachment he took with him was quite equal to the march, and that he had acted for the best in his journey, to save his men at Fort Wallace from threatened starvation. He showed how, when he arrived at Fort Harker, he found that General Hancock had actually closed the campaign and retired to Fort Leavenworth, and how all his labor had been useless. He showed how he had received express permission from his district commander to go to Fort Riley. He showed in fact, in his written defence, that, whatever the appearance of his actions, he had done all in the very spirit as well as letter of the last verbal orders he had received from General Sherman, and he asserted that he should certainly do the like again, were he placed in a similar dilemma with similar orders. He pointed out how he might certainly have been charged with cowardice and inefficiency had he remained idly at Fort Wallace, letting his command rot away piecemeal.

All his defence was in vain. The Indian campaign of 1867 was a ridiculous failure, and every army officer in the department felt sore and angry. It was necessary to find a victim, a scapegoat, some one to court-martial, some one to hold up as the cause of failure. In this instance Custer was the man selected. For very decency, the court could not find any criminality in his manner of treating the mutineers of the Seventh, but on the first charge and all its important specifications they found him guilty of making the journey on private business, and therefore of a serious breach of discipline. Consequently he was sentenced to be suspended from rank and pay for a whole year.

Either this sentence was too severe or too light. Had all the accusations been true, and had Custer really made the journey he did on private business, he ought to have been dismissed the service, no matter what his previous record. The lives of brave soldiers are too precious to be sacrificed for the private business of any one, however distinguished. That such could have been his motive is contradicted alike by his earnest protest, and his previous and subsequent record. He never had done such a thing before, and never did after. No man was ever found more thorough and devoted to his ideas of duty. True, he was given to exercising his own judgment and discretion as to the proper mode of executing an order, a privilege allowed to all general officers, especially those of the cavalry. At Winchester and at Sailor's Creek, when receiving an order to charge at a wrong place or an unpropitious moment, he had assumed the responsibility of choosing his own time, and events had justified him fully. He had the example of the great Prussian cavalry chief, Seydlitz, as a precedent, and that of many another great cavalry officer. Seydlitz, waiting for his moment at Rossbach (1757), received an order from the king, Frederick the Great, to charge; and sent back word that he would prefer to choose his own moment if his majesty would permit him. His conduct was approved by the king, and has since been justified by the customs of war.

In Custer's present case the worst that could be alleged of him on the evidence was an error of judgment, for it was obvious that he fully believed, all the while, that he was doing right and obeying orders. Such an error of judgment would have been amply covered by a reprimand; while a willful disobedience of orders, prompted only by private business, could not have been punished too severely. As it was, the court-martial, like all similar bodies, took a middle course. It was necessary to punish some one to silence public sneers, and Custer was the most convenient scapegoat; so they degraded him, on a flimsy pretence, in 1867, as he was again degraded on a still more flimsy pretext, nine years later, by another person. They found him guilty of the charges involving disobedience of orders, and gave him such an inadequate sentence for such a heinous offence, that even General Grant, reviewing the sentence at a distance, was compelled to notice the fact, and announced that he presumed the court had been so merciful on account of the past services rendered by the accused.

So Custer was degraded, and his enemies were for a brief space triumphant. Every elderly respectability in the army, every fossil with the sole merit of long service, every senior who had enjoyed the sweets of bureau duty during the war, every envious drunkard in the army, crowed over the victory, and hugged himself to think that this pushing Custer, this desperate marcher and fighter, this incarnation of restless activity, was out of the way at last, for a year at all events.

His absence then was a wonderful relief, as his death is now, to that numerous class of officers who " make a convenience of the service," who are always studying how little they can do with respectability, to whom such men as Custer are a constant silent reproach. How they chuckled over the disgrace of this "lucky fellow" this "favorite," this "pet." Truly their turn had come at last and for a while they were happy.

After a few months, however, things began to look a little less smooth for "convenience men." Unluckily for them, behind the army lies the great body of tax-payers, who do not admire the "convenience men," and even apply to them such ignominious slang terms as "dead beats" and "useless soldiers." The great body of tax-payers began to growl, through the medium of some impudent newspapers, and the criticisms on the management of the Indian campaign were the reverse of complimentary. The result was that General Sheridan was ordered to take command of this Indian country, and he arrived at Fort Leavenworth, where Custer was tried, just after the promulgation of the sentence. Sheridan, as we well know, had a pretty fair acquaintance with the merits of Custer, and was likely to understand his case. What he thought of it is evinced by a single circumstance, though etiquette closed his lips from criticism of trial or sentence.

When he arrived, he found Custer a disgraced man, out of the service for a year, with no right to quarters and no apparent resource but to go away to Monroe. Sheridan, as department commander, possessed a suite of apartments at Fort Leavenworth, and he insisted on Custer's occupation of these, just as long as he pleased; so that instead of being sent home in disgrace, the young culprit found himself just where he was before, with the sole exception that he was free from duty. Hardly could Sheridan have displayed in a more pointed manner, without speaking, his conviction of the injustice and malice of the action in Custer's case than he thus did, and the action is one of the bravest and most creditable of all the brave deeds of that frank, outspoken soldier, whose motto, like Custer's, might well be "*Nescio mentire.*"

With Sheridan for his friend, possessing the active sympathy of every good officer in his own regiment, and finally seeing the remorse even of his reckless accuser, Custer could well afford to

pass the winter at Leavenworth.   It was not till the spring that
he began to experience the real miseries of his position.   When
the Indian campaign came on, and he was compelled to see the
regiment depart for active service, while he staid behind, then
indeed he could no longer bear his position at the scene of action.
He broke up his household and returned to Monroe, which he
reached in June.   The time was coming, though he knew it
not, for the greatest triumph of his life.   Hitherto, the seniority
element had had its own way.   This summer was to prove
whether seniority or merit is the best ally in fighting an
active enemy.

CHAPTER VI.

THE WINTER CAMPAIGN.

IT can hardly be said that Custer did penance for his misdeeds in leaving Fort Wallace, by indulgence in sackcloth and ashes to any great extent. He retained, at this period of his life, a great deal of the boy's nature with which he had started. He had gone into his troubles regardless of the consequences, and having encountered them, was bound to make the best of it. As he tells us, while his regiment, under command of General Sully, as part of a large expedition, was studying how to kill Indians, Custer himself was trying to kill time. He pursues with his usual naivette :

" My campaign was a decided success. I established my base of operations in a most beautiful little town on the western shores of Lake Erie, from which I projected various hunting, fishing, and boating expeditions. With abundance of friends and companions, and ample success, time passed pleasantly enough ; yet with all there was a constant longing to be with my comrades in arms in the far West, even while aware of the fact that their campaign was not resulting in any material advantage. I had no reason to believe that I would be permitted to rejoin them until the following winter."

During the time of Custer's enforced retirement, the Indian war languished. In the summer of 1868 General Sully, with the Seventh Cavalry and some infantry, marched against the combined Cheyennes, Arapahoes and Kiowas, whom he struck near the present site of Camp Supply. After quite an animated fight, General Sully gave up the attempt to proceed further, and retired, substantially defeated.   This was in the Indian Territory, not far from the north-western border of Texas.   At the same time that Sully was operating down there, General " Sandy " Forsyth, with a company of scouts and plainsmen, enlisted for special purposes, was scouting to the north round the Forks of the Republican, the same country where Custer had met Pawnee Killer the previous year.   After some successes, Forsyth's party was at last surrounded by the Sioux, and besieged in a little island, where the scouts lost all their horses, six men killed, eight crippled for life, and twelve more wounded, out of a total of fifty-one men, the rest being only saved from total annihilation by the arrival of reinforcements.

Altogether, the summer campaign against both Northern and Southern Indians had been a failure.   The troops had lost men and prestige, the Indians had lost nothing but men killed in action.   The fight with Forsyth took place the third week in September, and the fact of his being desperately wounded rendered it impossible to rely on him for any more work, while General Sully was getting too old for real active service against such foes as the Indians.   It was on the 24th of September that Custer, who was then at Monroe, received the following telegram :

"HEADQUARTERS DEPARTMENT OF THE MISSOURI,
IN THE FIELD, FORT HAYS, KANSAS, September 24, 1868.

"General G. A. CUSTER, Monroe, Michigan:
Generals Sherman, Sully, and myself, and nearly all the officers of your regiment, have asked for you, and I hope the application will be successful.   Can you come at once ?   Eleven companies of your regiment will move about the 1st of October against the hostile Indians, from Medicine Lodge creek towards the Wichita mountains.
P. H. SHERIDAN, Major-General Commanding."

It may surprise the reader to hear that Custer, if he obeyed this request, disobeyed the letter of the law just as much as when he left Fort Wallace without orders, a proceeding which cost him a year's retirement, owing to the strictures of red tape. He had been by the War Department especially enjoined from taking command of his regiment; and his sentence had been approved by the President. No less authority could give him leave to go into the field. However, he decided to take the risk of Sheridan's application being refused, and accordingly started at once. It was almost worth a court-martial and a year's retirement to receive such a despatch. Red tape and envy had sent him home, and tried to get along without him, but red tape and envy were found unequal to the tasks of war. Like law, red tape is all very nice while people choose to submit to it, but it depends on the consent of the governed. In the case of the Indians, as in the case of the Confederates, it proved useless, for both spurned it. A *man* was wanted, and they had to send for Custer.

He telegraphed to Sheridan that he was coming by the next train, and by the next train he went. He was overtaken at a way station by a telegram from the adjutant-general of the army, directing him to report to Sheridan, so that, for this once, red tape yielded gracefully, and legalized his journey. The rest of his story we shall tell briefly and as much in his own words as possible.

"Arriving at Fort Hays," says Custer, "on the morning of the 30th, I found General Sheridan, who had transferred his headquarters temporarily from Fort Leavenworth to that point, in order to be nearer the field of operations. My regiment was at that time on or near the Arkansas River, in the vicinity of Fort Dodge, and about three easy marches from Fort Hays. After remaining at General Sheridan's headquarters one day and receiving his instructions, I set out with a small escort across the country to Fort Dodge to resume command of my regiment. Arriving at Fort Dodge without incident, I found General Sully, who at that time was in command of the district in which my regiment was serving. With the exception of a few detachments, the main body of the regiment was encamped on Bluff

Creek, a small tributary of the Arkansas, the camp being some thirty miles southeast from Fort Dodge. Taking with me the detachment at the fort, I proceeded to the main camp, arriving there in the afternoon."

He found his regiment practically in a state of siege, the Indians having become so impudent that they fired into the pickets almost every afternoon, and made the vicinity of the camp decidedly dangerous.

His arrival changed matters materially. All that the troops needed was a man like Custer at their head, one who was not afraid of the enemy. The afternoon of his arrival was distinguished by a skirmish, and the very same night he inaugurated the first scout against the Indians in which the regiment had indulged since General Sully's repulse. Four squadrons were sent out in different directions, each accompanied by scouts, and it is on this occasion that we are first introduced to Custer's great subsequent ally and friend, California Joe, whom he here appointed chief of scouts. He thus describes the meeting, in which Joe received news of his promotion:

"After the official portion of the interview had been completed, it seemed proper to Joe's mind, that a more intimate acquaintance between us should be cultivated, as we had never met before. His first interrogatory, addressed to me in furtherance of this idea, was frankly put as follows:

"'See hyar, Gineral, in order that we hev no misonderstandin', I'd jest like to ask ye a few questions.'

"Seeing that I had somewhat of a character to deal with, I signified my perfect willingness to be interviewed by him.

"'Air you an ambulance man, ur a hoss man?'

"Pretending not to discover his meaning, I requested him to explain.

"'I mean do you b'leve in catchin' Injuns in ambulances or on hossback?'

"Still assuming ignorance, I replied, 'Well, Joe, I believe in catching Indians wherever we can find them, whether they are found in ambulances or on horseback.' This did not satisfy him.

"'That ain't what I'm drivin' at. S'pose you're after Injuns and really want to hev a tussle with 'em, would ye start after 'em on hossback, or would ye climb into an ambulance and be hauled after 'em? That's the pint I'm headin' fur.'

"I answered that I would prefer the method on horseback, provided I really desired to catch the Indians; but if I wished them to catch me, I would adopt the ambulance system of attack.

"This reply seemed to give him complete satisfaction.

"'You've hit the nail squar on the hed. I've bin with 'em on the plains whar they started out after the Injuns on wheels, jist as ef they war goin' to a town funeral in the states, an' they stood 'bout as many chances uv catchin' Injuns az a six-mule team wud uv catchin' a pack of thievin' Ki-o-tees, jist as much. Why that sort uv work is only fun fur the Injuns; they don't want anything better. Ye ort to've seen how they peppered it to us, an' we a doin' nuthin' a' the time. Sum uv 'em wuz 'fraid the mules war goin' to stampede and run off with the train an' all our forage and grub, but that wuz impossible; fur besides the big loads uv corn an' bacon an' baggage the wagons hed in them, thar war from eight to a dozen infantry men piled into them besides. Ye ort to hev heard the quartermaster in charge uv the train tryin' to drive the infantry men out of the wagons and git them into the fight. I 'spect he wuz an Irishman by his talk, fur he sed to them, "Git out uv thim wagons; yez'll hev me tried fur disobadience uv ordhers fur marchin' tin min in a wagon whin I've ordhers but fur ait!"'"

Joe's career as a chief scout was cut short. He got drunk the very first night, and another man was put in his place, but as a scout, pure and simple, he remained with Custer the rest of the campaign, and did good service.

The first night's expeditions found no Indians. They served however, to accustom the regiment to taking the aggressive

27

once more; and the Indians, finding the trails of the four parties, realized the fact that their enemies had ceased to fear
them.   The next move was to transfer the regiment from Bluff
Creek to Medicine Lodge Creek, which was done the day after.
The reason for the move was that the war-parties that annoyed
the camp were said to come from the direction of Medicine
Lodge Creek, and it was always Custer's instinct to beat up his
enemies in their own quarters.   As soon as he started out, the
waiting Indians charged his wagon train, which was in the
rear, and compelled him to detach two companies for a rear-
guard to repel their attacks.   Having driven them off without
halting, they abandoned the attempt to stop his march, and he
established a temporary camp at Medicine Lodge Creek.   After
scouting a few days in that vicinity, he marched the regiment
to Fort Dodge, on the Arkansas River, and put them into camp
on the 21st of October, 1868, where they remained till November 12th, when they started on the soon-to-be-famous Washita
campaign.

Custer made this halt in his movement for one purpose.
He had found on his arrival in camp, that the Seventh Cavalry
was not what it used to be.   So many of the old men had
deserted, encouraged by the fact that their commander had
been court-martialed for stopping desertion, and so many
recruits had been put in, that the regiment, as a whole, was
greener than when it started.   It was full enough as to numbers, but the men had not been drilled: they could not ride,
they could not shoot, and they were to be pitted against "the
best light cavalry in the world."   He saw plainly, that if he
wanted to get a regiment fit to fight the Indians, he must give it
a little training.   The three weeks' encampment at Fort Dodge
was accordingly devoted to the individual instruction of the
men in rifle shooting and riding; and, to secure emulation, he organized a picked body of forty men, to be called the sharpshooters, and to be selected from the men showing the best records of
shooting in the command.   These were commanded by Colonel

Cook, the same young officer who with Robbins, had defended the train the previous year. The horses of the regiment were then divided off into squadrons, each of a single color, and the result of all the preparations was that, on the 12th of November, 1868, Custer led out of camp a smart regiment of horse, able to give a good account of themselves. He had entirely remade the Seventh Cavalry, and he had laid the foundations of a regimental pride which was soon to be consolidated by the triumph of the Washita.

The question may now be asked, what was the object of moving out of camp into the Indian country at the very beginning of winter. Custer tells the reason in a few words. It was the policy of Sheridan, founded on rude common sense.

" We had crossed weapons with the Indians," says Custer, " time and again during the mild summer months, when the rich verdure of the valleys served as bountiful and inexhaustible granaries in supplying forage to their ponies, and the immense herds of buffalo and other variety of game roaming undisturbed all over the plains supplied all the food that was necessary to subsist the war parties, and at the same time to allow their villages to move freely from point to point ; and the experience of both officers and men went to prove that in attempting to fight Indians in the summer season we were yielding to them the advantages of climate and supplies—we were meeting them on ground of their own selection, and at a time when every natural circumstance controlling the result of a campaign was wholly in their favor; and as a just consequence the troops, in nearly all these contests with the red men, had come off second best.

" During the fall, when the buffaloes are in the best condition to furnish food, and the hides are suitable to be dressed as robes, or to furnish covering for the lodges, the grand annual hunts of the tribes take place, by which the supply of meat for the winter is procured. This being done, the chiefs determine upon the points at which the village shall be located ; if the tribe is a large one, the village is often subdivided, one portion or band remaining at one point, other portions choosing localities within a circuit of thirty or forty miles.

"Even during a moderate winter season, it is barely possible for the Indians to obtain sufficient food for their ponies to keep the latter in anything above a starving condition. Many of the ponies actually die from want of forage, while the remaining ones become so weak and attenuated that it requires several weeks of good grazing in the spring to fit them for service—particularly such service as is required from the war ponies. Guided by these facts, it was evident that if we chose to avail ourselves of the assistance of so exacting and terrible an ally as the frosts of winter—an ally who would be almost as uninviting to friends as to foes—we might deprive our enemy of his points of advantage, and force him to engage in a combat in which we should do for him what he had hitherto done for us; compel him to fight upon ground and under circumstances of our own selection. To decide upon making a winter campaign against the Indians was certainly in accordance with that maxim in the art of war which directs one to do that which the enemy neither expects nor desires to be done. At the same time it would dispel the old-fogy idea, which was not without supporters in the army, and which was confidently relied on by the Indians themselves, that the winter season was an insurmountable barrier to the prosecution of a successful campaign."

This policy of a winter campaign was inaugurated by General Sheridan; and Custer, with his old eager assent to anything requiring action, coöperated with him heartily. The regiment being in good trim, thirteen of the Osage Indians, a semi-civilized tribe living on their reservations, were engaged as scouts and the expedition started from Fort Dodge, November 12th.

It was well planned for success. A train of four hundred wagons, with a guard of infantry, was to accompany the Seventh Cavalry to the edge of the Indian country, and then establish a depot of supplies, from which the cavalry could move

out on a three or four days' march, with a secure basis on which
to fall back in "Camp Supply," as the new station was named.
Custer was not in command of the whole expedition, but General
eral Sully conducted the march in such a manner as to encounter
ter the least possible danger from any Indians that should attack
them while encumbered with this enormous supply train. Custer
ter thus describes the arrangements:

"The country over which we were to march was favorable to
us, as we were able to move our trains in four parallel columns
formed close together. This arrangement shortened our flanks
and rendered them less exposed to attack. The following
morning after reaching Mulberry Creek the march was resumed
soon after daylight, the usual order being: the four hundred
wagons of the supply train and those belonging to the troops
formed in four equal columns; in advance of the wagons at a
proper distance rode the advance guard of cavalry; a corresponding cavalry force formed the rear-guard. The remainder
of the cavalry was divided into three equal detachments; these
six detachments were disposed of along the flanks of the column, three on a side, maintaining a distance between themselves
and the train of from a quarter to a half mile, while each
of them had flanking parties thrown out opposite the train,
rendering it impossible for an enemy to appear in any direction
without timely notice being received. The infantry on beginning the march in the morning were distributed throughout the
train in such manner that should the enemy attack, their services could be rendered most effective. Unaccustomed, however, to field service, particularly marching, the infantry apparently were only able to march for a few hours in the early part
of the day, when, becoming weary, they would straggle from
their companions and climb into the covered wagons, from
which there was no determined effort to rout them. In the
afternoon there would be little evidence perceptible to the eye
that infantry formed any portion of the expedition, save here
and there the butt of a musket or point of a bayonet peeping

out from under the canvas wagon covers, or perhaps an officer of infantry, " treading alone his native heath," or better still, mounted on an Indian pony—the result of some barter with the Indians when times were a little more peaceable, and neither wars nor rumors of wars disturbed the monotony of garrison life."

Nothing of interest occurred, however, till the command reached Camp Supply, where it lay some days, when General Sheridan arrived. His arrival was the signal for Custer's emancipation from the control of General Sully, whose age and extreme caution had served as a continual curb on the fiery young chief of horse; and he narrates it with evident glee.

" Hearing of his near approach, I mounted my horse and was soon galloping beyond the limits of camp to meet him. If there were any persons in the command who hitherto had been in doubt as to whether the proposed winter campaign was to be a reality or otherwise, such persons soon had cause to dispel all mistrust on this point. Selecting from the train a sufficient number of the best teams and wagons to transport our supplies of rations and forage, enough to subsist the command upon for a period of thirty days, our arrangements were soon completed, by which the cavalry, consisting of eleven companies and numbering between eight and nine hundred men, were ready to resume the march. In addition, we were to be accompanied by a detachment of scouts, among the number being California Joe ; also our Indian allies from the Osage tribe, headed by Little Beaver and Hard Rope. As the country in which we were to operate was beyond the limits of the district which constituted the command of General Sully, that officer was relieved from further duty with the troops composing the expedition, and in accordance with his instructions withdrew from Camp Supply and returned to his headquarters at Fort Harker, Kansas, accompanied by Colonel Keogh, Seventh Cavalry, then holding the position of staff officer at district headquarters.

" After remaining at Camp Supply six days, nothing was re-

quired but the formal order directing the movement to commence. This came in the shape of a brief letter of instructions
from Department headquarters. Of course, as nothing was
known positively as to the exact whereabouts of the Indian villages, the instructions had to be general in terms. In substance,
I was to march my command in search of the winter hiding-
places of the hostile Indians, and wherever found, to administer
such punishment for past depredations as my force was able to.
On the evening of November 22d, orders were issued to be in
readiness to move promptly at daylight the following morning.
That night, in the midst of other final preparations for a long
separation from all means of communication with absent friends,
most of us found time to hastily pen a few parting lines, informing them of our proposed expedition, and the uncertainties
with which it was surrounded, as none of us knew when or
where we should be heard from again, once we bade adieu to
the bleak hospitalities of Camp Supply. It began snowing the
evening of the 22d, and continued all night, so that when the
shrill notes of the bugle broke the stillness of the morning air
at reveille on the 23d, we awoke at four o'clock to find the
ground covered with snow to a depth of over one foot, and the
storm still raging in full force. Surely this was anything but
an inviting prospect as we stepped from our frail canvas shel-
ters and found ourselves standing in the constantly and rapidly
increasing depth of snow which appeared in every direction.

"'How will this do for a winter campaign?' was the half
sarcastic query of the adjutant, as he came trudging back to
the tent through a field of snow extending almost to the top of
his tall troop boots, after having received the reports of the
different companies at reveille. 'Just what we want,' was the
reply. Little grooming did the shivering horses receive from
the equally uncomfortable troopers that morning. Breakfast
was served and disposed of more as a matter of form and regulation than to satisfy the appetite. It still lacked some minutes
of daylight when the various commanders reported their com-

mands in readiness to move, save the final act of saddling the horses. While they were thus employed, I improved the time to gallop through the darkness across the narrow plain to the tents of General Sheridan, and say good-by. I found the headquarter tents wrapped in silence, and at first imagined that no one was yet stirring except the sentinel in front of the General's tent, who kept up his lonely tread, apparently indifferent to the beating storm. But I had no sooner given the bridle-rein to my orderly than the familiar tones of the General called out, letting me know that he was awake, and had been an attentive listener to our notes of preparation. His first greeting was to ask what I thought about the snow and the storm. To which I replied that nothing could be more to our purpose. We could move and the Indian villages could not. With an earnest injunction from my chief to keep him informed, if possible, should anything important occur, and many hearty wishes for a successful issue to the campaign, I bade him adieu. By the time I rejoined my men they had saddled their horses and were in readiness for the march. ' To horse' was sounded, and each trooper stood at his horse's head. Then followed the commands 'Prepare to mount' and 'Mount,' when nothing but the signal 'Advance' was required to put the column in motion. The band took its place at the head of the column, preceded by the guides and scouts, and when the march began it was to the familiar notes of that famous old marching tune, ' The girl I left behind me.' "

The Washita campaign was begun.

THE BATTLE OF THE WASHITA.

CHAPTER VII.

BATTLE OF THE WASHITA.

THE march of the Seventh Cavalry was begun in the face of the blinding snowstorm; and before they had gone many miles, even the Indian guides owned that they had lost their way and could not recognize the country till the snow ceased. It had been intended to encamp at Wolf Creek, fifteen miles from Camp Supply, but the guides could not find it. Most men would have stopped, in the face of such obstacles. Not so Custer. He took his course by the pocket compass, became his own guide, and reached Wolf Creek in the afternoon. Next morning at dawn the column started, with eighteen inches of snow on the ground, but a clear sky overhead, with a cold north wind. The march was continued with little incident except the cold, through a country abounding in game, where they found plenty of buffalo. At last they crossed the Canadian River. The crossing with the wagons occupied the best part of a day, and during that time Major Elliot, with three troops, was despatched on a scout down the Canadian to hunt for Indian sign. So far the column had met no Indians. Bad as the storm was for the soldiers, the Indians had found it still worse. It had made them hug their lodges.

The last wagon of the Seventh Cavalry had crossed the ford, and was parked on the plains to the south, when a courier from Major Elliot came dashing in, to report to Custer that Elliot had found the fresh trail of a war party, 150 strong, leading nearly due south, with a trifle of easting. It was evidently that of the last war-party of the season, going home, disgusted with the cold weather; and the snow had given it into Custer's hands. There was no more difficulty about finding the Indian village. Custer's perseverance and pluck in marching away in the midst of a blinding snow storm had been rewarded by "Custer's luck." A little earlier start, and the war party would have probably found him, not he them. As it was, he had the advantage of a surprise: he was in the heart of the Indian country, and as yet unperceived: the snow had proved his salvation. The pursuit was almost immediately taken up. Custer gave the regiment just twenty minutes to prepare: then, leaving eighty men, with the poorest horses, as a guard for the wagons, he started with the rest, provided only with what supplies could be carried on the horses, to intercept Major Elliot's party. The train was ordered to follow the trail of the regiment.

Custer struck off at an angle, to intercept Elliot's supposed course. That officer, having started the Indian trail twelve miles down the river, and at right angles thereto, it was probable that if Custer moved off to the south-east, he would cut the line of march. Just about sunset he found it, but it was not till nine o'clock at night that the whole command overtook Elliot's party, in camp on the trail of the Indians. Then the whole regiment, 800 strong, was reunited at last. They remained an hour in camp, getting supper and feeding the horses; and at ten resumed the march. They were already in the valley of the Washita River, and so close to their enemies that henceforth we must let Custer tell the story his own way. He says:

As soon as each troop was in readiness to resume the pursuit, the troop commander reported that fact at headquarters. Ten o'clock came and found us in our saddles. Silently the command stretched out its long length as the troopers filed off four abreast. First came two of our Osage scouts on foot: these were to follow the trail and lead the command: they were our guides; and the panther, creeping upon its prey, could not have advanced more cautiously or quietly than did these friendly Indians, as they seemed to glide rather than walk over the snow-clad surface. To prevent the possibility of the command coming precipitately upon our enemies, the two scouts were directed to keep three or four hundred yards in advance of all others; then came, in single file, the remainder of our Osage guides and the white scouts—among the rest California Joe. With these I rode, that I might be as near the advance guard as possible. The cavalry followed in rear, at the distance of a quarter or half a mile; this precaution was necessary, from the fact that the snow, which had thawed slightly during the day, was then freezing, forming a crust which, broken by the tread of so many hundreds of feet, produced a noise capable of being heard at a long distance. Orders were given prohibiting even a word being uttered above a whisper. No one was permitted to strike a match or light a pipe—the latter a great deprivation to the soldier. In this silent manner we rode mile after mile. Occasionally an officer would ride by my side and whisper some inquiry or suggestion, but aside from this our march was unbroken by sound or deed. At last we discovered that our two guides in front had halted, and were awaiting my arrival. Word was quietly sent to halt the column until inquiry in front could be made. Upon coming up with the two Osages we were furnished an example of the wonderful and peculiar powers of the Indian. One of them could speak broken English, and in answer to my question as to "What is the matter?" he replied, "Me don't know, but me smell fire." By this time several of the officers had quietly ridden up, and upon being informed of the Osage's remark, each endeavored, by sniffing the air, to verify or disprove the report. All united in saying that our guide was mistaken. Some said he was probably frightened, but we were unable to shake the confidence of the Osage warrior in his first opinion. I then directed him and his companion to advance even more cautiously than before, and the column, keeping up the interval, resumed its march. After proceeding about half a mile, perhaps further, again our guides halted, and upon coming up with them I was greeted with the remark, uttered in a whisper, "Me told you so;" and sure enough, looking in the direction indicated, were to be seen the embers of a wasted fire, scarcely a handful, yet enough to prove that our guide was right, and to cause us to feel the greater confidence in him. The discovery of these few coals of fire produced almost breathless excitement. The distance from where we stood was from seventy-five to a hundred yards, not in the line of our march, but directly to our left, in the edge of the timber. We knew at once that none but Indians, and they hostile, had built that fire. Where were they at that moment? Perhaps sleeping in the vicinity of the fire.

It was almost certain to our minds that the Indians we had been pursuing were the builders of the fire. Were they still there and asleep? We were too near already to attempt to withdraw undiscovered. Our only course was to determine the facts at once, and be prepared for the worst. I called for a few volunteers to quietly approach the fire and discover whether there were Indians in the vicinity; if not, to gather such information as was obtainable, as to their numbers and departure. All the Osages, and a few of the scouts quickly dismounted, and with rifles in readiness and fingers on the triggers, silently made their way to the nearest point of the timber, Little Beaver and Hard Rope leading the way. After they had disappeared in the timber, they still had to pass over more than half the distance, before reaching the fire. These moments seemed like hours, and those of us who were left sitting on our horses, in the open moonlight, and within easy range from the spot where the fire was located, felt anything but comfortable during this suspense. If Indians, as then seemed highly probable, were sleeping around the fire, our scouts would arouse them and we would be in a fair way to be picked off without being in a position to defend ourselves. The matter was soon determined. Our scouts soon arrived at the fire, and discovered it to be deserted. Again did the skill and knowledge of our Indian allies come in play. Had they not been with us, we should undoubtedly have assumed that the Indians who had had occasion to build the fire and those we were pursuing constituted one party. From examining the fire and observing the great number of pony tracks in the snow, the Osages arrived at a different conclusion, and were convinced that we were then on the ground used by the Indians for grazing their herds of ponies. The fire had been kindled by the Indian boys, who attend to the herding, to warm themselves by, and in all probability we were then within two or three miles of the village. I will not endeavor to describe the renewed hope and excitement that sprang up. Again we set out, this time more cautiously if possible, than before, the command and scouts moving at a greater distance in rear.

In order to judge of the situation more correctly, I this time accompanied the two Osages. Silently we advanced, I mounted, they on foot, keeping at the head of my horse. Upon nearing the crest of each hill, as is invariably the Indian custom, one of the guides would hasten a few steps in advance, and peer cautiously over the hill. Accustomed to this, I was not struck by observing it until once, when the same one who had discovered the fire advanced cautiously to the crest, and looked carefully into the valley beyond. I saw him place his hand above his eyes as if looking intently at some object, then crouch down and come creeping back to where I waited for him. " What is it ?" I inquired as soon as he reached my horse's side. "Heaps Injuns down there," pointing in the direction from which he had just come. Quickly dismounting and giving the reins to the other guide, I accompanied the Osage to the crest, both of us crouching low so as not to be seen in the moonlight against the horizon. Looking in the direction indicated, I could indistinctly recognize the presence of a large body of animals of some kind in the valley below, and at a distance which then seemed not more than half a mile. I looked at them long and anxiously, the guide uttering not a word, but was unable to discover anything in their appearance different from what might be presented by a herd of buffalo under similar circumstances. Turning to the Osage, I inquired in a low tone why he thought there were Indians there. " Me heard dog bark," was the satisfactory reply. Indians are noted for the large number of dogs always found in their villages, but never accompanying their war parties. I waited quietly to be convinced; I was assured, but wanted to be doubly so. I was rewarded in a moment by hearing the barking of a dog in the heavy timber off to the right of the herd, and soon after I heard the tinkling of a small bell; this convinced me that it was really the Indian herd I then saw, the bell being one worn around the neck of some pony who was probably the leader of the herd. I turned to retrace my steps when another sound was borne to my ear through the cold, clear atmosphere of the valley—it was the distant cry of an infant; and savages though they were, and justly outlawed by the number and atrocity of their recent murders and depredations on the helpless settlers of the frontier, I could but regret that in a war such as we were forced to engage in, the mode and circumstances of battle would possibly prevent discrimination.

Leaving the two Osages to keep a careful lookout, I hastened back until I met the main party of the scouts and Osages. They were halted and a message sent back to halt the cavalry, enjoining complete silence, and directing every officer to ride to the point we then occupied. The hour was past midnight. Soon they came, and after dismounting and collecting in a little circle, I informed them of what I had seen and heard; and in order that they might individually learn as much as possible of the character of the ground and the location of the village, I proposed that all should remove their sabres, that their clanking might make no noise, proceed gently to the crest and there obtain a view of the valley beyond. This was done; not a word was spoken until we crouched together and cast our eyes in the direction of the herd and village. In whispers I briefly pointed out everything that was to be seen, then motioned all to return to where we had left our sabres; then, standing in a group upon the ground or crust of snow, the plan of the attack was explained to all and each assigned his part. The general plan was to employ the hours between then and daylight to completely surround the village, and, at daybreak, or as soon as it was barely light enough for the purpose, to attack the Indians from all sides. The command, numbering as has been stated, about eight hundred mounted men, was divided into four nearly equal detachments. Two of them set out at once, as they had each to make a circuitous march of several miles in order to arrive at the points assigned them from which to make their attack. The third detachment moved to its position about an hour before day, and until that time remained with the main or fourth column. This last, whose movements I accompanied, was to make the attack from the point from which we had first discovered the herd and village. Major Elliot commanded the column embracing G, H and M troops, Seventh Cavalry, which moved around from our left to a position almost in rear of the village; while Colonel Thompson commanded the one consisting of B and F troops, which moved in a corresponding manner from our right to a position which was to connect with that of Major Elliot. Colonel Myers commanded the third column, composed of E and I troops, which was to take position in the valley and timber a little less than a mile to my right. By this disposition it was hoped to prevent the escape of every inmate of the village. That portion of the command which I proposed to accompany consisted of A, C, D, and K troops, Seventh Cavalry, the Osages and scouts, and Colonel Cook with his forty sharpshooters. Captain Hamilton commanded one of the squadrons, Colonel West the other. After the first two columns had departed for their posts—it was still four hours before the hour of attack—the men of the other two columns were permitted to dismount, but much intense suffering was unavoidably sustained. The night grew extremely cold towards morning; no fires of course could be permitted, and the men were even ordered to desist from stamping their feet and walking back and forth to keep warm, as the crushing of the snow beneath produced so much noise that it might give the alarm to our wily enemies.

During all these long weary hours of this terribly cold and comfortless night each man sat, stood, or lay on the snow by his horse, holding to the rein of the latter. The officers, buttoning their huge overcoats closely about them, collected in knots of four or five, and, seated or reclining upon the snow's hard crust, discussed the probabilities of the coming battle—for battle we knew it would be, and we could not hope to conquer or kill the warriors of an entire village without suffering in return more or less injury. Some, wrapping their capes about their heads, spread themselves at full length upon the snow and were apparently soon wrapped in deep slumber. After being satisfied that all necessary arrangements were made for the attack, I imitated the example of some of my comrades, and gathering the cavalry cape of my great coat about my head, lay down and slept soundly for perhaps an hour. At the end of that time I awoke, and on consulting my watch found there remained nearly two hours before we would move to the attack. Walking about among the horses and troopers, I found the latter generally huddled at the feet of the former in squads of three and four, in the endeavor to keep warm. Occasionally I would find a small group engaged in conversation, the muttered tones and voices strangely reminding me of those heard in the death-chamber. The officers had disposed of themselves in similar but various ways ; here at one place were several stretched out together upon the snow, the body of one being used by the others as a pillow. Nearly all were silent ; conversation had ceased, and those who were prevented by the severe cold from obtaining sleep were no doubt fully occupied in their minds with thoughts upon the morrow and the fate that might be in store for them. Seeing a small group collected under the low branches of a tree which stood a little distance from the ground occupied by the troops, I made my way there to find the Osage warriors, with their chiefs, Little Beaver and Hard Rope. They were wrapped up in their blankets, sitting in a circle, and had evidently made no effort to sleep during the night. It was plain to be seen that they regarded the occasion as a momentous one, and that the coming battle had been the sole subject of their conference. What the views expressed by them were, I did not learn until after the engagement was fought, when they told me what ideas they had entertained regarding the manner in which the white men would probably conduct and terminate the struggle next day. After the success of the day was decided, the Osages told me that, with the suspicion so natural and peculiar to the Indian nature, they had, in discussing the proposed attack upon the Indian village, concluded that we would be outnumbered by the occupants of the village, who of course would fight with the utmost desperation in defence of their lives and lodges, and to prevent a complete defeat of our forces or to secure a drawn battle, we might be induced to engage in a parley with the hostile tribe, and on coming to an agreement we would probably, to save ourselves, offer to yield up our Osage allies as a compromise measure between our enemies and ourselves. They also mistrusted the ability of the whites to make a successful attack upon a hostile village, located—as this one was known to be—in heavy timber, and aided by the natural banks of the stream. Disaster seemed certain in the minds of the Osages to follow us, if we attacked a force of unknown strength and numbers; and the question with them was to secure such a position in the attack as to be able promptly to detect any move disadvantageous to them. With this purpose they came to the conclusion that the standard-bearer was a very important personage, and neither he nor his standard would be carried into danger or exposed to the bullets of the enemy. They determined therefore to take their station immediately behind my standard-bearer when the lines became formed for attack to follow him during the action,

28

and thus be able to watch our movements, and if we were successful over our foes to aid us; if the battle should go against us, then they, being in a safe position, could take advantage of circumstances and save themselves as best they might.

Turning from our Osage friends, who were, unknown to us, entertaining such doubtful opinions as to our fidelity to them, I joined another group near by, consisting of most of the white scouts. Here were California Joe and several of his companions. One of the latter deserves a passing notice. He was a low, heavy-set Mexican, with features resembling somewhat those of the Ethiopian—thick lips, depressed nose, and low forehead. He was quite a young man, probably not more than twenty-five years of age, but had passed the greater portion of his life with the Indians, had adopted their habits of life and modes of dress, and had married among them. Familiar with the language of the Cheyennes and other neighboring tribes, he was invaluable both as a scout and interpreter. His real name was Romero, but some of the officers of the command, with whom he was a sort of favorite, had dubbed him Romeo, and by this name he was always known, a sobriquet to which he responded as readily as if he had been christened under it; never protesting, like the original Romeo:

> Tut, I have lost myself; I am not here;
> This is not Romeo, he's some other where.

The scouts, like nearly all the other members of the command, had been interchanging opinions as to the result of the movements of the following day. Not sharing the mistrust and suspicion of the Osage guides, yet the present experience was in many respects new to them, and to some the issue seemed at least shrouded in uncertainty. Addressing the group, I began the conversation with the question as to what they thought of the prospect of our having a fight. "Fight!" responded California Joe; "I havn't nary doubt concernin' that part uv the business; what I've been tryin' to get through my topknot

all night is whether we'll run aginst more than we bargain fur."
"Then you do not think the Indians will run away, Joe?"
"Run away! How in creation can Injuns or anybody else run
away when we'll have 'em clean surrounded afore daylight?"
"Well, suppose then that we succeed in surrounding the village, do you think we can hold our own against the Indians?"
"That's the very pint that's been botherin' me ever since we
planted ourselves down here, and the only conclusion I kin
come at is that it's purty apt to be one thing or t'other; if we
jump these Injuns at daylight, we're either goin' to make a
spoon or spile a horn, an' that's my candid judgment, sure.
One thing's sartin, ef them Injuns doesn't har anything uv us
till we open on 'em at daylight, they'll be the most powerful
'stonished redskins that's been in these parts lately—they will,
sure. An' ef we git the bulge on 'em and keep puttin' it to 'em
sort a lively like, we'll sweep the platter—thar won't be nary
trick left for 'em. As the deal stands now, we hold the keerds
and are holdin' over 'em; they've got to straddle our blind or
throw up their hands. Howsomever, thar's a mighty sight in
the draw."

The night passed in quiet. I anxiously watched the opening signs of dawn in order to put the column in motion. We
were only a few hundred yards from the point from which we
were to attack. The moon disappeared about two hours before
dawn, and left us enshrouded in thick and utter darkness, making the time seem to drag even slower than before.

At last faint signs of approaching day were visible, and I
proceeded to collect the officers, awakening those who slept.
We were standing in a group near the head of the column, when
suddenly our attention was attracted by a remarkable sight, and
for a time we felt that the Indians had discovered our presence.
Directly beyond the crest of the hill which separated us from
the village, and in a line with the supposed location of the latter,
we saw rising slowly but perceptibly, as we thought, up from
the village, and appearing in bold relief against the dark sky as

a background, something which we could only compare to a signal
rocket, except that its motion was slow and regular. All eyes were
turned to it in blank astonishment, and but one idea seemed to
be entertained, and that was that one or both of the attacking
columns under Elliot or Thompson had encountered a portion
of the village, and this that we saw was the signal to other portions of the band near at hand. Slowly and majestically it continued to rise above the crest of the hill, first appearing as a
small brilliant flaming globe of bright golden hue. As it ascended still higher it seemed to increase in size, to move more
slowly, while its colors rapidly changed from one to the other,
exhibiting in turn the most beautiful combinations of prismatic
tints. There seemed to be not the shadow of a doubt that we
were discovered. The strange apparition in the heavens maintained its steady course upward. One anxious spectator, observing it apparently at a standstill, exclaimed, " How long it
hangs fire ! why don't it explode ? " still keeping the idea of a
signal rocket in mind. It had risen perhaps to the height of
half a degree above the horizon as observed from our position,
when, lo ! the mystery was dispelled. Rising above the mysti-
fying influences of the atmosphere, that which had appeared so
suddenly before us, and excited our greatest apprehensions, developed into the brightest and most beautiful of morning stars.
Often since that memorable morning have I heard officers remind each other of the strange appearance which had so excited
our anxiety and alarm. In less perilous moments we probably
would have regarded it as a beautiful phenomenon of nature, of
which so many are to be witnessed through the pure atmosphere of the plains.

All were ordered to get ready to advance ; not a word to
officer or men was spoken above undertone. It began growing
lighter in the east, and we moved forward toward the crest of
the hill. Up to this time two of the officers and one of the
Osages had remained on the hill overlooking the valley beyond,
so as to detect any attempt at a movement on the part of the

village below. These now rejoined the troops. Colonel West's squadron was formed in line on the right, Captain Hamilton's squadron in line on the left, while Colonel Cook with his forty sharpshooters was formed in advance of the left, dismounted. Although the early morning air was freezingly cold, the men were directed to remove their overcoats and haversacks, so as to render them free in their movements. Before advancing beyond the crest of the hill, strict orders were issued prohibiting the firing of a single shot until the signal to attack should be made. The other three detachments had been informed before setting out that the main column would attack promptly at daylight, without waiting to ascertain whether they were in position or not. In fact it would be impracticable to communicate with either of the first two until the attack began. The plan was for each party to approach as closely to the village as possible without being discovered, and there await the approach of daylight. The regimental band was to move with my detachment, and it was understood that the band should strike up the instant the attack opened. Colonel Myers, commanding the third party, was also directed to move one-half of his detachment dismounted. In this order we began to descend the slope leading down to the village. The distance to the timber in the valley proved greater than it had appeared to the eye in the darkness of the night. We soon reached the outskirts of the herd of ponies. The latter seemed to recognize us as hostile parties and moved quickly away. The light of day was each minute growing stronger, and we feared discovery before we could approach near enough to charge the village. The movement of our horses over the crusted snow produced considerable noise, and would doubtless have led to our detection, but for the fact that the Indians, if they heard it at all, presumed it was occasioned by their herd of ponies. I would have given much at that moment to know the whereabouts of the two columns first sent out. Had they reached their assigned positions, or had unseen and unknown obstacles delayed or misled them ? These were questions which could not then be answered. We had now reached the level of the valley, and began advancing in line toward the heavy timber in which, and close at hand, we knew the village was situated.

Immediately in rear of my horse came the band, all mounted, and each with his instrument in readiness to begin playing the moment their leader, who rode at their head, and who kept his cornet to his lips, should receive the signal. I had previously told him to play " Garry Owen " as the opening piece. We had approached near enough to the village now to plainly catch a view here and there of the tall white lodges as they stood in irregular order among the trees. From the openings at the top of some of them we could perceive faint columns of smoke ascending, the occupants no doubt having kept up their feeble fires during the entire night. We had approached so near the village that from the dead silence which reigned I feared the lodges were deserted, the Indians having fled before we advanced. I was about to turn in my saddle and direct the signal for attack to be given—still anxious as to where the other detachments were—when a single rifle shot rang sharp and clear on the far side of the village from where we were. Quickly turning to the band leader, I directed him to give us " Garry Owen." At once the rollicking notes of that familiar marching and fighting air sounded forth through the valley, and in a moment were re-echoed back from the opposite sides by the loud and continued cheers of the men of the other detachments, who, true to their orders, were there and in readiness to pounce upon the Indians the moment the attack began. In this manner the battle of the Washita commenced. The bugle sounded the charge, and the entire command dashed rapidly into the village. The Indians were caught napping; but realizing at once the dangers of their situation, they quickly overcame their first surprise, in an instant seized their rifles, bows, and arrows, and sprang behind the nearest trees, while some leaped into the stream, nearly waist deep, and using the bank as a rifle-pit, began a vigorous and determined defence. Mingled with the exultant cheers of my men could be heard the defiant war-whoop of the warriors, who from the first fought with a desperation and courage which no race of men could surpass. Actual possession of the village and its lodges was ours within a few moments after the charge was made, but this was an empty victory unless we could vanquish the late occupants, who were then pouring in a rapid and well-directed fire from their stations behind trees and banks. At the first onset a considerable number of the Indians rushed from the village in the direction from which Elliot's party had attacked. Some broke through the lines, while others came in contact with the mounted troopers, and were killed or captured.

We had gained the centre of the village, and were in the midst of the lodges, while on all sides could be heard the sharp crack of the Indian rifles and the responses from the carbines of the troopers. After disposing of the smaller and scattering parties of warriors, who had attempted a movement down the valley, and in which some were successful, there was but little opportunity left for the successful employment of mounted troops. As the Indians by this time had taken cover behind logs and trees, and under the banks of the stream which flowed through the centre of the village, from which stronghold it was impracticable to dislodge them by the use of mounted men, a large portion of the command was at once ordered to fight on foot, and the men were instructed to take advantage of the trees and other natural means of cover, and fight the Indians in their own style. Cook's sharpshooters had adopted this method from the first, and with telling effect. Slowly but steadily the Indians were driven from behind the trees, and those who escaped the carbine bullets posted themselves with their companions who were already firing from the banks. One party of troopers came upon a squaw endeavoring to make her escape, leading by the hand a little white boy, a prisoner in the hands of the Indians, and who doubtless had been captured by some of their war parties during a raid upon the settlements. Who or where his parents were, or whether still alive or murdered by the Indians, will never be known, as the squaw, finding herself and prisoner about to be surrounded by the troops, and her escape cut off, determined, with savage malignity, that the triumph of the latter should not embrace the rescue of the white boy. Casting her eyes quickly in all directions, to convince herself that escape was impossible, she drew from beneath her blanket a huge knife and plunged it into the almost naked body of her captive. The next moment retributive justice reached her in the shape of a well-directed bullet from one of the troopers' carbines. Before the men could reach them life was extinct in the bodies of both the squaw and her unknown captive.

The desperation with which the Indians fought may be inferred from the following: Seventeen warriors had posted themselves in a depression in the ground, which enabled them to protect their bodies completely from the fire of our men, and it was only when the Indians raised their heads to fire that the troopers could aim with any prospect of success. All efforts to drive the warriors from this point proved abortive, and resulted in severe loss to our side. They were only vanquished by our men securing position under cover and picking them off by sharpshooting as they exposed themselves to get a shot at the troopers. Finally the last one was despatched in this manner. In a deep ravine near the suburbs of the village the dead bodies of thirty-eight warriors were reported after the fight terminated. Many of the squaws and children had very prudently not attempted to leave the village when we attacked it, but remained concealed inside their lodges. All these escaped injury, although when surrounded by the din and wild excitement of the fight, and in close proximity to the contending parties, their fears overcame some of them, and they gave vent to their despair by singing the death song, a combination of weird-like sounds which were suggestive of anything but musical tones. As soon as we had driven the warriors from the village, and the fighting was pushed to the country outside, I directed "Romeo," the interpreter, to go around to all the lodges and assure the squaws and children remaining in them that they would be unharmed and kindly cared for; at the same time he was to assemble them in the large lodges designated for that purpose, which were standing near the centre of the village. This was quite a delicate mission, as it was difficult to convince the squaws and children that they had any thing but death to expect at our hands.

It was perhaps ten o'clock in the forenoon, and the fight was still raging, when to our surprise we saw a small party of Indians collected on a knoll a little over a mile below the village, and in the direction taken by those Indians who had effected an escape through our lines at the commencement of the attack. My surprise was not so great at first, as I imagined that the Indians we saw were those who had contrived to escape, and having procured their ponies from the herd, had mounted them, and were then anxious spectators of the fight, which they felt themselves too weak in numbers to participate in. In the meantime the herds of ponies belonging to the village, on being alarmed by the firing and shouts of the contestants, had, from a sense of imagined security or custom, rushed into the village, where details of troopers were made to receive them. California Joe, who had been moving about in a promiscuous and independent manner, came galloping into the village, and reported that a large herd of ponies was to be seen near by, and requested authority and some men to bring them in. The men were otherwise employed just then, but he was authorized to collect and drive in the herd if practicable. He departed on his errand, and I had forgotten all about him and the ponies, when in the course of half an hour I saw a herd of nearly three hundred ponies coming on the gallop toward the village, driven by a couple of squaws, who were mounted, and had been concealed near by, no doubt; while bringing up the rear was California Joe, riding his favorite mule, and whirling about his head a long lariat, using it as a whip in urging the herd forward. He had captured the squaws while endeavoring to secure the ponies, and very wisely had employed his captives to assist in driving the herd. By this time the group of Indians already discovered outside our lines had increased until it numbered upwards of a hundred. Examining them through my field glass, I could plainly perceive that they were all mounted warriors; not only that, but they were armed and caparisoned in full war costume, nearly all wearing the bright-colored war-bonnets and floating their lance pennants. Constant accessions to their numbers were to be seen arriving from beyond the hill on which they stood. All this seemed inexplicable. A few Indians might have escaped through our lines when the attack on the village began, but only a few, and even these must have gone with little or nothing in their possession save their rifles and perhaps a blanket. Who could these new parties be, and from whence came they? To solve these troublesome questions I sent for "Romeo," and taking him with me to one of the lodges occupied by the squaws, I interrogated one of the latter as to who were the Indians to be seen assembling on the hill below the village. She informed me, to a surprise on my part almost equal to that of the Indians at our sudden appearance at daylight, that just below the village we then occupied, and which was a part of the Cheyenne tribe, were located in succession the winter villages of all the hostile tribes of the southern plains with which we were at war, including the Arapahoes, Kiowas, the remaining band of Cheyennes, the Comanches, and a portion of the Apaches; that the nearest village was about two miles distant, and the others stretched along through the timbered valley to the one furthest off, which was not over ten miles.

What was to be done?—for I needed no one to tell me that we were certain to be attacked, and that, too, by greatly superior numbers, just as soon as the Indians below could make their arrangements to do so; and they had probably been busily employed at these arrangements ever since the sound of firing had reached them in the early morning, and been reported from village to village. Fortunately, affairs took a favorable turn in the combat in which we were then engaged, and the firing had almost died away. Only here and there where some warrior still maintained his position was the fight continued. Leaving as few men as possible to look out for these, I hastily collected and re-formed my command, and posted them in readiness for the attack which we all felt was soon to be made; for already at different points and in more than one direction we could see more than enough warriors to outnumber us, and we knew they were only waiting the arrival of the chiefs and warriors from the lower villages before making any move against us. In the meanwhile our temporary hospital had been established in the centre of the village, where the wounded were receiving such surgical care as circumstances would permit. Our losses had been severe; indeed we were not then aware how great they had been. Hamilton, who rode at my side as we entered the village, and whose soldierly tones I heard for the last time as he calmly cautioned his squadron, "Now, men, keep cool, fire low, and not too rapidly," was among the first victims of the opening charge, having been shot from his saddle by a bullet from an Indian rifle. He died instantly. His lifeless remains were tenderly carried by some of his troopers to the vicinity of the hospital. Soon afterward I saw four troopers coming from the front bearing between them, in a blanket, a wounded soldier; galloping to them, I discovered Colonel Barnitz, another troop commander, who was almost in a dying condition, having been shot by a rifle bullet directly through the body in the vicinity of the heart. Of Major Elliot, the officer second in rank, nothing had been seen since the attack at daylight, when he rode with his detachment into the village. He, too, had evidently been killed, but as yet we knew not where or how he had fallen. Two other officers had received wounds, while the casualties among the enlisted men were also large. The sergeant-major of the regiment, who was with me when the first shot was heard, had not been seen since that moment. We were not in as effective condition by far as when the attack was made, yet we were soon to be called upon to contend against a force immensely superior to the one with which we had been engaged during the early hours of the day. The captured herds of ponies were carefully collected inside our lines, and so guarded as to prevent their stampede or recapture by the Indians. Our wounded, and the immense amount of captured property in the way of ponies, lodges, etc., as well as our prisoners, were obstacles in the way of our attempting an offensive movement against the lower villages. To have done this would have compelled us to divide our forces, when it was far from certain that we could muster strength enough united to repel the attacks of the combined tribes. On all sides of us the Indians could now be seen in considerable numbers, so that from being the surrounding party, as we had been in the morning, we now found ourselves surrounded and occupying the position of defenders of the village. Fortunately for us, as the men had been expending a great many rounds, Major Bell, the quartermaster, who with a small escort was endeavoring to reach us with a fresh supply of ammunition, had by constant exertion and hard marching succeeded in doing so, and now appeared on the ground with several thousand rounds of carbine ammunition, a reinforcement greatly needed. He had no sooner arrived safely than the Indians attacked from the direction from which he came. How he had managed to elude their watchful eyes, I never could comprehend, unless their attention had been so completely absorbed in watching our movements inside as to prevent them from keeping an eye out to discover what might be transpiring elsewhere.

Issuing a fresh supply of ammunition to those most in want of it, the fight soon began generally at all points of the circle, for such in reality had our line of battle become—a continuous and unbroken circle, of which the village was about the centre. Notwithstanding the great superiority in numbers of the Indians, they fought with excessive prudence and a lack of that confident manner which they usually manifest when encountering greatly inferior numbers—a result due, no doubt, to the fate which had overwhelmed our first opponents. Besides, the timber and the configuration of the ground enabled us to keep our men concealed until their services were actually required. It seemed to be the design and wish of our antagonists to draw us away from the village; but in this plan they were foiled. Seeing that they did not intend to press the attack just then, about two hundred of my men were ordered to pull down the lodges in the village and collect the captured property in huge piles preparatory to burning. This was done in the most effectual manner. When everything had been collected the torch was applied, and all that was left of the village were a few heaps of blackened ashes. Whether enraged at the sight of this destruction or from other cause, the attack soon became general along our entire line, and was pressed with so much vigor and audacity that every available trooper was required to aid in meeting these assaults. The Indians would push a party of well-mounted warriors close up to our lines in the endeavor to find a weak point through which they might venture, but in every attempt were driven back. I now concluded, as the village was off our hands and our wounded had been collected, that offensive measures might be adopted. To this end several of the squadrons were mounted and ordered to advance and attack the enemy wherever force sufficient was exposed to be a proper object of attack, but at the same time to be cautious as to ambuscades. Colonel Weir, who had succeeded to the command of Hamilton's squadron, Colonels Benteen and Myers with their respective squadrons, all mounted, advanced and engaged the enemy. The Indians resisted every step taken by the troops, while every charge made by the latter was met or followed by a charge from the Indians, who continued to appear in large numbers at unexpected times and places.   The squadrons acting in support of each other, and the men in each being kept well in hand, were soon able to force the line held by the Indians to yield at any point assailed.   This being followed up promptly, the Indians were driven at every point and forced to abandon the field to us. Yet they would go no further than they were actually driven. It was now about three o'clock in the afternoon.   I knew that the officer left in charge of the train and eighty men would push after us, follow our trail, and endeavor to reach us at the earliest practicable moment.   From the tops of some of the highest peaks or round hills in the vicinity of the village I knew the Indians could reconnoitre the country for miles in all directions. I feared if we remained as we were then until the following day, the Indians might in this manner discover the approach of our train and detach a sufficient body of warriors to attack and capture it ; and its loss to us, aside from that of its guard, would have proven most serious, leaving us in the heart of the enemy's country, in midwinter, totally out of supplies for both men and horses.

By actual count we had in our possession eight hundred and seventy-five captured ponies, so wild and unused to white men that it was difficult to herd them.   What we were to do with them was puzzling, as they could not have been led had we been possessed of the means of doing this ; neither could we drive them as the Indians were accustomed to do.   And even if we could take them with us, either the one way or the other, it was anything but wise and desirable on our part to do so, as such a large herd of ponies, constituting so much wealth in the eyes of the Indians, would have been too tempting a prize to the warriors who had been fighting us all the afternoon, and to effect their recapture they would have waylaid us day and night, with every prospect of success, until we should have arrived at a place of safety.   Besides, we had upwards of sixty prisoners in our hands, to say nothing of our wounded, to embarrass our movements.   We had achieved a great and important success over the hostile tribes ; the problem now was how to retain our advantage and steer safely through the difficulties which seemed to surround our position. The Indians had suffered a telling defeat, involving great losses in life and valuable property. Could they succeed, however, in depriving us of the train and supplies, and in doing this accomplish the killing or capture of the escort, it would go far to offset the damage we had been able to inflict upon them and to render our victory an empty one. We did not need the ponies, while the Indians did. If we retained them they might conclude that one object of our expedition against them was to secure plunder, an object thoroughly consistent with the red man's idea of war. Instead, it was our desire to impress upon their uncultured minds that our every act and purpose had been simply to inflict deserved punishment upon them for the many murders and other depredations committed by them in and around the homes of the defenceless settlers on the frontier. Impelled by these motives, I decided neither to attempt to take the ponies with us nor to abandon them to the Indians, but to adopt the only measure left—to kill them. To accomplish this seemingly—like most measures of war—cruel but necessary act, four companies of cavalrymen were detailed dismounted, as a firing party. Before they reluctantly engaged in this uninviting work, I took Romeo, the interpreter, and proceeded to the few lodges near the centre of the village which we had reserved from destruction, and in which were collected the prisoners, consisting of upward of sixty squaws and children. Romeo was directed to assemble the prisoners in one body, as I desired to assure them of kind treatment at our hands, a subject about which they were greatly wrought up ; also to tell them what we should expect of them, and to inform them of our intention to march probably all that night, directing them at the same time to proceed to the herd and select therefrom a suitable number of ponies to carry the prisoners on the march. When Romeo had collected them in a single group, he, acting as interpreter, acquainted them with my purpose in calling them together, at the same time assuring them that they could rely confidently upon the fulfilment of any promises I made them, as I was the "big chief." The Indians refer to all officers of a command as "chiefs," while the officer in command is designated as the "big chief." After I had concluded what I desired to say to them, they signified their approval and satisfaction by gathering around me and going through an extensive series of hand-shaking. One of the middle-aged squaws then informed Romeo that she wished to speak on behalf of herself and companions.

So far we have followed Custer's direct narrative and now resume our own. This squaw last mentioned, turned out to be the sister of Black Kettle, chief of the band Custer had struck; she bemoaned the wickedness of Black Kettle, and told Custer how only that night the last war-party returned with white scalps and plunder, and how they got so drunk that the white man was able to ride into their lodges next morning, before they woke up. She concluded by reminding him that it was his duty to help the helpless, and offered him a young girl in marriage. As soon as the general found from the interpreter what she was doing, he declined the honor, though not till Mahwissa—the old squaw's name—had performed the whole of the Indian part of the ceremony, which consisted in placing the girl's hand in Custer's, and invoking the Great Spirit on the union. The general asked Romeo the scout what could have been Mahwissa's object in this marriage, and received the following very plain reply:

"Well, I'll tell ye; ef you'd 'a married that squaw, then she'd 'a told ye that all the rest of 'em were her kinfolks, and as a nateral sort of a thing you'd 'a been expected to kind o' provide and take keer of your wife's relations. That's jist as I tell it to you—fur don't I know? Didn't I marry a young Cheyenne squaw, and give her old father two of my best ponies for her, and it wasn't a week till ever tarnal Injun in the village, old and young, came to my lodge, and my squaw tried to make me b'lieve they were all relations of hern, and that I ought to give 'em some grub; but I didn't do nothin' of the sort." " Well, how did you get out of it, Romeo?" " Get out of it? Why, I got out by jist takin' my ponies and traps, and the first good chance I lit out; that's how I got out. I was satisfied to marry one or two of 'em, but when it come to marryin' an intire tribe, 'scuse me."

The end of the matter was that the squaws took their ponies from the herd, and that the rest of the animals were shot. Search was then made for the killed, wounded and missing of the command, of which all, except Major Elliot and nineteen troopers, were found. These last were never heard of again till their bodies were discovered some weeks later. It seems that a party of Indians, at the beginning of the attack on the village, had escaped through a gap in the lines of the cavalry, that Elliot had pursued them, and run into the large force that was then hovering round Custer, fearing to attack him. Having fruitlessly searched for the major, it was rightly concluded that he and his party had been attacked and killed, and Custer prepared for his return march.

Placing his prisoners in the centre, he first deployed his forces and marched straight down the river at the threatening parties of Indians from the other villages, with colors displayed and band playing. His intention was to strike consternation into their hearts, and make them think he was about to serve them as he had served Black Kettle's band. The movement had all the effect he desired. The Indians fled in confusion, leaving only a few warriors to hover around him and watch him. He did not start till within an hour of sunset, and his feint diverted Indian attention from his wagon train, which he knew must be pretty near him by this time. About an hour after dark, he reached the abandoned villages of the alarmed tribes, where he halted, and at ten o'clock retraced his steps, marching rapidly for the wagons. At two o'clock he halted in the valley of the Washita, and went into bivouac, the men

29

building huge fires to supply the loss of their overcoats, which the Indians had captured during the fight. They had been left in a heap on the ground. Secrecy was no longer necessary now, and the men enjoyed themselves hugely. Next day they reached the wagons and pushed on, encamping at night at the place where the regiment first struck Elliot's trail. From thence, California Joe and another scout were despatched to Camp Supply, to carry the news to General Sheridan. The two scouts made the journey in safety. The country was apparently denuded of Indians, the blow on the Washita having demoralized them. California Joe met Custer's column with a return despatch, before the regiment could reach Camp Supply. It was read at the head of the troops, and repaid them for all their hardships. It was as follows:

HEADQUARTERS DEPARTMENT OF THE MISSOURI, IN THE FIELD, DEPOT ON
    THE NORTH CANADIAN, AT THE JUNCTION OF BEAVER CREEK, INDIAN
    TERRITORY,   November 29, 1868.

GENERAL FIELD ORDERS No. 6.—The Major-General commanding announces to this command the defeat by the Seventh regiment of cavalry, of a large force of Cheyenne Indians, under the celebrated chief Black Kettle, re-enforced by the Arapahoes under Little Raven, and the Kiowas under Satanta, on the morning of the 27th instant, on the Washita River, near the Antelope Hills, Indian Territory, resulting in a loss to the savages of one hundred and three warriors killed, including Black Kettle, the capture of fifty-three squaws and children, eight hundred and seventy-five ponies, eleven hundred and twenty-three buffalo robes and skins, five hundred and thirty-five pounds of powder, one thousand and fifty pounds of lead, four thousand arrows, seven hundred pounds of tobacco, besides rifles, pistols, saddles, bows, lariats, and immense quantities of dried meat and other winter provisions, the complete destruction of their village, and almost total annihilation of this Indian band.

The loss to the Seventh Cavalry was two officers killed, Major Joel H. Elliot and Captain Louis McL. Hamilton, and nineteen enlisted men ; three officers wounded, Brevet Lieutenant-Colonel Albert Barnitz (badly), Brevet Lieutenant-Colonel T. W. Custer, and Second Lieutenant T. Z. March (slightly), and eleven enlisted men.

The energy and rapidity shown during one of the heaviest snow-storms that has visited this section of the country, with the temperature below freezing point, and the gallantry and bravery displayed, resulting in such signal success, reflect the highest credit upon both the officers and men of the Seventh Cavalry ; and the Major-General commanding, while regretting the loss of such gallant officers as Major Elliot and Captain Hamilton, who fell while gallantly leading their men, desires to express his thanks to the officers and men engaged in the battle of the Washita, and his special congratulations are tendered to their distinguished commander, Brevet Major-General George A. Custer, for the efficient and gallant services rendered, which have characterized the opening of the campaign against hostile Indians south of the Arkansas.

By command of

Major-General P. H. SHERIDAN,

J. SCHUYLER CROSBY, Brevet Lieutenant-Colonel,

A. D. C., A. A. A. General.

We cannot terminate the campaign better than by the description in Custer's own words of the review which closed it. General Sheridan was so much pleased with the success of the expedition that he personally honored the regiment by reviewing it, a great condescension, in military etiquette, from a major-general to a single regiment. Custer describes it thus:

" In many respects the column we formed was unique in appearance. First rode our Osage guides and trailers, dressed and painted in the extremest fashions of war, according to their rude customs and ideas. As we advanced, these warriors chanted their war songs, fired their guns in triumph, and at intervals gave utterance to their shrill war-whoops. Next came the scouts riding abreast, with California Joe astride his faithful mule bringing up the right, but unable, even during this ceremonious and formal occasion, to dispense with his pipe. Immediately in rear of the scouts rode the Indian prisoners under guard, all mounted on Indian ponies, and in their dress, conspicuous by its bright colors, many of them wearing the scarlet blanket so popular with the wild tribes, presenting quite a contrast to the dull and motley colors worn by the scouts. Some little distance in the rear came the troops formed in column of platoons, the leading platoon preceded by the band playing "Garry Owen," being composed of the sharpshooters under Colonel Cook, followed in succession by the squadrons in the regular order of march. In this order and arrangement we marched proudly in front of our chief, who, as the officers rode by, giving him the military salute with the sabre, returned their formal courtesy by a graceful lifting of his cap and a pleased look of recognition from his eye, which spoke his approbation in language far more powerful than studied words could have done. In speaking of the review afterwards, General Sheridan said the appearance of the troops, with the bright rays of the sun reflected from their burnished arms and equipments, as they advanced in beautiful order and precision down the slope, the band playing, and the blue of the soldiers' uniforms slightly relieved by the gaudy colors of the Indians, both captives and Osages, the strangely fantastic part played by the Osage guides, their shouts, chanting their war songs, and firing their guns in air, all combined to render the scene one of the most beautiful and highly interesting he remembered ever having witnesssd."

So closed the Washita campaign December 2d, 1868. It will be observed, however, that General Sheridan's congratulatory order calls the battle only "the opening of the campaign against the hostile Indians south of the Arkansas." Such it was meant to be. Five days later, December 7th, the regiment, with thirty days' rations in the wagons, started for the Washita once more, accompanied by General Sheridan and staff. Along with Sheridan were the Nineteenth Kansas Volunteer cavalry, a special force, just raised for Indian hostilities, and the whole expedition numbered about fifteen hundred men.

CHAPTER VIII.

CLOSING OPERATIONS.

THE Seventh Cavalry reached their old battle ground in safety without adventure. What California Joe thought of the renewed winter campaign is characteristic.

" I'd jist like to see the streaked count'nances of Satanta, Medicine Arrow, Lone Wolf, and a few others o 'em, when they ketch the fust glimpse of the outfit. They'll think we're comin' to spend an evenin' with 'em sure, and hev brought our knittin' with us. One look'll satisfy 'em. Thar 'll be sum of the durndest kickin' out over these plains that ever war heern tell uv. One good thing, it's goin' to cum as nigh killin' uv 'em to start 'em out this time uv year as ef we hed an out an' out scrummage with 'em. The way I looks at it they hev jist this preference : them as don't like bein' shot to deth kin take ther chances at freezin'."

After a careful search around the battle-ground they came on the bodies of Major Elliot's party, all horribly mutilated in a manner similar to that which is recorded of the Kidder party. The bodies were tenderly buried. The position of affairs in the neighborhood is thus described by Custer :

" The forest along the banks of the Washita, from the battle-ground a distance of twelve miles, was found to have been one continuous Indian village. Black Kettle's band of Cheyennes was above ; then came other hostile tribes camped in the following order : Arapahoes under Little Raven ; Kiowas under Satanta and Lone Wolf ; the remaining bands of Cheyennes, Comanches, and Apaches. Nothing could exceed the disorder and haste with which the tribes had fled from their camping grounds. They had abandoned thousands of lodge poles, some of which were still standing, as when last used. Immense numbers of camp kettles, cooking utensils, coffee-mills, axes, and several hundred buffalo robes were found in the abandoned camps adjacent to Black Kettle's village, but which had not been visited before by our troops. By actual examination, it was computed that over six hundred lodges had been standing along the Washita during the battle, and within five miles of the battle-ground, and it was from these villages, and others still lower down the stream, that the immense number of warriors came who, after our rout and destruction of Black Kettle and his band, surrounded my command and fought until defeated by the Seventh Cavalry."

The ground having been examined, the campaign was resumed as follows, according to Custer's account:

"At daylight on the following morning the entire command started on the trail of the Indian villages, nearly all of which had moved down the Washita toward Fort Cobb, where they had good reason to believe they would receive protection. The Arapahoes and remaining band of Cheyennes left the Washita valley and moved across in the direction of Red River. After following the trail of the Kiowas and other hostile Indians for seven days, over an almost impassable country, where it was necessary to keep two or three hundred men almost constantly at work with picks, axes, and spades, before being able to advance with our immense train, my Osage scouts came galloping back on the morning of the 17th of December, and reported a party of Indians in our front bearing a flag of truce."

The party turned out to be the Kiowas, under Satanta and Lone Wolf. They were accompanied by a scout who said that he came from Fort Cobb, Indian Territory, a station on the Washita, one hundred miles below the battle-ground. At this fort was stationed General Hazen, who had been placed by General Sherman in control of the Kiowas and Comanches. The scout bore the following note:

HEADQUARTERS SOUTHERN INDIAN DISTRICT, FORT COBB,
9 P. M. December 16, 1868.

To the officer, commanding troops in the Field.

Indians have just brought in word that our troops to-day reached the Washita some twenty miles above here. I send this to say that all the camps this side of the point reported to have been reached are friendly, and have not been on the war path this season. If this reaches you, it would be well to communicate at once with Satanta or Black Eagle, chiefs of the Kiowas, near where you now are, who will readily inform you of the position of the Cheyennes and Arapahoes, also of my camp.

Respectfully,

(Signed) W. B. HAZEN, Brevet Major-General.

"This scout," says Custer, "at the same time informed me that a large party of the Kiowa warriors, under Lone Wolf, Satanta, and other leading chiefs, were within less than a mile of my advance, and notwithstanding the above certificate regarding their friendly character, they had seized a scout who accompanied the bearer of the despatch, disarmed him, and held him a prisoner of war. Taking a small party with me, I proceeded beyond our lines to meet the flag of truce. I was met by several of the leading chiefs of the Kiowas, including those above named. Large parties of their warriors could be seen posted in the neighboring ravines and upon the surrounding hill-tops. All were painted and plumed for war, and nearly all were armed with one rifle, two revolvers, bow and arrow, some of their bows being strung, and their whole appearance and conduct plainly indicating that they had come for war."

Very unwillingly, Custer was restrained from attacking the Kiowas, but the presence of Sheridan compelled him to submit to the assurance of Hazen's note and refrain from war.

"After meeting the chiefs, who with their bands had approached our advance under flag of truce, and compelling the release of the scout whom they had seized and held prisoner, we continued our march toward Fort Cobb, the chiefs agreeing to ride with us and accompany my command to that place.

Every assurance was given me that the villages to which
these various chiefs belonged would at once move to Fort Cobb
and there encamp, thus separating themselves from the hostile
tribes, or those who preferred to decline this proposition of
peace, and to continue to wage war; and as an evidence of the
sincerity of their purpose, some eighteen or twenty of the most
prominent chiefs, generally Kiowas, voluntarily proposed to
accompany us during the march of the day and the next, by
which time it was expected that the command would reach
Fort Cobb. The chiefs only requested that they might send
one of their number, mounted on a fleet pony, to the villages,
in order to hasten their movement to Fort Cobb."

Custer consented to this cheerfully, but as he was exceedingly suspicious of the Indians, watched them closely. On the
next day's march, the chiefs, on one pretext or another, began
to drop out of the column, and Custer became convinced that
they were fooling him, to gain time to send their villages away
from, not towards Fort Cobb. Feeling sure of this, he waited
until the inferior chiefs had departed, leaving only Satanta and
Lone Wolf, when the officers at the head of the column drew
their revolvers, and the two chiefs were informed they were
prisoners, and hostages. Custer did not need two lessons in
Indian diplomacy. Pawnee Killer had fooled him once, but
Satanta and Lone Wolf were not equal to repeating the trick.

Here it is necessary to notice a dispute which arose at the
time between Custer and General Hazen, which turned on the
identity of the Indians engaged in the late battle. Custer,
relying on the statements of Mahwissa and the other squaws of
Black Kettle's band, was convinced that he had been fighting
the Kiowas of Satanta and Lone Wolf. Mahwissa even pointed
out Satanta's camp, close to that of Black Kettle. General
Hazen, on the other hand, was convinced that Satanta and
Lone Wolf were not in the battle, that the major part of the
Kiowas were in camp at Fort Cobb, a hundred miles from the
battle field, and that only a small band of either Kiowas or

SATANTA.

Comanches, who had not come in, could possibly have been in the battle.

Not for six years was the difficulty cleared up. It was then settled by the production of various affidavits from the disbursing officers and agents at Fort Cobb, which proved conclusively, that Satanta and Lone Wolf visited and slept at the officers' quarters in Fort Cobb, on the 27th November, the same night that Custer fought Black Kettle, a hundred miles away, and that rations were issued to nine-tenths of the Kiowas on the 26th of November, at the same place. General Hazen's statement was published in brief in the *Army and Navy Journal* of March 30, 1874, and settles the question. It seems, however, that the Kiowas, knowing that a small band of their friends had been in the battle, were naturally frightened to death when they heard of Custer's return, a fortnight later. They at once scattered, and left Fort Cobb, fearing to be punished for past misdeeds; and the embassy of Lone Wolf and Satanta probably had just the intention which Custer divined, that of giving the lodges time to get away safe.

At all events, the capture of the two chiefs as hostages had the happiest effect. The column continued its march to Fort Cobb. On the way they were met by Satanta's son, who was allowed to come and go within the lines, as a medium of communication between the whites and the Kiowas. For a long time the Indians tried to procrastinate and avoid yielding to Custer's demands. These were simple, that the Indians should come in and settle once more on their reservations by the fort, in the power of the troops. At last General Sheridan's rapid decision cut the knots of diplomacy in a very effectual manner. He told Custer, through whom he conducted all the negotiations, to assure Lone Wolf and Satanta, that if their bands were not in camp before sunset of the following day, both chiefs *would be hung at that hour, and troops sent after Kiowas.* This settled the question very quickly. Satanta's son was sent off, full speed, to the tribes, and long before the said sunset the Kiowas were quietly settled under the guns of Fort Cobb.

The next tribe that needed subduing was the Arapahoes. The Cheyennes had been humbled, the Kiowas pacified without bloodshed, thanks to Custer's seizure of Satanta, the Arapahoes must also be brought on their reservations. To do this required either hard fighting and marching, or the exercise of finesse. General Sheridan, who had so far left the fighting and negotiation entirely to Custer, continued to do so. The young lieutenant-colonel found him a very different chief, sympathetic and appreciative, to the others by whom he had been commanded since the war. Sheridan continued to let him have his own way, and it was crowned with the same triumphant success which had marked it hitherto. Briefly, Custer succeeded in bringing the Arapahoes as he had the Kiowas, but by a different method.

First, a friendly chief of the Apaches, named Iron Shirt, who volunteered for the office, was selected as an ambassador in the cause of peace to both Cheyennes and Arapahoes. With him was dispatched Mahwissa, the sister of Black Kettle, and both were well supplied with presents. Their instructions were to go to the Cheyennes and Arapahoes, see the chiefs, tell them that if they chose to come in and settle on their reservations they should be well treated, and to remind them that if they did not come in, they might get the same treatment as Black Kettle.

The departure of the envoys made an end of all hope of a winter campaign, for which, no doubt, the officers of the Seventh Cavalry were not sorry. It was late in January before Iron Shirt returned, without Mahwissa. He brought the news that the distance was too great and the ponies too thin for the tribes to move, and that the Cheyennes had detained Mahwissa from returning. He reported however that Little Robe, chief of the Cheyennes, and Yellow Bear, second chief of the Arapahoes, were both very anxious to accept the government's proposition, and would themselves visit the camp shortly.

A few days after, sure enough, Little Robe and Yellow Bear arrived and were handsomely received. The latter was about the least cruel and most sensible of the chiefs on the plains, a great contrast to the peculiarly savage and insolent Satanta. He was the one good Indian whom Custer appears to have met. The sequel to the visit is thus told by Custer:

" They reported that their villages had had under consideration the question of accepting our invitation to come in and live at peace in the future, and that many of their people were strongly in favor of adopting this course, but for the present it was uncertain whether or not the two tribes would come in. The two tribes would probably act in concert, and if they intended coming, would make their determination known by despatching couriers to us in a few days. In spite of the sincerity of the motives of Little Robe and Yellow Bear, whom I have always regarded as two of the most upright and peaceably inclined Indians I have ever known, and who have since that time paid a visit to the President at Washington, it was evident that the Cheyennes and Arapahoes, while endeavoring to occupy us with promises and pretences, were only interested in delaying our movements until the return of spring, when the young grass would enable them to recruit the strength of their winter-famished ponies and move when and where they pleased.

" After waiting many long weary days for the arrival of the promised couriers from the two tribes, until even Little Robe and Yellow Bear were forced to acknowledge that there was no longer any reason to expect their coming, it occurred to me that there was but one expedient yet untried which furnished even a doubtful chance of averting war. This could only be resorted to with the approval of General Sheridan, whose tent had been pitched in our midst during the entire winter, and who evidently proposed to remain on the ground until the Indian question in that locality should be disposed of. My plan was as follows:

" After weighing the matter carefully in my own mind, I

decided that with General Sheridan's approval I would select from my command forty men, two officers, and a medical officer, and, accompanied by the two chiefs, Little Robe and Yellow Bear, who regarded my proposition with favor, I would set out in search of the hostile camp, there being but little doubt that with the assistance of the chiefs I would have little difficulty in discovering the whereabouts of the villages; while the smallness of my party would prevent unnecessary alarm or suspicion as to our intentions. From my tent to General Sheridan's was only a few steps, and I soon submitted my proposition to the General, who from the first was inclined to lend his approval to my project. After discussing it fully, he gave his consent by saying that the character of the proposed expedition was such that he would not order me to proceed upon it, but if I volunteered to go, he would give me the full sanction of his authority and every possible assistance to render the mission a successful one; in conclusion urging me to exercise the greatest caution against the stratagems or treachery of the Indians, who no doubt would be but too glad to massacre my party in revenge for their recent well-merited chastisement. Returning to my tent, I at once set about making preparations for my journey, the extent or result of which now became interesting subjects for deliberation. The first thing necessary was to make up the party which was to accompany me.

" As the number of men was to be limited to forty, too much care could not be exercised in their selection. I chose the great majority of them from the sharpshooters, men who, in addition to being cool and brave, were experienced and skillful marksmen. My standard-bearer, a well-tried sergeant, was selected as the senior non-commissioned officer of the party. The officers who were to accompany me were my brother Colonel Custer, Captain Robbins, and Dr. Renick, Acting Assistant Surgeon U. S. Army. As guide I had Neva, a Blackfoot Indian, who had accompanied General Fremont in his explorations, and who could speak a little English. Little Robe and Yellow Bear were also to be relied upon as guides, while Romeo accompanied us as interpreter. All were well armed and well mounted. We were to take no wagons or tents ; our extra supplies were to be transported on pack-mules. We were to start on the evening of the second day, the intervening time being necessary to complete our preparations. It was decided that our first march should be a short one, sufficient merely to enable us to reach a village of friendly Apaches, located a few miles from our camp, where we would spend the first night and be joined by Little Robe and Yellow Bear, who at that time were guests of the Apaches. I need not say that in the opinion of many of our comrades our mission was regarded as closely bordering on the imprudent, to qualify it by no stronger term.

So confident did one of the most prudent officers of my command feel in regard to our annihilation by the Indians, that in bidding me good-bye, he contrived to slip into my hand a small pocket Derringer pistol, loaded, with the simple remark, "You had better take it, general ; it may prove useful to you." As I was amply provided with arms, both revolvers and rifle, and as a pocket Derringer may not impress the reader as being a very formidable weapon to use in Indian warfare, the purpose of my friend in giving me the small pocket weapon may not seem clear. It was given me under the firm conviction that the Indians would overwhelm and massacre my entire party ; and to prevent my being captured, disarmed, and reserved for torture, that little pistol was given me in order that at the last moment I might become my own executioner— an office I was not seeking, nor did I share in my friend's opinion.

"Everything being ready for our departure, we swung into our saddles, waved our adieus to the comrades who were to remain in camp, and the next moment we turned our horses' heads westward."

We do not intend to enlarge on the incidents of the journey which ensued, which are fully recorded in "Life on the

Plains," to which the reader is referred. Suffice it to say that it was successful, that Custer reached the Arapahoe camp in safety, and that the expedition ended in the quiet location of the whole tribe under the guns of the fort on their reservation. The Cheyennes however were not so tractable. The destruction of Black Kettle's band had only exasperated, not cowed them, and they needed another lesson. It was soon given them by Custer.

General Sheridan departed for Camp Supply as soon as the Kiowas and Arapahoes were settled, while Custer, taking with him the Seventh Cavalry and Nineteenth Kansas, started, on the 2d of March, 1869, on the search after the Cheyennes. The story of his march is so well and succinctly told in his official report, that we give it nearly entire.

On the morning of the 2d March, my command, composed of eleven troops of the Seventh U. S. Cavalry, and ten troops of the Nineteenth Kansas Cavalry, left its camp on Medicine Bluff Creek, about thirty miles due south from Fort Cobb. My course was via Camp Radziminski, mouth of Elk Creek, to a point on the North Fork of Red River, a few miles above the mouth of Salt Creek. Here I divided my command into two columns. Selecting about eight hundred of the most effective men from both regiments, I directed Brevet Lieutenant-Colonel Myers, Seventh Cavalry, to proceed in command of the remainder and surplus train up the North Fork, and across to a point on the Washita, near the late battle-ground; and there await further orders.

With that portion of the command selected for the purpose, I left our camp on the North Fork on the morning of the 6th instant, and marched due west, striking the Salt Fork after a few hours' march. About noon we struck a fresh trail of a single lodge and fourteen animals heading up the Salt Fork. Taking up the pursuit we followed the trail three days and one night, and on the afternoon of the third day surprised the party we were pursuing, while seeking shelter from an approaching storm, capturing their lodge, cooking utensils, provisions, and eleven of their ponies, the party, which consisted of nine Cheyennes, barely making their escape into one of the many ravines near by. This was one of the small parties which the Cheyennes had sent to the vicinity of our camps on Medicine Bluff Creek to observe and report our movements, and was then on its way to the main village to report that we were again on the move. The point at which the capture was made was in Texas, on a small fresh water tributary of Salt Fork.

On the morning of the 9th we moved in a westerly direction; marched all day, but were unable to find water, and were forced to make a dry camp on the prairie. Before daylight next morning we resumed the march, changing our course to the south, and by noon reached camp on Middle Fork, a stream which, on some maps, is designated as Gypsum Creek.

On the following morning we moved toward the southwest, crossing Mulberry Creek. Our march was continued until we came in sight of the banks of the main Red River. Here we discovered the trail of one lodge leading north-west. The trail was nearly one month old, but with the hope that it would lead to others, we took it up, and before pursuing many miles had the satisfaction of seeing the trail increased by that of eleven lodges, all about the same time.

That night we encamped on the head-waters of Mulberry Creek, occupying the ground selected for the same purpose by the Indians. From this point the trail led northward. Notwithstanding the trail was very old, I felt confident that with due precautions, and knowing the lazy manner in which Indians moved when not pursued, we could overhaul them, or at least get very near them, before our proximity was discovered. Thanks to their superior geographical knowledge I was not troubled by routes, water or camping grounds. The trail led us by easy marches to good water, plenty of timber, and the best camping grounds that could be selected.

On the morning of the 12th the pursuit was resumed. Early in the day the trail was found to be enlarged by the addition of forty-two lodges, and before night about as many more joined, making the trail one of over a hundred lodges, and so plain we could follow it at a gallop, could our horses have kept up the gait. That night we encamped on Middle Fork.

The morning of the 13th we observed fresher signs of Indians than we had yet seen, indicating that they had left the Middle Fork not more than a week previous. This will be understood when it is known that in the ordinary manner of moving the village remains from three days to a week in each camp, and then moves but about ten miles before making another camp.

We moved without delay, and one of our marches equaled two or three made by the Indians. As the trail grew warmer it became necessary to adopt additional precautions to insure success. No bugle calls or discharges of fire-arms were permitted. Fires were lighted after dark and covered with earth before daylight. Tents were burned, and all blankets in excess of one per man, and all clothing shared the same fate.

Daily the pursuit was continued until the morning of the 15th, when we reached a camp ground on the North Fork which had been abandoned only two days before. Encouraged by the prospect, we pressed forward, and by noon the advance had made twenty miles.

Hard Rope, the war chief of the Osages, and who at this moment was running the trail, discovered, about one mile in advance, a herd of forty or fifty ponies, grazing and herded by two Indians. The latter discovered us at the same time, and drove the herd rapidly in the direction of a timber stream which could be seen some two or three miles beyond.

I at once sent orders back to the column, which was still a considerable distance in the rear, to close up at a rapid gait.

The deep sand and the exhausted condition of horses and

men prevented this being done promptly. I was uncertain as to whether the village was in our front, or whether the herd seen driven off was merely on the move. If the latter, desiring to effect its capture, I advanced with the few men then in front in the direction taken by the herd. After proceeding about two miles, Indians could be seen in front, partially concealed behind the sand hills, and watching our movements. Taking my orderly with me, I advanced to learn their character and intentions. After considerable signaling and parleying, eight Indians came forward to meet me. From them I learned that the entire Cheyenne tribe, numbering two hundred and sixty lodges, was encamped at different points within ten or fifteen miles from where we then were. A few moments afterward thirty or forty Indians rode up to us, including Medicine Arrow, the head chief of the Cheyennes and several other noted chiefs of the same tribe. From the latter I learned that over two hundred lodges were encamped on the stream directly in our front, the remainder, under Little Robe, being some ten or fifteen miles lower down.

Included in the two hundred lodges were nearly all the lodges belonging to the Dog Soldiers, the most mischievous, bloodthirsty and barbarous band of Indians that infest the Plains.

Here, then, was the opportunity we had been seeking, to administer a well-merited punishment to the worst of all Indians. My intentions were formed accordingly, and as I rode with Medicine Arrow in the direction of the village, I made my plans for surrounding the village and attacking as soon as the troops came up. I did not pursue this course, however, and for the following reasons: On my way to the village I learned that the two white women captured in Kansas last autumn—one Mrs. Morgan, on the Solomon; the other, Miss White, on the Republican—were then held captive in the Cheyenne village. It was then out of the question to assume a hostile attitude, at least until every peaceable means for their recovery had been exhausted. The opening of our attack would

30

have been the signal for their murder by their captors, as we very well knew. I therefore determined to encamp my command, as soon as it arrived, near the village. In the meantime I accompanied Medicine Arrow to his lodge in the centre of his village, where all the principal chiefs and the medicine man of the tribe soon assembled.

Before entering the village I observed the greatest excitement prevailed; the entire herd was collected; the squaws had everything except their lodges packed, and their ponies were saddled ready for a precipitate flight. So that, had my intention to attack been carried out, it is doubtful whether, with the timely warning they had received, and considering the jaded condition of my animals, we could at that time have inflicted any very serious injury beyond the capture of their lodges. The recovery of the captive white women was now my first object. The squaws and children remained seated upon their ponies, until the troops approached the village, when their fears, coupled with the remembrance of the crimes of the tribe and their deserved punishment, got the better of them, and, like a herd of frightened sheep, old and young squaws, papooses, ponies and mules, started in the direction of Little Robe's village, abandoning to us their lodges and poles, and immense numbers of camp kettles, robes, shields and ponies. I ordered my men not to fire upon the fugitives, but caused four of their principal men, two of them noted chiefs of the Dog Soldiers—"Big Head" and "Dull Knife"—to be seized and held under guard, intending through them to compel the release of the two white women. At the same time, to prevent the Cheyennes from breaking up into small parties and renewing hostilities, I sent word to them to return and take their lodges with them, adding that if they would all agree to encamp near Little Robe and his band, I would not permit their abandoned village to be disturbed until the lodges had been removed.

This proposition was generally accepted. I then sent a runner to Little Robe, who was well known to me, and whose in-

fluence with his tribe was great, to come and see me, promising
him safe passport back to his village. He accepted my invitation, came to my camp, and after a long talk promised to use
his influence for the best. No promise to deliver up the captives into our hands without the payment of a large ransom
could be obtained. I was determined to secure their release,
and that unconditionally, and thereby discourage the custom of
ransoming captives from Indians, which is really nothing more
or less than offering the latter a premium upon every captive.

To obtain a better camp, and at the same time accomplish
my purpose, I told Little Robe I would change my camp the
following day, moving in the direction of his village, but that I
had no desire to approach its immediate vicinity, and that, after
my arrival in camp, if he and the other chiefs would visit me
I would talk with them.

On the evening of the second day a chief who had accompanied Little Robe the first day came to my camp to learn
what I had to say, and to procure, if possible, the release of the
chiefs and warriors held by me. No satisfactory statement
could be gotten from him regarding the return of the white
women or the intentions of the chiefs. I, therefore, determined
not to be put off any longer, and told him we had then waited
three days for them to give us the white women, and had obtained no satisfactory response; that I should wait one day
longer, but if by sunset the following day the white women
were not delivered up, I would hang to a tree, which was there
designated, three of the men held captive by me (the fourth one
having been sent as a runner to Little Robe), and that the following day I would follow and attack the village. With this
message the chief departed. The next day was one of no little
anxiety to all, and to none more than to the three captive Cheyennes whom I certainly intended to hang if their people failed
to accede to our demands. The ropes were ready, and the limb
selected when, about three o'clock P. M. a small party of Indian
warriors were seen approaching camp. They halted on a knoll

about one mile distant, while one of their number came forward with the welcome intelligence that the women were with them and would be given up; but this was coupled with the proposition that I should exchange the three men, or two of them, for the women. This was refused, and the return of the women demanded at once, and unconditionally. A reluctant assent to this was given. The Indians, however, feared to come inside of our lines. Lieutenant-Colonel Moore, and Majors Jones and Jenkins were, therefore, detailed to go out and receive them.

[The matter ended by the release of the women, and their restoration to their friends, and the sequel of the story is thus told by Custer]:

"After the momentary excitement consequent upon the arrival of the girls in camp had subsided, officers, particularly of the Kansas volunteers, came to me with the remark that when we first overtook the Cheyenne village, and I failed to order an attack when all the chances were in our favor, they mentally condemned my decision as a mistake; but with the results accomplished afterward they found ample reason to amend their first judgment, and frankly and cordially admit that the release of the two captives was far more gratifying than any victory over the Indians could have been if purchased by the sacrifice of their lives.

"With this happy termination of this much of our negotiations with the Indians, I determined to march in the morning for Camp Supply, Indian Territory, satisfied that with the three chiefs in our possession, and the squaws and children captured at the Washita, still held as prisoners at Fort Hays, Kansas, we could compel the Cheyennes to abandon the war-path and return to their reservation. The three chiefs begged to be released, upon the ground that their people had delivered up the two girls; but this I told them was but one of the two conditions imposed; the other required the tribe to return to their reservation, and until this was done, they need not hope for freedom; but in the meanwhile I assured them of kind treatment at our hands.

"Before dark a delegation of chiefs from the village visited camp to likewise urge the release of the three chiefs. My reply to them was the same that I had given to the captives. I assured them, however, that upon complying with their treaty obligations, and returning to their reservation, the three chiefs would be restored to their people, and we would return to them also the women and children captured at the Washita. Seeing that no modification of these terms could be obtained, they finally promised to accede to them, saying that their ponies, as I knew to be the fact, were in no condition to travel, but as soon as practicable they would surely proceed with their entire village to Camp Supply, and abandon the war-path forever; a promise which, as a tribe, they have adhered to, from that day to this, with strict faith, so far as my knowledge extends."

The settlement of the Cheyennes closed Custer's services on the southern plains. His command proceeded to Camp Supply and thence to Fort Hays, where the Nineteenth Kansas was mustered out. From and after the Washita campaign, the frontiers of Kansas were untroubled by any considerable depredations. Pawnee Killer, and the single campaign of 1867, had taught Custer all he needed to know of Indian fighting. In 1868–9, he showed the fruits of his lesson in the first thoroughly successful campaign that had yet been prosecuted against the Indians of the plains.

As many of our readers may feel an interest in the various characters introduced in these southern campaigns of Custer, a short summary of the fate of his best scouts may not be uninteresting. It seems that Romeo, true to his amorous name, and not deterred by his previous experience in Indian marriages, took to himself one more Cheyenne wife, when the tribe came in on their reservation, and that he became and is an Indian trader.

California Joe disappeared for several years, till in 1874, when Custer was in command at Fort Lincoln, he sent the general this letter:

SIERRE NEVADE MOUNTAINS, CALEFORNIA, March 16, 1874.

Dear General after my respets to you and Lady i thought that i tell you that i am still on top of land yit i hev been in the rockey mountain the most of the time sence last I seen you but i got on the railroad and started west and the first thing I knew I landed in san Francisco so I could not go any further except goin by water and salt water at that so i turned back and headed for the mountains once more resolved never to go railroading no more i drifted up with the tide to sacramento city and i landed my boat so i took up through town they say thar is 20 thousand people living thar but it looks to me like to be 100 thousand counting chinaman and all i cant describe my wolfish feeling but i think that i look just like i did when we was chasing Buffalo on the cimarone so i struck up through town and i come to a large fine building crowded with people so i bulged in to see what was going on and when i got in to the counsil house i took a look around at the crowd and i seen the most of them had bald heads so i thought to myself i struck it now that they are indian peace commissioners so i look to see if i would know any of them but not one so after while the smartess lookin one got up and said gentleman i introduce a bill to have speckle mountain trout and fish eggs imported to california to be put in the american Bear and yuba rivers— those rivers is so muddy that a tadpole could not live in them caused by mining—did any body ever hear of speckle trout living in muddy water and the next thing was the game law and that was very near as bad as the Fish for they aint no game in the country as big as mawking bird i heard some fellow behind me ask how long is the legislaturs been in session then i dropt on myself it wuzent Indian commissioners after all so i slid out took across to chinatown and they smelt like a kiowa camp in August with plenty buffalo meat around—it was gettin late so no place to go not got a red cent so i happen to think of an old friend back of town that i knowed 25 years ago so i lit out and sure enough he was thar just as i left him 25 years ago baching [leading the life of bachelor—G. A. C.] so i got a few seads i going to plant in a few days give my respects to the 7th calvery and except the same yoursly

CALIFORNIA JOE.

Joe subsequently turned up again as a miner in the Black Hills, where he probably is to-day. He still smokes.

CHAPTER IX.

LOUISVILLE TO THE YELLOWSTONE.

THE final submission of the Cheyennes completed the work of Custer in the southwest, and set on him the stamp of complete success. He had done what no other officer in the American army had yet succeeded in doing, beaten tribe after tribe of Indians, completely and decisively; and his exploits had justly earned the reputation for him of being the best Indian fighter on the plains. For a time, his bitterest enemies were silent. They could not alter the facts by their sneers, and their animus was too palpable when they tried to belittle his exploits. The *facts* were Custer's best eulogy.

A hostile and prejudiced court had sentenced him to disgrace on a frivolous pretext, and his enemies had tried their best to get along without him. They had all the United States army to pick from, and yet they had done nothing all the summer but get into trouble and fail. The stage routes were deserted, travel stopped, and only the line of the railway, as far as built, was safe. At last Custer's worst enemies were compelled to acquiesce silently in the request of Sherman and Sheridan to be given back Custer himself as the only hope of success. Every officer of the Seventh, enemies and all, joined in the request. A few months' experience of being made ridiculous under another leader, brought them to that. Custer might be severe on drunkards, he might be a hard marcher, but he never made a fool of the regiment, and his worst enemies in that regiment had been conscious that he was unjustly treated in his court-martial.

They knew that the principal instigator of the charges against him had since been compelled to leave the army on account of habitual drunkenness, and that all the really good and valuable officers who had ever served under Custer were unanimous in his praise. They joined in that request, the like of which had never been known before. A whole department formally asked for the return to command of an officer whom a year before the powers had tried their utmost to disgrace. He came, and what was the result? Before the winter had fairly turned into spring, Custer had ended the whole war and placed the frontier in peace, alone and unassisted, *just because he was given his own way.* In seven months he had closed the campaign which commenced in 1867, when Hancock let the Cheyennes slip from between his fingers, and when Custer saw his first Indian chief. He learned the mysteries of Indian warfare pretty quickly after that.

The close of this seven months' campaign gave Custer a long and well-earned rest, during the summer of 1869. During the whole winter campaign he had been separated from his wife, who had remained at Fort Leavenworth; but now that hostilities were closed, she rejoined him. The Seventh Cavalry was encamped during the whole summer in the neighborhood of Fort Hays, at Big Creek, where the very perfection of prairie life was the portion of all. This period and the next year may be called one of the very happiest of Custer's life, wherein he enjoyed himself as much as when in Texas after the close of the war. His whole military life seems to have been passed in a series of these changes, from periods of the hardest, most protracted and vigorous labor, to periods of rest and pleasure, enjoyed with the keenest zest by himself and wife.

The summer of 1869 was a perfect round of pleasurable excitement, hunting excursions taking place almost every week, parties of tourists from the east or from Europe coming to visit the camp, attracted by the fame of Custer the successful Indian-fighter, and anxious to see him. Every week or so, a single squadron would be sent off on a scout through southern Kansas, to look after any small parties of Indians that might sneak out of the agencies on a cattle lifting raid; but there was no fighting or danger. The main body of Indians was really and truly at peace, cowed by Custer's successes. The campaign had made them respect him, and they all held him in deep reverence. Already, showing the thoroughness of his character, he had mastered the Indian sign language, and was able to converse with Indians from any tribe on the plains, by this universal medium of communication.

The summer being passed in entertaining eastern visitors, private and public, camp was struck in October, and the winter passed in Fort Leavenworth, where Custer began to write his War Memoirs, in a slightly different form from that in which they afterwards appeared, but he gave them up when they had reached no further than the battle of Williamsburg in the Peninsular Campaign. He was always very diffident as to his literary abilities, being keenly sensible of the deficiencies of a West Point education in that direction, and it was this diffidence which probably caused him to give up the War Memoirs so early. People had accused him so often of vanity, that he had become painfully sensitive on the subject of mentioning himself, and strove hard to keep his own name out of the War Memoirs, as well as, later, in the Life on the Plains. This is, in fact, the gravest literary fault possessed by either. Almost all the interest they possess is that which appertains to Custer personally, as the most romantic figure of the war, and instead of this he thought himself obliged to give us historical sketches of others, not possessing half the same charm.

His literary labors at Fort Leavenworth were varied, late in the winter, by a leave of absence, spent in a trip to New York with the little wife, still as fresh and childish in mind and heart as ever, a matter in which she and Custer were exactly alike. All the summer they would be saving up their money for the eastern trip in the winter, and when the time came, they started off like two happy children, determined to have a good time, seeing all the sights, going to all the theatres, laughing at Dundreary and weeping over the simulated sorrows of Clara Morris, enjoying themselves to the very utmost. From that time thereafter, every winter saw the same little trip, and every spring saw them returning to the rough frontier life, having spent all their spare cash, but having had a splendid trip, full of enjoyment.

The spring and summer of 1870 were merely a repetition of those of 1869, with more visitors. By this time, Custer's fame as a cavalry general was completely overshadowed by his more recent triumphs as an Indian fighter, and his still more recent exploits as a mighty hunter. His Scotch deerhounds had increased in number till he owned quite a large pack, his rifles were growing numerous, his sporting letters to the *Turf, Field and Farm* had made him a friend of every hunter in the United States, and the English noble and gentle tourists, out for a buffalo hunt, always stopped at Fort Hays and brought letters to General Custer, who was supposed to know everything about the plains and buffalo. Even the great humbug Barnum came out west to have a buffalo hunt, and was indulged with a run. It was of course a good deal of trouble entertaining all these greenhorns, and especially taking care of them in a buffalo hunt. It was necessary to send out a mounted orderly with each, to see he did not get lost, and as soon as the chase separated the hunters, the orderly used to kill the buffalo for his particular tourist, while the latter fired off all the barrels of his revolver into the carcass and then cut off the tail and claimed the beast as his own spoil. The orderlies found it a paying business to sell silence, while the amateurs took home their buffalo tails in triumph and hung them up in their studies. There are a good many such trophies in the Eastern States to-day, which might not be such a cause of pride to their owners were the true story to leak out.

October, 1870, again took Custer to Fort Leavenworth, where

the whole regiment was reunited, under the command of General Sturgis, its new colonel. General A. J. Smith had gone on the retired list, and Sturgis had succeeded him, as being the senior lieutenant-colonel of the army. It was now determined, in view of the peculiar exigencies of the U. S. regular army, that the Seventh Cavalry should be broken up and moved elsewhere, while another regiment relieved it in the West. Custer was thus likely to find himself, like many another officer, put in garrison at some one or two company post in the States and he wished to avoid this, as he was beginning to love his wild life on the plains. He therefore made a formal application to headquarters, requesting to be assigned to duty at Fort Hays, or else at headquarters of his regiment.

The endorsement on this communication will show what at that time was General Sturgis' opinion on Custer's merits as an Indian fighter, which he has since so strenuously denied. It runs thus :

HEADQUARTERS SEVENTH CAVALRY, CAMP NEAR FORT HAYS, KAS.
August 13th, 1869.

In forwarding this communication approved, I would respectfully ask for it that favorable consideration to which it would appear to be entitled, not only in view of General Custer's worth and former services, but also of the arduous and important services rendered by him against the Indians of this department, while in command of the Seventh Cavalry. *There is perhaps, no other officer of equal rank on this line who has worked more faithfully against the Indians, or who has acquired the same degree of knowledge of the country and of the Indian character.* If however, it should be deemed impracticable to give him the command he desires, I would respectfully recommend that he be permitted to accompany the Headquarters of the Regiment.

S. D. STURGIS, *Col. Seventh Cavalry,*
Bvt. Maj. Gen. U. S. A. Comd. Regt.

This was Sturgis's free and unbiased opinion on Custer, fresh from the experience of his Indian warfare. It reads well to-day, since he has tried to change his opinion, now that Custer is dead.

The application was unsuccessful. There was no longer an urgent necessity for a first class Indian fighter at Fort Hays, and any old seniority fossil would do. Custer had done his work very well, no doubt, better than any other man who had been put out there, but that was a year before. It was necessary to give some other regiment a chance at the plains, so the Seventh was ordered away into the States, and broken up into detachments at small posts. Under these circumstances, the position of the field officers of a regiment, if they are inclined to be lazy, is very pleasant. There is really nothing for them to do. They become mere ornamental appendages tacked on to a post, to sign their names to requisitions and reports. It was so far pleasant to Custer that he got all the leaves he wanted, and was able to go to Monroe early in 1871, while his extended leave finally took him to New York on private business. In March, the Seventh was ordered partly to Kentucky, partly to South Carolina, Custer being assigned to a two company post at Elizabethtown, Kentucky, a small place, some forty miles south of Louisville. Here the husband and wife settled down in June for the next two years to a monotonous existence, especially irksome to Custer. Nine officers out of ten, of the common pattern, which aims at earning its money easily, would have been delighted with this snug billet, but to Custer it was the reverse of pleasant. All that saved him from unhappiness was his literary work, in writing for the Galaxy the papers entitled "My Life on the Plains," which were begun and finished during his Kentucky residence. Part of the time he was detailed in Louisville on a board for buying horses for the regiment, which naturally brought him in contact with all the smart horse-dealers of the "horsey" state. This horse purchasing business also took him out to the Blue Grass country at times, and while there he invested much of his private funds in race-horses, on which he expected to realize handsomely. Just as his "luck" in war had been good, however, just so was his "luck" in horse-buying during peace time decidedly bad.

No sooner had he paid his money for a valuable mare, than the mare would be kicked by another, and get a leg broken, or fall sick or die; and in this way his horse ventures all came to grief and he lost some ten thousand dollars in a few years. The fact was, Custer was too honest and frank, too much of a knight of romance, he loved his horses too well, to succeed in trade with them. To be a successful horse trader, a man must be thoroughly callous, and regard his horses as mere objects of trade, which Custer never would do. Only one of his purchases now remains alive, and that one has been nearly ruined by the carelessness of the person in whose care it was left.

During his Louisville residence, Custer only caught one glimpse of his beloved plains—in the winter of 1872. During that year the Russian Grand Duke Alexis came to the United States on a tour, and it was judged civil to show him a buffalo hunt. General Sheridan, still in command of the great western division, and now moreover a lieutenant-general, was getting rather too stout for that kind of thing himself, and yet it was necessary to find some officer of high rank and national reputation to escort the Grand Duke, and to show him the honors as well as the buffalo. No one was judged so fit for the purpose as Custer, and accordingly he received a telegraphic order to report at Omaha in January, 1872, where he joined Alexis, the renowned scout William Cody ("Buffalo Bill") being also ordered there. The Grand Duke was delighted with his hunt and with Custer, whom he saw for the first time in the picturesque buckskin hunting-shirt which the General always wore on the plains. The hunt over, the duke insisted that Custer must accompany him on his further trip through the west, which the latter did, returning with Alexis to Louisville. Here they were joined by Mrs. Custer, and the party visited Mammoth Cave, and finally started on a regular trip through the south, which terminated March, 1872, at New Orleans, where Alexis took ship for Russia. Nothing of note transpired during the summer of 1872, during which the Life on the Plains was fairly begun, and nearly completed during the rest of the year. In March 1873, the Seventh Cavalry was once more ordered to the Plains, this time up in Dakota.

This order perfectly delighted Custer. He was getting heartily sick of the useless life he had been leading, and he knew that work was coming, real work. When the whole Seventh Cavalry was ordered out in a body, it meant business. Once before they had been ordered out, and had ended in con- quering the southwest. Now it was necessary to overrun the northwest. When Custer pacified the Kiowas, Arapahoes, and Cheyennes by force, physical and moral, the Sioux of the northwest had fared very differently. They had frightened the Government into a treaty, the treaty of 1868, by which the United States had promised to give up to them forever a large expanse of country, and not to trespass thereon.

Now that the danger was over, and the Pacific Railroad safely completed to the south, thanks to Custer, the treaty with the Northern Indians became irksome. It was all well enough to *promise* a lot of naked savages to give them up so much land, but it could not be expected that such a promise should be *kept* a moment longer than was necessary to secure a quiet building of the railroad. It was now time to break the treaty. A north- ern Pacific road had become necessary, and its route was to lie right through the very midst of the territory solemnly prom- ised the Indians by the treaty of 1868. As a practical measure to provoke an Indian war, there is nothing so certain as the commencement of a railroad. With the power to run it through, however, a different state of things ensues, as Custer himself forcibly illustrates, in narrating the events of the Yellowstone expedition, the last in which we are able to follow his words.

" The experience of the past," says Custer, " particularly that of recent years, has shown too that no one measure so quickly and effectually frees a country from the horrors and devastations of Indian wars and Indian depredations generally

as *the building and successful operation of a railroad* through
the region overrun."

Nothing can be truer than this, when once the railroad is
completed, but the trouble is that while it is being built, the
war has to be paid for at the same time, for the Indians, recognizing that the railroad will be their ruin, do all they can to
hinder it.

Knowing this, the Seventh Cavalry was ordered to Dakota
in March, 1873. Custer, overjoyed, left Louisville with his two
companies, and was joined at Memphis by the rest of the regiment, all delighted to be together. There was Tom Custer, who
had been down in South Carolina, hunting whiskey distillers,
and was heartily sick of the nauseous business; there were Cook,
Yates, Calhoun, Smith and all the fellows, glad to see each other
and anxious for work.

What with friends and relatives, the little group of officers
nearest to Custer seemed like one family. There was Calhoun,
the young boyish-looking Apollo of the regiment, who had
married Maggie Custer a year before, and who was now acting
as adjutant. There was Tom Custer, who had risen from the
ranks of the volunteers, as Calhoun did from those of the regulars, and whose only privilege as the general's brother, was to
get put in arrest for the little breaches of discipline oftener
than any officer in the regiment. There was "Queen's Own"
Cook, with his high-bred face and long Dundreary whiskers,
and sturdy business-like Yates, who kept the "band-box troop"
of the regiment. How glad all the boys were to see each other,
and how they delighted in the prospect of work!

The regiment was taken by boat to Yankton on the Missouri, where it was put ashore, and remained a week or so, being
finally organized again April 10th, 1873. Then the whole
Seventh Cavalry, in regular old style, took up their march
along the banks of the Missouri all the way to Fort Rice, 600
miles off, which they reached in six weeks. In regular old
style, Mrs. Custer rode on her horse at the head of the column,

and this time she had the company of more than one lady. Mrs. Calhoun, Mrs. Yates, Mrs. Smith and several other of the officers' wives went with her, and all accomplished the journey in safety. They passed through the Cheyenne, Brule, Yanktonnais and Standing Rock Agencies, seeing for the first time, the Northern Indians, and finally went into camp at Fort Rice late in May.

There, however, the ladies found themselves, very unwillingly, compelled to turn back. The regiment was ordered to accompany the Yellowstone Expedition. Mrs. Custer and her friends returned to Monroe, while Custer proceeded on that expedition which he shall henceforth tell in his own words.

In the early spring of '73, says Custer, the officials of the Northern Pacific railroad applied to the Government authorities at Washington for military protection for a surveying party to be sent out the ensuing summer to explore and mark out the uncompleted portion of the road extending from the Missouri River in Dakota to the interior of Montana, west of the Yellowstone.

To extend encouragement and aid to the projectors and builders of the Northern Pacific road, the Government granted the application of the road for a military escort, and gave authority for the organization of what was afterward designated as the Yellowstone expedition. The troops composing the expedition numbered about seventeen hundred men, consisting of cavalry, infantry, an improvised battery of artillery, and a detachment of Indian scouts, the whole under command of Brevet Major-General D. S. Stanley. Fort Rice, Dakota, on the Missouri River, was selected as the point of rendezvous and departure of the expedition.

It was not until July that the Yellowstone expedition assumed definite shape, and began its westward movement from Fort Rice. The engineers and surveyors of the Northern Pacific railroad were under the direction and management of General Thomas L. Rosser. He and I had been cadets together at the Military Academy at West Point, occupying adjoining rooms, and being members of the same company, often marching side by side in the performance of our various military duties while at the Academy. When the storms of secession broke upon the country in '61, Rosser, in common with the majority of the cadets from the Southern States, resigned his warrant, and hastened to unite his personal fortunes with those of his State—Texas. He soon won distinction in the Confederate army, under Lee, and finally rose to the rank and command of major-general of cavalry.

When the war was ended, Rosser, like many of his comrades from the South who had staked their all upon the issue of the war, at once cast about him for an opportunity to begin anew the battle, not of war, but of life. Possessing youth, health, many and large abilities, added to indomitable pluck, he decided to trust his fortunes amidst his late enemies, and repaired to Minnesota, where he sought employment in one of the many surveying parties acting under the auspices of the Northern Pacific road. Upon applying to the officer of the road for a position as civil engineer, he was informed that no vacancy existed to which he could be appointed. Nothing daunted, he persisted, and finally accepted a position among the axemen, willing to work, and proved to his employers not only his industry, but his fitness for promotion. He at once attracted the attention of his superiors, who were not slow to recognize his merit. Rosser was advanced rapidly from one important position to another, until in a few months he became the chief engineer of the surveying party accompanying the expedition. In this capacity I met him on the plains of Dakota, in 1873, nearly ten years after the date when in peaceful scabbards we sheathed the swords which on more than one previous occasion we had drawn against each other. Omitting the incidents of the march from our starting point, Fort Rice, on the Missouri, we come to the time when we found ourselves encamped on the east bank of the beautiful and swift flowing Yellowstone, about a hundred

31

miles from its mouth. At this point the expedition was met by a steamer, sent for that purpose up the Missouri, hundreds of miles above Fort Rice, then up the Yellowstone to the point of junction. From it fresh supplies of forage and subsistence stores were obtained. This being done, the entire expedition, save a small detachment left at this point to guard our surplus stores, intended for our return march, was ferried by the steamer across the Yellowstone River. Our course for several days carried us up that stream; our tents at night being usually pitched on or near the river bank. The country to be surveyed, however, soon became so rough and broken in places that we encountered serious delays at times in finding a practicable route for our long and heavily laden wagon trains, over rocks and through canons hitherto unexplored by white men. So serious did these embarrassments become, and so much time was lost in accomplishing our daily marches, that I suggested to General Stanley that I should take with me each day a couple of companies of cavalry and a few of the Indian scouts, and seek out and prepare a practicable road in advance, thereby preventing detention of the main command. This proposition being acceded to, it was my custom thereafter to push rapidly forward in the early morning, gaining an advance of several miles upon the main expedition, and by locating the route relieving the troops and trains in rear of a great amount of fatigue and many tedious detentions. One result of this system was that I and my little party, who were acting as pioneers, usually arrived at the termination of our day's march, our camp ground for the night, at an early hour in the day, several hours in advance of the main portion of the expedition.

On the morning of August 4th, with two companies of the Seventh Cavalry, commanded by Captain Moylan and Colonel Custer—who, with my adjutant, Lieutenant Calhoun, and Lieutenant Varnum, composed the officers of the party, and guided by my favorite scout, Bloody Knife, a young Arickaree warrior, the entire party numbering eighty-six men and five officers, I left camp at five o'clock in the morning, and set out as usual to explore the country and find a practicable route for the main column. Soon after we left camp, Bloody Knife's watchful eyes discovered fresh signs of Indians. Halting long enough to allow him to examine the trail, Bloody Knife was soon able to gather all the information attainable. A party of Indians had been prowling about our camp the previous night, and had gone away, travelling in the direction in which we were then marching.

This intelligence occasioned no particular surprise, as we had been expecting to discover the presence of Indians for several days. Bloody Knife's information produced no change in our plans. The hostile party of whose presence we had become aware, numbered nineteen ; our party numbered over ninety.

Over rock-ribbed hills, down timbered dells, and across open, grassy plains, we wended our way without unusual interest, except at intervals of a few miles to discover the trail of the nineteen prowling visitors of the previous night, showing that our course, which was intended to lead us again to the Yellowstone, was in the same direction as theirs. Bloody Knife interpreted this as indicating that the village from which the nineteen had probably been sent to reconnoitre and report our movements, was located somewhere above us in the Yellowstone valley. About ten o'clock we reached the crest of the high line of bluffs bordering the Yellowstone valley, from which we obtained a fine view of the river and valley extending above and beyond us as far as the eye could reach.

After halting upon the crest of the bluffs long enough to take in the pleasures of the scene, and admire the beautiful valley spread out like an exquisite carpet at our feet, we descended to the valley and directed our horses' heads toward a particularly attractive and inviting cluster of shade trees standing on the river bank, and distant from the crest of the bluffs nearly two miles. First allowing our thirsty horses to drink from the clear, crystal water of the Yellowstone, which ran murmuringly by in its long tortuous course to the Missouri, we then picketed them out to graze.

Precautionary and necessary measures having been attended to, looking to the security of our horses, the next important and equally necessary step was to post half a dozen pickets on the open plain beyond, to give timely warning in the event of the approach of hostile Indians. This being done, the remainder of our party busied themselves in arranging each for his individual comfort, disposing themselves on the grass beneath the shade of the wide-spreading branches of the cotton woods that grew close to the river bank. For myself, so oblivious was I to the prospect of immediate danger, that after selecting a most inviting spot for my noonday nap, and arranging my saddle and buckskin coat in the form of a comfortable pillow, I removed my boots, untied my cravat, and opened my collar, prepared to enjoy to the fullest extent, the delight of the outdoor siesta.

I did not omit, however, to place my trusty Remington rifle within easy grasp—more from habit, it must be confessed, than from anticipation of danger. Near me, and stretched on the ground sheltered by the shade of the same tree, was my brother, the colonel, divested of his hat, coat, and boots; while close at hand, wrapped in deep slumber, lay the other three officers, Moylan, Calhoun, and Varnum. Sleep had taken possession of us all—officers and men—excepting of course the watchful pickets into whose keeping the safety, the lives, of our little detachment was for the time entrusted. How long we slept I scarcely know—perhaps an hour, when the cry of "Indians! Indians!" quickly followed by the sharp ringing crack of the pickets' carbines, aroused and brought us—officers, men, and horses—to our feet. There was neither time nor occasion for questions to be asked or answered. Catching up my rifle, and without waiting to don hat or boots, I glanced through the grove of trees to the open plain or valley beyond, and saw a small party of Indians bearing down toward us as fast as their ponies could carry them.

" Run to your horses, men ! Run to your horses ! " I fairly yelled as I saw that the first move of the Indians was intended to stampede our animals and leave us to be attended to afterward.

At the same time the pickets opened fire upon our disturbers, who had already emptied their rifles at us as they advanced as if boldly intending to ride us down. As yet we could see but half a dozen warriors, but those who were familiar with stratagems knew full well that so small a party of savages unsupported would not venture to disturb in open day a force the size of ours. Quicker than I could pen the description, each trooper, with rifle in hand, rushed to secure his horse, and men and horses were soon withdrawn from the open plain and concealed behind the clump of trees beneath whose shade we were but a few moments before quietly sleeping. The firing of the pickets, the latter having been reinforced by a score of their comrades, checked the advance of the Indians and enabled us to saddle our horses and be prepared for whatever might be in store for us.

A few moments found us in our saddles and sallying forth from the timber to try conclusions with the daring intruders. We could only see half a dozen Sioux warriors galloping up and down in our front, boldly challenging us by their manner to attempt their capture or death. Of course it was an easy matter to drive them away, but as we advanced it became noticeable that they retired, and when we halted or diminished our speed they did likewise. It was apparent from the first that the Indians were resorting to stratagem to accomplish that which they could not do by an open, direct attack. Taking twenty troopers with me headed by Colonels Custer and Calhoun, and directing Moylan to keep within supporting distance with the remainder, I followed the retreating Sioux up the valley, but with no prospect of overtaking them, as they were mounted upon the fleetest of ponies. Thinking to tempt them within our grasp, I being mounted on a Kentucky thoroughbred in

whose speed and endurance I had confidence, directed Colonel
Custer to allow me to approach the Indians, accompanied only
by my orderly, who was also well mounted; at the same time
to follow us cautiously at a distance of a couple of hundred
yards. The wily redskins were not to be caught by any such
artifice. They were perfectly willing that my orderly and myself should approach them, but at the same time they carefully
watched the advance of the cavalry following me, and permitted
no advantage. We had by this time almost arrived abreast of
an immense tract of timber growing in the valley and extending
to the water's edge, but distant from our resting place, from
which we had been so rudely aroused, about two miles.

The route taken by the Indians, and which they evidently
intended us to follow, led past this timber, but not through it.
When we had arrived almost opposite the nearest point, I sig-
nalled to the cavalry to halt, which was no sooner done than the
Indians also came to a halt. I then made the sign to the latter
for a parley, which was done simply by riding my horse in a
circle. To this the savages only responded by looking on in
silence for a few moments, then turning their ponies and moving off slowly, as if to say, "Catch us if you can." My suspicions were more than ever aroused, and I sent my orderly
back to tell Colonel Custer to keep a sharp eye upon the heavy
bushes on our left and scarcely three hundred yards distant
from where I sat on my horse. The orderly had delivered his
message, and had almost rejoined me, when judging from our
halt that we intended to pursue no further, the real design and
purpose of the savages was made evident. The small party in
front had faced toward us and were advancing as if to attack.
I could scarcely credit the evidence of my eyes, but my astonishment had only begun when turning to the wood on my left
I beheld bursting from their concealment between three and
four hundred Sioux warriors mounted and caparisoned with all
the flaming adornments of paint and feathers which go to make
up the Indian war costume. When I first obtained a glimpse

of them—and a single glance was sufficient—they were dashing from the timber at full speed, yelling and whooping as only Indians can. At the same time they moved in perfect line, and with as seeming good order and alignment as the best drilled cavalry.

To understand our relative positions the reader has only to imagine a triangle whose sides are almost equal; their length in this particular instance being from three to four hundred yards, the three angles being occupied by Colonel Custer and his detachment, the Indians, and myself. Whatever advantage there was in length of sides fell to my lot, and I lost no time in availing myself of it. Wheeling my horse suddenly around, and driving the spurs into his sides, I rode as only a man rides whose life is the prize, to reach Colonel Custer and his men, not only in advance of the Indians, but before any of them could cut me off. Moylan with his reserve was still too far in the rear to render their assistance available in repelling the shock of the Indians' first attack. Realizing the great superiority of our enemies, not only in numbers, but in their ability to handle their arms and horses in a fight, and fearing they might dash through and disperse Colonel Custer's small party of twenty men, and having once broken the formation of the latter, despatch them in detail, I shouted to Colonel Custer at almost each bound of my horse, " Dismount your men !   Dismount your men !" but the distance which separated us and the excitement of the occasion prevented him from hearing me.

Fortunately, however, this was not the first time he had been called upon to contend against the sudden and unforeseen onslaught of savages, and although failing to hear my suggestion, he realized instantly that the safety of his little band of troopers depended upon the adoption of prompt means of defence.

Scarcely had the long line of splendidly mounted warriors rushed from their hiding place before Colonel Custer's voice rang out sharp and clear, " Prepare to fight on foot." This order required three out of four troopers to leap from their saddles and take their position on the ground, where by more deliberate aim, and being freed from the management of their horses, a more effective resistance could be opposed to the rapidly approaching warriors. The fourth trooper in each group of "fours" remained on his horse, holding the reins of the horses of his three comrades.

Quicker than words can describe, the fifteen cavalrymen, now on foot and acting as infantry, rushed forward a few paces in advance of the horses, deployed into open order, and dropping on one or both knees in the low grass, waited with loaded carbines—with finger gently pressing the trigger—the approach of the Sioux, who rode boldly down as if apparently unconscious that the small group of troopers were on their front. "Don't fire, men, till I give the word, and when you do fire, aim low," was the quiet injunction given his men by their young commander, as he sat on his horse intently watching the advancing foe.

Swiftly over the grassy plain leaped my noble steed, each bound bearing me nearer to both friends and foes. Had the race been confined to the Indians and myself the closeness of the result would have satisfied an admirer even of the Derby. Nearer and nearer our paths approached each other, making it appear almost as if I were one of the line of warriors, as the latter bore down to accomplish the destruction of the little group of troopers in front. Swifter seem to fly our mettled steeds, the one to save, the other to destroy, until the common goal has almost been reached—a few more bounds, and friends and foes will be united—will form one contending mass.

The victory was almost within the grasp of the redskins. It seemed that but a moment more, and they would be trampling the kneeling troopers beneath the feet of their fleet-limbed ponies; when, "Now men, let them have it!" was the signal for a well-directed volley, as fifteen cavalry carbines poured their contents into the ranks of the shrieking savages. Before the latter could recover from the surprise and confusion which followed, the carbines—thanks to the invention of breech-loaders—were almost instantly loaded, and a second carefully aimed discharge went whistling on its deadly errand. Several warriors were seen to reel in their saddles, and were only saved from falling by the quickly extended arms of their fellows. Ponies were tumbled over like butchered bullocks, their riders glad to find themselves escaping with less serious injuries. The effect of the rapid firing of the troopers, and the firm, determined stand, showing that they thought neither of flight nor surrender, was to compel the savages first to slacken their speed, then to lose their daring and confidence in their ability to trample down the little group of defenders in the front. Death to many of their number stared them in the face. Besides, if the small party of troopers in the front was able to oppose such plucky and destructive resistance to their attacks, what might not be expected should the main party under Moylan, now swiftly approaching to the rescue, also take part in the struggle? But more quickly than my sluggish pen has been able to record the description of the scene, the battle line of the warriors exhibited signs of faltering which soon degenerated into an absolute repulse. In a moment their attack was transformed into flight in which each seemed only anxious to secure his individual safety. A triumphant cheer from the cavalry-men as they sent a third installment of leaden messengers whistling about the ears of the fleeing redskins served to spur both pony and rider to their utmost speed. Moylan by this time had reached the ground and had united the entire force. The Indians in the mean time had plunged out of sight into the recesses of the jungle from which they first made their attack. We knew too well that their absence would be brief, and that they would resume the attack, but not in the manner of the first.

We knew that we had inflicted no little loss upon them—dead and wounded ponies could be seen on the ground passed over

by the Indians. The latter would not be satisfied without determined efforts to get revenge. Of this we were well aware.

A moment's hurried consultation between the officers and
myself, and we decided that as we would be forced to act entirely upon the defensive against a vastly superior force, it
would be better if we relieved ourselves as far as possible of the
care of our horses, and take our chances in the fight which was
yet to come, on foot. At the same time, we were then so far
out on the open plain and from the river bank, that the Indians could surround us. We must get nearer to the river,
conceal our horses or shelter them from fire, then with every
available man form a line or semicircle, with our backs to the
river, and defend ourselves until the arrival of the main body
of the expedition, an event we could not expect for several
hours. As if divining our intentions and desiring to prevent
their execution, the Indians now began their demonstrations
looking to a renewal of the fight.

Of course it was easy to see what had been the original plan
by which the Indians hoped to kill or capture our entire party.
Stratagem of course was to play a prominent part in the quarrel.
The few young warriors first sent to arouse us from our midday
slumber came as a decoy to tempt us to pursue them beyond
the ambush in which lay concealed the main body of the savages; the latter were to dash from their hiding place, intercept
our retreat, and dispose of us after the most approved manner
of barbarous warfare.

The next move on our part was to fight our way back to
the little clump of bushes from which we had been so rudely
startled. To do this Captain Moylan, having united his force
to that of Colonel Custer, gave the order " Prepare to fight on
foot." This was quickly obeyed. Three-fourths of the fighting force were now on foot armed with the carbines only.
These were deployed in somewhat of a circular skirmish line,
of which the horses formed the centre; the circle having a
diameter of several hundred yards. In this order we made our

way back to the timber; the Indians whooping, yelling, and firing their rifles as they dashed madly by on their fleet war ponies. That the fire of their rifles should be effective under these circumstances could scarcely be expected. Neither could the most careful aim of the cavalrymen produce much better results. It forced the savages to keep at a respectful distance, however, and enabled us to make our retrograde movement. A few of our horses were shot by the Indians in this irregular skirmish; none fatally, however. As we were falling back, contesting each foot of ground passed over, I heard a sudden sharp cry of pain from one of the men in charge of our horses; the next moment I saw his arm hanging helplessly at his side, while a crimson current flowing near his shoulder told that the aim of the Indians had not been entirely in vain. The gallant fellow kept his seat in his saddle, however, and conducted the horses under his charge safely with the rest to the timber. Once concealed by the trees, and no longer requiring the horses to be moved, the number of horseholders was reduced so as to allow but one trooper to eight horses; the entire remainder being required on the skirmish line. The redskins had followed us closely, step by step, to the timber, tempted in part by their great desire to obtain possession of our horses. If successful in this, they believed no doubt that, flight on our part being no longer possible, we must be either killed or captured.

Taking advantage of a natural terrace or embankment extending almost like a semicircle in front of the little grove in which we had taken refuge, and at a distance of but a few hundred yards from the latter, I determined by driving the Indians beyond to adopt it as our breastwork or line of defence. This was soon accomplished, and we found ourselves deployed behind a natural parapet or bulwark from which the troopers could deliver a carefully directed fire upon their enemies, and at the same time be protected largely from the bullets of the latter. The Indians made repeated and desperate efforts to dislodge us and force us to the level plateau. Every effort of this kind proved unavailing.

Rather a remarkable instance of rifle shooting occurred in the early part of the contest. I was standing in a group of troopers, and with them was busily engaged firing at such of our enemies as exposed themselves. Bloody Knife was with us, his handsome face lighted up by the fire of battle and the desire to avenge the many wrongs suffered by his people at the hands of the ruthless Sioux. All of us had had our attention drawn more than once to a Sioux warrior who, seeming more bold than his fellows, dashed repeatedly along the front of our lines, scarcely two hundred yards distant, and although the troopers had singled him out, he had thus far escaped untouched by their bullets. Encouraged by his success perhaps, he concluded to taunt us again, and at the same time exhibit his own daring, by riding along the lines at full speed, but nearer than before. We saw him coming. Bloody Knife, with his Henry rifle poised gracefully in his hands, watched his coming, saying he intended to make this his enemy's last ride. He would send him to the happy hunting ground. I told the interpreter to tell Bloody Knife that at the moment the warrior reached a designated point directly opposite to us, he, Bloody Knife, should fire at the rider and I at the same instant would fire at the pony.

A smile of approval passed over the swarthy features of the friendly scout as he nodded assent. I held in my hand my well-tried Remington. Resting on one knee and glancing along the barrel, at the same time seeing that Bloody Knife was also squatting low in the deep grass with rifle levelled, I awaited the approach of the warrior to the designated point. On he came, brandishing his weapons and flaunting his shield in our faces, defying us by his taunts to come out and fight like men. Swiftly sped the gallant little steed that bore him, scarcely needing the guiding rein. Nearer and nearer both horse and rider approached the fatal spot, when sharp and clear, and so simultaneous as to sound as one, rang forth the reports of the two

rifles. The distance was less than two hundred yards. The
Indian was seen to throw up his arms and reel in his saddle,
while the pony made one final leap, and both fell to the earth.
A shout rose from the group of troopers, in which Bloody Knife
and I joined. The next moment a few of the comrades of the
fallen warrior rushed to his rescue, and without dismounting
from their ponies, scarcely pulling rein, clutched up the body,
and the next moment disappeared from view.

Foiled in their repeated attempts to dislodge us, the Indians
withdrew to a point beyond the range of our rifles for the
apparent purpose of devising a new plan of attack. Of this we
soon became convinced. Hastily returning to a renewal of the
struggle, we saw our adversaries arrange themselves in groups
along our entire front. They were seen to dismount, and the
quick eyes of Bloody Knife detected them making their way
toward us by crawling through the grass. We were at a loss
to comprehend their designs, as we could not believe they intended to attempt to storm our position on foot. We were not
left long in doubt. Suddenly, and almost as if by magic, we
beheld numerous small columns of smoke shooting up all along
our front.

Calling Bloody Knife and the interpreter to my side, I inquired the meaning of what we saw. "They are setting fire
to the long grass, and intend to burn us out," was the scout's
reply, at the same time keeping his eyes intently bent on the
constantly increasing columns of smoke. His features wore a
most solemn look ; anxiety was plainly depicted there. Looking to him for suggestions and advice in this new phase of our
danger, I saw his face gradually unbend and a scornful smile
part his lips. "The Great Spirit will not help our enemies,"
was his muttered reply to my question. " See," he continued ;
"the grass refuses to burn." Casting my eyes along the line
formed by the columns of smoke, I saw that Bloody Knife
had spoken truly when he said, "The grass refuses to burn."

This was easily accounted for. It was early in the month

of August; the grass had not ripened or matured sufficiently to burn readily. A month later, and the flames would have swept us back to the river as if we had been surrounded by a growth of tinder. In a few moments the anxiety caused by the threatening of this new and terrible danger was dispelled. While the greatest activity was maintained in our front by our enemies, my attention was called to a single warrior who, mounted on his pony, had deliberately, and as I thought rashly, passed around our left flank—our diminished numbers preventing us from extending our line close to the river—and was then in rear of our skirmishers, riding slowly along the crest of the low river bank with as apparent unconcern as if in the midst of his friends instead of being almost in the power of his enemies. I imagined that his object was to get nearer to the grove in which our horses were concealed, and toward which he was moving slowly, to reconnoitre and ascertain how much force we held in reserve. At the same time, as I never can see an Indian engaged in an unexplained act without conceiving treachery or stratagem to be at the bottom of it, I called to Lieutenant Varnum, who commanded on the left, to take a few men and endeavor to cut the wily interloper off. This might have been accomplished but for the excessive zeal of some of Varnum's men, who acted with lack of caution, and enabled the Indian to discover their approach and make his escape by a hurried gallop up the river. The men were at a loss even then to comprehend his strange manœuvre, but after the fight had ended, and we obtained an opportunity to ride over and examine the ground, all was made clear, and we learned how narrowly we had escaped a most serious if not fatal disaster.

The river bank in our rear was from twenty to thirty feet high. At its base and along the water's edge ran a narrow pebbly beach. The redskins had hit upon a novel but to us most dangerous scheme for capturing our horses and at the same time throwing a large force of warriors directly on our rear. They had found a pathway beyond our rear, leading from the large tract of timber in which they were first concealed through a cut or ravine in the river bank. By this they were enabled to reach the water's edge, from which point they could move down the river, following the pebbly beach referred to, the height of the river bank protecting them perfectly from our observation. Thus they would have placed themselves almost in the midst of our horses before we could have become aware of their designs. Had they been willing, as white men would have been, to assume greater risks, their success would have been assured. But they feared that we might discover their movements and catch them while strung out along the narrow beach, with no opportunity to escape. A few men on the bank could have shot down a vastly superior force. In this case the Indians had sent on this errand about one hundred warriors. After the discovery of this attack and its failure, the battle languished for awhile, and we were surprised to notice, not very long after, a general withdrawal from in front of our right, and a concentration of their forces opposite our left. The reason for this was soon made clear to us. Looking far to the right and over the crest of the hills already described, we could see an immense cloud of dust rising and rapidly approaching. We could not be mistaken ; we could not see the cause producing this dust ; but there was not one of us who did not say to himself, "Relief is at hand." A few moments later a shout arose from the men. All eyes were turned to the bluffs in the distance, and there were to be seen, coming almost with the speed of the wind, four separate squadrons of Uncle Sam's best cavalry, with banners flying, horses' manes and tails floating on the breeze, and comrades spurring forward in generous emulation as to which squadron should land its colors first in the fight. It was a grand and welcome sight, but we waited not to enjoy it. Confident of support and wearied from fighting on the defensive, now was our time to mount our steeds and force our enemies to seek safety in flight, or to battle on more even terms. In a moment we were in our saddles and dashing after

them.   The only satisfaction we had was to drive at full speed
for several miles a force outnumbering us five to one.   In this
pursuit we picked up a few ponies which the Indians were compelled to abandon on account of wounds or exhaustion.   Their
wounded, of whom there were quite a number, and their killed,
as afterwards acknowledged by them when they returned to
the agency to receive the provisions and fresh supplies of ammunition which a sentimental government, manipulated and
directed by corrupt combinations, insists upon distributing annually, were sent to the rear before the flight of the main body.
The number of Indians and ponies killed and wounded in this
engagement, as shown by their subsequent admission, almost
equalled that of half our entire force engaged.

That night the forces of the expedition encamped on
the battle-ground, which was nearly opposite the mouth of
Tongue River.   My tent was pitched under the hill from
which I had been so unceremoniously disturbed at the commencement of the fight; while under the wide-spreading
branches of a neighboring cottonwood, guarded and watched
over by sorrowing comrades who kept up their lonely vigils
through the night, lay the mangled bodies of two of our companions of the march, who although not present nor participating in the fight, had fallen victims to the cruelty of our foes.

Thus closes Custer's account of this, his first fight with the
Northern Indians.   In it will be noticed the same coolness and
deliberately studied recklessness which made him so successful
an Indian fighter.   This was the first intimation that the Sioux
were on the war-path against the whites, and their first opposition to the running of the railroad.

In the last sentence of Custer's account of this action, which
closes his published articles on the plains, he mentions two victims of Indian cruelty.   It is necessary to explain the allusion,
because these two men were remotely the cause of Custer's own
death, three years later.

They were both unarmed men, the veterinary surgeon and

the sutler of the Seventh Cavalry. Dr. Houzinger, the first, was a corpulent old man of the quietest and most inoffensive habits, a great favorite with the regiment. Mr. Baliran, the sutler, was also an elderly man, and a great friend of Dr. Houzinger. The two were in the habit of straying off from the main body of the command, picking up natural curiosities, and so far had experienced no trouble. On the day of Custer's fight, these two quiet old men were somewhere about two miles behind his party, and ahead of the main body. Their bodies were found by the advance of the main expedition, where they had been swooped upon and killed by Indians, some out-lying members of the main party. Dr. Houzinger's skull was fractured as with some blunt instrument, but neither body was mutilated. Who had killed them was of course not known then. It came to light in a very strange manner, two years after, as we shall see in its place.

Another man, a soldier of Company F. Seventh Cavalry, was also found killed, where he had been surprised at a spring, and it was the discovery of these bodies, together with the reports of scouts and stragglers that the Indians were up, that had induced General Stanley to send on help to Custer, arriving in time as it did. Stanley mentions this fight in very handsome terms in his report.

For the next three days after the fight, Indians were to be seen hovering round the column, and on the 8th of August the appearance was explained. A lodge pole trail, evidently belonging to a very large village, was found leading up the Yellowstone, and Custer was sent out with all the cavalry and scouts to pursue it, starting at nine that night. The trail was followed for thirty-six hours, and on the 10th August, it was found that the Indians had crossed the Yellowstone in "bull boats," the old trapper name for the wicker coracle, covered with a bull's hide, which is the transport of the plains Indians. Custer tried all day to cross after them, but in vain ; the American horses would not swim the river. Next morning, he was attacked by

32

the Indians, who had been watching his discomfiture. Some came down and fired at him across the river, while another body, probably from a second village, came down behind him, firing from the rear. The place where they now were, was on the north bank of the Yellowstone, three miles below the mouth of the Big Horn. Then, as now, the valley of the Upper Yellowstone, especially the southern bank, was the headquarters of the hostile Indians, and then, as now, Sitting Bull seems to have been their leader. Such at least was the impression of men in the ranks at the time, as I learn from extracts from the diary of an old soldier, then of the Twenty-second infantry, and now in the marines. His name is Patrick Bresland, and he seems to have been a regular old warrior all over the world, having served in the English army in the Crimea and Indian Mutiny, and several enlistments in different corps of the United States Army. This brave fellow it seems, kept a diary, meagre and bare enough, but still recording the main facts during the Yellowstone Expedition, and his entry of the fight of the 4th August is that it was " between the Sioux under Sitting Bull and Companies A and B, Seventh Cavalry." He says further, "the Indians retreated, followed by the Seventh Cavalry, Twenty-second infantry, and the rest of the expedition under General Stanley. On the 10th August we struck their trail at the Yellowstone crossing. We lay in camp all night, or until 3 o'clock next morning, when the Indians, 1500 strong, who had recrossed to our side of the river, commenced an attack at a distance. General Custer ordered out two companies of his regiment as skirmishers, and they were joined by Companies C. I. F. and K. of the Twenty-second infantry. We were ordered by Custer to charge in a body. I was present on this occasion, and followed the Indians nine or ten miles, when they reached the hills and scattered. . . . From here we went to Mussel Shell River, which is the extreme point of the survey on the Northern Pacific Railroad. We remained here several days, when we returned to the Yellowstone, where we had several engagements with the Indians."

Bresland's account mentions the killing of Dr. Houzinger, Mr. Baliran, and Ball of the Seventh Cavalry, and is valuable as coming from an independent and unofficial source, confirming the main facts. General Stanley's report mentions that artillery was used in the fight, which caused a complete stampede of the Indians, they being very much afraid of shells. He also mentions that the soldiers found on the field citizens' clothing, coffee, sugar, bacon, two Winchester rifles and plenty of shells of patent ammunition, showing that the Indians must have been at the agencies recently, as those are the only places where Indians can get these articles.

The station where the expedition left the Yellowstone and crossed the divide to the Mussel-Shell, was named "Pompey's Pillar." This is a knoll on the south side of the Yellowstone, thirty miles from the Big Horn. It stands alone, separated by the water from the other bluffs, with perpendicular sides one hundred and fifty feet high, with a top of grass sod, an acre in extent. In fact, says Stanley, it looks like anything but a "pillar;" however, such it was named, and such it remains on the map to the present day. At this place several Indians came out and fired a volley into a number of soldiers belonging to the expedition, who were bathing, causing a great scattering of naked men. No further serious trouble was experienced, and Custer returned at the close of the trip to Fort Rice late in September. From thence he was ordered to Chicago to report to General Sheridan, with whom he went to Toledo to the reunion of the Army of the Tennessee, and thence to Monroe, where he again met his little wife.

He was now granted a leave, part of which was spent at Chicago, during which time the eldest son of President Grant, an officer on Sheridan's staff, was married to Miss Honoré, a wedding duly reported by the Jenkinses of that date. At the close of his leave, Custer was ordered to assume command of the post at which he spent the remaining years of his life, Fort Abraham Lincoln, on the right bank of the Missouri River, opposite to the little town of Bismarck, which is the present terminus of the Northern Pacific Railroad. He started, with Mrs. Custer and all his belongings, and went through to Bismarck on the very last train that ran that year. The next day, down came the first snow, and thenceforth Custer and his little post were practically cut off from the rest of the world, till the spring opened the country once more.

CHAPTER X.

THE BLACK HILLS.

THE close of the Yellowstone expedition left Custer in quiet for the winter, and it was not till the year 1874 that he was called on for active service. This time it was in connection with the Black Hills expedition, an enterprise that was to prove the cause of much trouble and ultimate war, while its first inception was founded in injustice and cupidity.

The Black Hills, from the time of the first overland travel down to the establishment of the Pacific Railroad, had been an unknown land to the whites. The region that passed by that name lay only some sixty or seventy miles to the north of Fort Laramie, which was the oldest fort on the plains, but it was out of the regular line of travel, and had never been visited by white men so as to be thoroughly explored. The Indians, when questioned about it, were very mysterious, and refused to give definite information, and the few trappers who professed to have visited it, reported it as a land of wonders. Little dependence could be placed on their stories, however. Trappers are, like sailors, given to spinning long yarns, and it was seriously doubted whether any of them had ever been near the hills, as it was known that the Indians guarded the place with great jealousy.

In 1857 a small exploring party, led by Lieutenant Warren of the Engineers—the same who afterwards, as General Warren, had trouble with Sheridan at Five Forks—started from Fort Laramie to explore the Black Hills. Warren's party found the travelling very bad, but succeeded in reaching the

western verge of the hills, near a lofty mountain which the
Indians named Inyan Kara.   Here the party was met by a
number of Sioux chiefs, then at peace with the government,
and warned that it could not proceed further into the hills,
which the Indians regarded as sacred property.   Warren, who
states in his report that he believed the Indians to be justified
in their demands, obeyed them and turned back.   He went off
to the south, and then turned to the east, keeping the hills in
view all the time, and skirting them till he came to the other
side, where another lofty hill was found and marked Bear
Butte.   Warren's expedition and a previous one from another
quarter, led by Captain, afterwards General Reynolds, determined the general figure of the unknown region, but left its
interior as mysterious as ever.

The Black Hills region was found to be a great oval, with
the long axis running nearly north and south, about a hundred
miles by fifty.   It served as a watershed to divide the South
Fork and the Belle Fourche or North Fork of the Cheyenne
River.   So far as it could be seen from the plains around, it
seemed to be a nest of hills covered with dark pines, whence
its name.

From the time of Warren to the running of the Pacific
Railroad, no further efforts were made to penetrate the Black
Hills.   By the treaty of 1868 (already referred to) with the
Sioux Indians, that region, in common with others, was declared an inviolable part of Indian reservations, not to be tres-
passed on by white men, and such it remained for many years.
At last some Indians, coming to a trading post, brought in
some gold dust and nuggets, which they admitted came from
the Black Hills.   The story, like that of the gold dust in Sut-
ter's mill-race in California, spread like wild-fire, and the government was importuned to sanction trespasses on the Indians'
land.

Parties of miners began to organize for the Black Hills, and
the gold excitement waxed high in the west.   Under these cir-

cumstances it was, that the government ordered the Custer expedition of 1874. It was determined to send a strong column to explore the hills and ascertain whether there was any gold to be found there. Accordingly on the first day of July, 1874, the village of Bismarck in Dakota Territory, in the vicinity of Fort Lincoln, was all alive with troops as the expedition started, under command of Custer himself.

The column consisted of ten companies of the Seventh Cavalry, Company I. Twentieth infantry, and Company G. Seventeenth infantry, with sixty Indian scouts, and four Gatling guns. General "Sandy" Forsyth was with the column, and the President's son, Lieutenant Fred. Grant of the Second Cavalry, accompanied Custer on the staff. The whole force was over 1200 strong, and accompanied by a huge wagon train, full of provisions. It was to move southwest from Fort Lincoln, nearly two hundred miles, striking the Black Hills from the north. There was little or no danger to the powerful column, either real or apprehended. It started on a romantic and mysterious expedition, as if for a picnic, and as such it found the whole journey. The progress of the expedition is best told by a few extracts from Custer's reports. He writes from Prospect Valley, a few miles to the north of the Belle Fourche, on the 15th July, 1874:

"This expedition reached this point yesterday, having marched since leaving Fort Lincoln 227½ miles. We are now 170 miles in a direct line from Lincoln within five miles of the "Little Missouri" River, and within about twelve miles from the Montana boundary, our bearing from Fort Lincoln being south 62° west. After the second day from Lincoln we marched over a beautiful country; the grazing was excellent and abundant, wood sufficient for our wants, and water in great abundance every ten miles. When we struck the tributaries of Grand River we entered a less desirable portion of the country : nearly all the streams flowing into Grand River being more or less impregnated with alkali, rendering the crossings difficult.

We found a plentiful supply of grass, wood, and water, however, even along this portion of our route. Upon leaving the head-waters of the Grand River, we ascended the plateau separating the water-shed of the " Little Missouri " from that running into the Missouri, and found a country of surpassing beauty and richness of soil. The pasturage could not be finer, timber is abundant, and water both good and plentiful.

" Our march thus far has been made without molestation upon the part of the Indians. We discovered no signs indicating the recent presence of Indians until day before yesterday, when Captain McDougall, Seventh Cavalry, who was on the flank, discovered a small party of about twenty Indians, watching our movements; the Indians scampered off as soon as discovered. Yesterday the same or a similar-sized party made its appearance along our line of march, and was seen by Captain Moylan, Seventh Cavalry, who was in command of the rear guard. Soon after several signals of smoke were sent up, which our Indian guides interpret as carrying information to the main body of our presence and movements."

At the time that the expedition started, there were strong indications that the Sioux contemplated opening a general war of small parties, such as had greeted Custer in 1867 when he first went on the plains; but the presence of his column and the uncertainty of the Indians as to its destination served one good purpose. It kept the greater part of the Sioux forces busy watching Custer, till he entered the Black Hills, and the knowledge of its presence deterred the Indians from overt war that year. Once in the hills, the Sioux seem to have been re-assured, for he was watched no further, and seems to have quite taken the denizens of the hills, such few as there were, by surprise. A second despatch, dated August 2d, gives the result of two weeks further progress. It seems to have been a regular pic-nic still.

Having taken up his march from Prospect Valley, he pursues :—

" After leaving that point this expedition moved in a south-westerly direction until it reached the valley of the Little Missouri River, up which we moved twenty-one miles. Finding this valley almost destitute of grazing along our line of march I ordered the water-kegs filled, and a supply of wood placed on the wagons, and left the valley in search of a better camp-ground. During our passage up the valley of the Little Missouri we had entered and were about to leave the Territory of Montana. Our course was near due south. After a further march of nine miles we arrived before sundown at a point capable of furnishing us good grazing and water for our animals, having marched over thirty miles since breaking camp in the morning. From this point to the valley of the Belle Fourche on the 18th of July, encamped where good grass, wood and water were abundant, at a point just west of the line separating Dakota from Wyoming.

" The following day was spent in camp. On the 20th we crossed the Belle Fourche and began, as it were, skirmishing with the Black Hills. We began by feeling our way carefully along the outlying ranges of the hills, seeking a weak point through which we might make our way to the interior. We continued from the time we ascended from the valley of the Belle Fourche, to move through a very superior country, covered with the best of grazing and abundance of timber, principally pine, poplar, and several varieties of oak. As we advanced, the country skirting the Black Hills to the south-west became each day more beautiful. On the evening of the 22d we halted and encamped east of and within four miles of the base of Inyan Kara. Desiring to ascend that peak the following day, it being the highest in the western range of the Black Hills, I did not move camp the following day, but taking a small party with me, proceeded to the highest point of this prominent landmark, whose height is given as 6,600 feet. The day was not favorable for obtaining distant views, but I decided on the following morning to move due east and attempt the passage of the hills. We experienced considerable delay from fallen timber which lay in our pathway. With this exception, and a very little digging, rendered necessary in descending into a valley, the pioneers prepared the way for the train, and we reached camp by two o'clock, having marched eleven miles. We here found grass, water and wood of best quality and in great abundance. On the following day we resumed our march up this valley, which I had explored several miles the preceding evening, and which led us by an easy ascent almost southeast. After marching nearly twelve miles we encamped at an early hour in the same valley. This valley in one respect presented the most wonderful as well as beautiful aspect. Its equal I have never seen, and such, too, was the testimony of all who beheld it. In no public or private park have I ever seen such a profuse display of flowers. Every step of our march that day was amidst flowers of the most exquisite colors and perfume. So luxuriant in growth were they that men plucked them without dismounting from the saddle. Some belonged to new or unclassified species. It was a strange sight to glance back at the advancing column of cavalry, and behold the men with beautiful bouquets in their hands, while the head gear of their horses was decorated with wreaths of flowers fit to crown a queen of May. Deeming it a most fitting appellation, I named this Floral Valley. General Forsyth, at one of our halting places, chosen at random, plucked seventeen beautiful flowers belonging to different species, and within a space of twenty feet square. The same evening, while seated at the mess table, one of the officers called attention to the carpet of flowers strewn under our feet, and it was suggested that it be determined how many different flowers could be plucked without leaving our seats at the dinner table. Seventeen beautiful varieties were thus gathered. Professor Donaldson, the botanist of the expedition, estimated the number of flowers in bloom in Floral Valley at fifty, while an equal number of varieties had bloomed or were yet to bloom. The number of trees, shrubs, and grasses was twenty-five, making the total flora of the valley embrace 125 species.

"Through this beautiful valley meanders a stream of crystal water so cold as to render ice undesirable even at noonday. The temperature of two of the many springs found flowing into it was taken and ascertained to be 44 and 44½ deg. respectively.

"The next morning, although loath to leave so enchanting a locality, we continued to ascend this valley until gradually, almost imperceptibly, we discovered that we were on the crest of the western ridge of the Black Hills; and instead of being among barren, rocky peaks, as might be supposed, we found ourselves wending our way through a little park, whose natural beauty may well bear comparison with the loveliest portions of Central Park. Favored as we had been in having Floral Valley for our roadway to the west of the Black Hills, we were scarcely less fortunate in the valley which seemed to me to meet us on the interior slope. The rippling stream of clear cold water, the counterpart of that we had ascended the day before, flowed at our feet and pointed out the way before us, while along its banks grew beautiful flowers, surpassed but little in beauty and profusion by their sisters who had greeted us the day before. After advancing down this valley about fourteen miles, our course being almost southeast, we encamped in the midst of grazing, whose only fault, if any, was its great luxuriance. Having preceded the main column, as usual, with our escort of two companies of cavalry, E and C, and Lieutenant Wallace's detachment of scouts, I came upon an Indian camp-fire still burning, and which with other indications showed that a small party of Indians had encamped there the previous night, and had evidently left that morning in ignorance of our close proximity. Believing they would not move far, and that a collision might take place at any time unless a friendly understanding was arrived at, I sent my head scout, Bloody Knife, and twenty of his braves to advance a few miles and reconnoitre the valley. The party had been gone but a few minutes when two of Bloody Knife's young men came galloping back and informed me that they had discovered five Indian lodges a few miles down the valley, and that Bloody Knife, as directed, had concealed his party in a wooded ravine, where they awaited further orders. Taking E Company with me, which was afterward reinforced by the remainder of the scouts and Colonel Hart's company, I proceeded to the ravine where Bloody Knife and his party lay concealed, and from the crest beyond obtained a full view of the five Indian lodges, about which a considerable number of ponies were grazing. I was enabled to place my command still nearer to the lodges undiscovered. I then despatched Agard, the interpreter, with a flag of truce, accompanied by two of our Sioux scouts, to acquaint the occupants of the lodges that we were friendly disposed and desired to communicate with them. To prevent either treachery or flight on their part, I galloped the remaining portion of my advance and surrounded the lodges. This was accomplished almost before they were aware of our presence. I then entered the little village and shook hands with its occupants, assuring them through the interpreter that they had no cause to fear, as we were not there to molest them. I invited them to visit our camp, and promised presents of flour, sugar, and coffee to all who would accept. This invitation was accepted. At the same time I entered into an agreement with the leading men that they should encamp with us a few days and give us such information concerning the country as we might desire, in return for which service I was to reward them with rations. With this understanding I left them. The entire party numbered twenty-seven. Later in the afternoon four of the men, including the chief, "One Stab," visited our camp and desired the promised rations, saying their entire party would move up and join us the following morning, as agreed upon. I ordered presents of sugar, coffee, and bacon to be given them ; and to relieve their pretended anxiety for the safety of their village during the night, I ordered a party of fifteen of my command to return with them and protect them during the night. But from their great disinclination to wait a few minutes until the party could saddle up, and from the fact that two of the four had already slipped away, I was of the opinion that they were not acting in good faith. In this I was confirmed when the two remaining ones set off at a gallop in the direction of the village. I sent a party of our scouts to overtake them and request their return ; not complying with the request I sent a second party with orders to repeat the request, and if not complied with to take hold of the bridles of their ponies and lead them back, but to offer no violence. When overtaken by our scouts one of the two Indians seized the musket of one of the scouts and endeavored to wrest it from him. Failing in this he released his hold after the scout became dismounted in the struggle, and set off as fast as his pony could carry him but not before the musket of the scout was discharged. From blood discovered afterward it was evident that either the Indian or his pony was wounded.

" ' One Stab,' the chief, was brought back to camp. The scouts galloped down the valley to the site of the village, when it was discovered that the entire party had packed up their lodges and fled, and the visit of the four Indians to our camp was not only to obtain the rations promised them in return for future services but to cover the flight of their lodges. I have effected arrangements by which the chief ' One Stab ' remains with us as guide three days longer, when he will take his departure and rejoin his band.' "

From this point the march through the hills was continued without opposition or further incident. The small party of Indians seems to have found the white man's method of offering friendship not to its taste, for which we can hardly blame the poor savages. The major part of the despatch is taken up with a description of the country, which Custer found delightful. It was not till September that he returned, further explorations having confirmed his first glowing impression of the beauties and advantages of the country, and made his final report, which

was mainly an enlargement of the passages already quoted.
Then the fever of excitement commenced, as also a fever of
controversy, Custer's statements being stigmatized by some officers who had not been with him as baseless and exaggerated.

Especially there arose between him and General Hazen a
warm dispute as to the value of the Northwest, which was carried on with some acrimony in the western papers. There
seemed to be a fate that was always bringing Hazen and Custer
into collision, whenever they came near each other. It began
at West Point, when Hazen's inopportune presence cost Custer
a court-martial. After that, they did not meet for seven years
more. When they did, it was to get into a dispute about Satanta and the Kiowas, in which each insisted that the other was
wrong, and which was not decided for six years more. Now,
in a second seven years, they came into violent collision on another question of fact, Hazen insisting that the greater portion
of the Northwest along the line of the Rocky Mountains was a
barren waste, utterly unfit for human habitation, and incapable
of permanent amelioration, Custer insisting that it was the very
garden of America, only needing cultivation to develop into a
Paradise. As usual in such cases, the truth lies between the
two. The majority of the seasons in Hazen's "Barren Belt"
appear to be dry, but when a wet season comes, as it does every
few years, the fertility of the land seems to be amazing.

A more serious dispute arose as to the mining value of the
Black Hills, which the geologists who accompanied Custer reported in an unsatisfactory manner. To settle the dispute, a
second expedition under Professor Jenney, with a military escort under Lieutenant Colonel Dodge, Ninth Infantry, was sent
from Fort Laramie the following year. This expedition after
trying in vain to enter from the south-west, finally effected an
entrance near the point where Custer went in, and spent some
time in the hills. Arriving a month earlier than Custer, the
expedition found "Floral Valley" in a miserable state, the
snow hardly melted, the buds hardly started, not a flower to be

seen, but a violent storm of sleet in progress. By the time the expedition was over, however, the Black Hills revealed themselves as a perfect garden, and the gold region was carefully explored, turning out to be not as rich as expected, but enough so to attract miners. Several camps of these enterprising individuals were found, one of twenty-two people having passed the whole of the previous winter there, untroubled by Indians. The two expeditions revealed one fact, that the Indians rarely visited the interior of the Black Hills, which they regard with superstitious feelings. Game was not very plentiful, but it was very tame. The soil was as fertile as Custer represented it, but the extreme shortness of the summer season made it improbable that the country could ever become valuable for arable purposes, though as a stock farm country it offered every inducement to settlers. Such was the final report on the subject of the Black Hills, and by that time it was full of miners, who came there in defiance of treaties.

Dodge's expedition and the troops under General Crook made several trips into the Black Hills during the summer of 1875, to maintain the faith of the government, and half compelled, half persuaded, the miners to leave, escorting them to the military post, where they were delivered over to the " civil authority "—the territorial government of Dakota—to be punished for disobedience to the law. In every case the miners seem to have willingly complied with the injunctions of the military authority, though themselves far superior in numbers to the small force of troops, and well armed besides. Just as soon, however, as the civil authority took them in hand, the whole proceeding turned out to be a farce. The miners were invariably released, without even the formality of bail, and as invariably went straight back to the Black Hills. In August there were over six hundred men there, who had started a " city " which they called " Custer City," laid it out in lots, and staked out their claims, as if the land belonged to them. They were removed and others took their places, so that to-day the Black

Hills are fuller than last year. In all this, the rights of the Indians to retain their property and the obligation of the United States to keep its word have been wantonly violated, as a natural and inevitable consequence of the expedition of 1874. Had it not been for the rumors of the presence of gold in that region, the expedition would never have started. As long as the Black Hills were regarded as worthless, the Indians were allowed to retain them. As soon as it was discovered that gold was there, all restraints of treaties were thrown aside, and Custer was ordered on the Black Hills expedition. That was the first wrong act, and from it flowed all the rest. Afterwards, when the miners began to crowd in, the government tried to keep its word by putting them out, but the first interlopers, the men who made the first trouble, were the troopers of Custer's column who started from Fort Lincoln July 1, 1874, in obedience to the orders of the United States Government.

It is a sad and humiliating confession to be made, but the irresistible logic of truth compels it, that all the subsequent trouble of the Sioux war really sprang from the deliberate violation by the United States Government of its own freely plighted faith, when Custer was ordered to lead his column from Fort Lincoln to the Black Hills. The avowed purpose of the journey was to find out whether gold existed there, a matter which concerned no one but the owners. All the subsequent efforts of the government were mere palliations of its own first fault, and perfectly useless. Strange, but an illustration of poetic justice, that the very man, who, in obeying his orders, became the instrument of injustice towards the Indians, should fall a victim in the contest which ensued.

Strange but true! Yet we cannot blame Custer, as we approach the tragic close of so bright and hopeful a career. He was a soldier, bound to obey orders, and a mere instrument in the hand of power. He was ordered to explore the Black Hills, and he went there. He was ordered on the trail of the Sioux, and he went. None the less, the pleasant-seem-

ing and roseate hues of that long picnic party called the Black
Hills Expedition close the brightness of his career. From
thenceforth clouds began to gather, and the time was swiftly
coming when his sun should set in death.

The close of the Black Hills Expedition sent Custer back to
Fort Lincoln, where he remained during the whole of the
winter, his usual eastern leave being enjoyed before the snow
closed in, and in New York as usual.

Happily ignorant of the coming storm, the last years of
Custer's life were happy ones, so long as he was untrammeled
by official difficulties or enmities. The reader will remember
that he had always possessed a disposition remarkably cheerful,
and a tendency to make the best of things : this tendency seemed
to become more and more confirmed as he grew older, spite of
all surrounding difficulties, sobered as it was by the earnest
Christianity which had marked his private character ever since
the period of his marriage engagement. To many men Custer's
lot and that of his little wife seemed hard at the best, but they
seemed to enjoy it to the full. Where others would have been
complaining of the isolation of a frontier post, of the lack of
society, of the privation of luxuries, Custer and his wife seemed
perfectly happy. A fire came and burned down their house,
so that they lost everything save what was on the lower story,
which the men helped to carry out, including, fortunately, most
of the General's papers : Custer and the little wife made light
of the misfortune, and passed the bitter cold winter of the
Northwest in slight temporary quarters, laughing at their discomforts. Nothing seemed to ruffle either, and they even
made the accident a source of subsequent congratulation, when
the new quarters were put up.

If their life was pleasant, if they were happy, it was their
own sunny temperaments that made them so. They were
happy, where others would have been miserable. An air of
luxury and good taste pervaded the " General's room," where
he wrote and received his visitors. What gave it that air?

33

The furniture was of the plainest, and much of it old and worn. But over every old chair or sofa, covering all deficiencies, were beautiful furs and skins that money could hardly have purchased, the spoils of Custer's rifle, and all around the walls hung grand heads of buffalo, of ahsata or "big horn," graceful antelope heads, prepared by Custer himself, the fierce faces of wolf, bear or panther, giving a wild and peculiar grace to the lofty room, lit up by the glow from yonder ample fire-place, with its blazing logs.

There Custer was perfectly happy. Often he would say to his wife, when all alone with her:

"How happy we are, and how God has blessed us! It seems to me we have everything so good. Our horses are the best, our dogs are the best, our regiment is the best, our home is the best in all the land. God be thanked for his goodness."

In all this was no boasting. The man seemed to feel to the very core of his heart that his lot in life left him nothing to wish for: he was perfectly happy and devoutly grateful. And yet, had he known it, the end was coming, and the very happiest years of his life at Fort Lincoln were to bring him forth one more enemy, the man who finally slew him. Who he was, the next chapter will show.

RAIN-IN-THE-FACE.

CHAPTER II.

RAIN-IN-THE-FACE.

IT will be remembered that in a previous chapter we recorded the murder of two inoffensive old men, Dr. Honzinger and Mr. Baliran, on the Yellowstone expedition. They were killed it was supposed, by "hostiles," but the discovery of agency property on the field of battle subsequently revealed that among these hostiles were some so called "good Indians" who drew rations at the agencies and received property from the government. No hope was felt that the names of the Indians who killed the two unarmed old men would be found out. During the winter of 1875, however, their identity came out in a very strange manner.

Charley Reynolds, one of Custer's scouts, who afterwards was killed at the Little Horn battle, happened to be at Standing Rock Agency, a place some seventy miles below Fort Lincoln, where the Indians were drawing rations. As usual at their rejoicings, they were having "a dance." The Indians appear to signalize every great event by a dance, and this dance is always made the occasion of boasting about all the valiant deeds they ever have done. In the course of this dance, Charley Reynolds heard one of the Indians boasting how he had killed two men at a time, white men, too, and then the savage went on with his pantomime dance and described how he did it, how one of them was a fat old man, and how he fell from his horse, how he, the Indian, finished him off by smashing his skull with a big stone, and then shot the other white man and took all they had. Then he proudly exhibited articles that Charley knew belonged to Dr.

Honzinger, and the scout knew that he had found the murderer. That Indian was named " Rain-in-the-Face."

The rest of his story was written at the time, January, 1875, by Mrs. Custer, and she shall tell it to the reader in her own words.

I have been so much interested, says the dear little lady, in the capture and present imprisonment of an Indian murderer, I cannot but think that the story might entertain others. Since so many of the " ready writers " of the present day make up their histories of Indian life and incidents, thousands of miles from the actual scene, I do not wonder that the true impression of the real wild Indian is confined mostly to those who live either with or near them. I must go back for a moment to the Yellowstone Expedition under General Stanley in the summer of 1873. Attached to the cavalry accompanying the expedition were two civilians who rode a great part of the time together. They were not obliged to submit to the regulation that compels soldiers to keep the ranks, and so they daily guided their horses where they chose. One day they stopped to water their steeds, and the main column was scarcely out of sight, hidden by a divide, before the two were surrounded and instantly murdered by Indians. A portion of the cavalry under General Custer had at the same time been surrounded and were fighting, but unable of course to go to the relief of the two poor victims. Dr. Honzinger was an honest, kind-hearted old man, who had followed the fortunes of the Seventh Cavalry for some years, as its veterinary surgeon. Mr. Baliran was the sutler for the cavalry. Both were favorites with the command and were much regretted. Both left families poorly provided for.

It is now over a year and a half since their death. A few weeks since, reliable information came from the Indian agency below here on the river, that the murderer of Dr. Honzinger and Mr. Baliran was at the agency drawing his rations, blankets, ammunition, etc., from government, and boasting of his foul deed of the two summers preceding.

This piece of news at once created the most intense excitement in our garrison, largely composed as it is of members of the Yellowstone expedition and friends of the slaughtered men. It really seemed too aggravating to endure the knowledge of the fact that the government should feed, clothe and equip Indians, to go out and fight and kill soldiers and others who were working to protect the frontier. So after the excitement had somewhat lulled, a detachment was quickly prepared to march to the agency. No one knew the object of their trip. Most persons supposed it was to capture another Indian murderer, belonging to the agency, who had killed a citizen on Red River of the North, last summer. Four officers and a hundred men left this post, one cold windy day, under sealed orders. The orders directed them to capture and bring back an Uncpapa Indian, called Rain-in-the-Face, the assassin of Dr. Honzinger and Mr. Baliran. Our next post is twenty miles distant, and had the orders not been sealed, General Custer knew that the Sioux scouts employed by government at Fort Rice, as soon as the troops arrived there and told their errand, would send out a runner to the agency below and inform the Indians of the intended arrest, giving time for the murderer to escape. So the orders were not opened until Rice was left behind twenty miles. As the troops neared the agency it was found necessary to observe the greatest care, to prevent the Indians from finding out the object of the visit. It was the day for our red brethren to draw beef from their generous Uncle Sam. Hundreds of them were there at the agency, of course armed to the teeth, as they always are. In the face of hundreds of fully armed Indians, though on the reservation, still most of them full of hate toward the white man, it seemed a very venturesome deed to appear in their midst and claim one of their number. The reservation Indians are constantly told that they will be fed, clothed, and armed, if they will consent never to make war on the white man, but if they do they must submit to the penalties of the law. But in the instance of this murderer he dared everything to prove his courage. He had been frequently to the agency, boasting of his base deed. One party of troops had been down to capture him earlier in the winter, but he had hidden and escaped them. So Captain Yates, who had charge of the troops, sent one of the lieutenants, with forty men, to the Indian camp ten miles below, to make inquiries for three Indians who had murdered citizens on Red River last summer.

This ruse succeeded in deceiving the Indians as to the real object of their presence among them. As the trader's store is the great place of resort for the Indians, it was presumed that in the course of the day Rain-in-the-Face would be there. Col. Custer (brother of the general) was directed to take five picked men and go to the store and capture the murderer, should the latter put in an appearance. He remained in the store for several hours. The day was cold and the Indians kept their blankets drawn about their heads, thus rendering it almost impossible to distinguish one from the other. At last one of them loosened his blanket and Col. Custer identified him as Rain-in-the-Face. Coming suddenly behind him, he threw his arms around him and seized the Winchester rifle that the Indian attempted in an instant to cock. The murderer was taken entirely by surprise. Stolid as their faces usually are, his, in this moment of amaze, was a study. No fear to be seen, but other emotions showed themselves with lightning rapidity on his countenance. Surprise, hate, revenge, then the final determination that he would show his brother warriors he was not afraid to die. He had been considered brave beyond precedent, to even enter the agency store and encounter this risk of arrest.

As soon as Rain-in-the-Face was actually captured and his hands tied, an old Indian orator of the tribe began exhorting the Indians, who had assembled in the store to the number of thirty or more, to recapture their comrade. He spoke in the key assumed by the Indian warriors, high and loud, but with no rising or falling inflections. The most intense excitement prevailed among the braves. The instant Rain-in-the-Face was arrested, Captain Yates, who had remained outside a close observer of affairs, gave the signal, and rallied his entire force in the immediate vicinity of the trader's store, prepared to repel any attempt to rescue the prisoner. These precautions were adopted none too quickly, for no sooner had news of the capture of Rain-in-the-Face been conveyed to the numerous groups of Indians to be seen in the vicinity of the agency, than a mass of armed warriors, estimated at over five hundred in number, rushed to the trader's store, and in loud, threatening, and excited tones, demanded the instant release of their comrade. The occasion was one requiring the exercise of the utmost prudence as well as the most determined courage upon the part of the little group of officers and men who stood with weapons in their hands, about the prisoner. Determined to resist to the very death any attempt at a rescue, Captain Yates, presenting a bold front to the Indians, enraged as they were, prevented the immediate recapture of his prisoner. By means of an interpreter, he then briefly explained to the Indians the cause of the arrest, and announced the determination of himself and men to maintain their hold over their captive. He at the same time urged the chiefs to withdraw with their followers, and thus avoid a collision that would only result in loss of life on both sides, without accomplishing any purpose. Seeing they could not carry out their end by intimidation or the display of greatly superior numbers, the Indians then resorted to parley and offers of compromise. They offered through an interpreter to sacrifice two Indians of the tribe, if Rain-in-the-Face could be released. He is a great warrior among them. He has five brothers at the agency, one of whom, Iron Horn, is a chief of influential standing in the tribe. It was not expected that Indians of any notoriety or rank would be offered as a sacrifice; only some who had not distinguished themselves in any way; and the selections were to be made by the great moguls of the tribe. These offers were of course refused, and Rain-in-the-Face was taken to the camp of the Cavalry. In an incredibly short time not an Indian was to be seen at the agency. All went to their camp, ten miles below. Later in the day, a party of fifty mounted Indians dashed by the agency on the road to be taken by our troops on the return. Of course our officers expected to be attacked by this party the next morning, but they were unmolested, and reached here after a march of three days, through cold and snow and winds such as only Dakota can furnish. It was explained to us afterward, that the party of fifty seen passing the agency were on their way to the camp of the chief " Two Bears " to try and induce him to urge his young braves to combine with them in the release of Rain-in-the-Face. But Two Bears is an old chief, and he opposed the attack. He has been a friend of the whites for a long time, but his age would induce one to think the motive of his friendship was policy.

After the officers had reported, General Custer sent for Rain-in-the-Face to interview him. He is a young man with an impenetrable countenance. This is as we saw him, but in a subsequent interview, when General Custer locked himself alone in a room with him, he showed some signs of agitation. After a time, when they had talked by signs as far as it was possible, the interpreter was admitted, and for hours General Custer attempted by every clever question he could invent, to induce Rain-in-the-Face to confess his crime. At last he succeeded in getting his account of the murder, and the next day in the presence of a number of the officers, Rain-in-the-Face made a full confession of his crime. He called Dr. Honzinger the old man, and says he shot him, but he rode some distance before falling from his horse. Mr. Baliran he described as being among some trees, and signaling to them by holding up his hand as an overture of peace. He says that Baliran gave them his hat when they reached him, but they shot him at once, first with a gun, then with arrows. One of the arrows entered his back and he tried to pull it through, but failed. They did not scalp their victims. Dr. Honzinger was bald, and Mr. Baliran had his hair closely cut. Neither of these gentlemen were armed when attacked by the Indians. This short but cruel story made our blood boil when we afterwards learned what Rain-in-the-Face had confessed.

The brother of the prisoner, " Iron Horn," and one other Indian, had followed the cavalry up from the agency and asked to see the captive before they went home. General Custer sent for Rain-in-the-Face, and he met his brother and had council with him. They expected it was a farewell interview, as the Indians all believed Rain-in-the-Face would be hung.

During the council, which was very solemn, Iron Horn took off his beautiful beaded blanket and put it on his brother, taking his common one in place of it. He also exchanged pipes with him, giving his highly ornamented one to Rain-in-the-Face, to present to General Custer. He charged his brother most solemnly not to try to escape, that should he get back to the reservation he would be recaptured, and he believed he would be kindly treated while a captive. He hoped the great Father would not hang him, and perhaps General Custer would intercede in his favor. The great Father rarely hung Indians. Asking him not to lose his spirits, they took a farewell smoke and he departed.

In about ten days he returned, bringing a party of Indians with him. Another interview with General Custer was obtained. After all the guests were seated, Rain-in-the-Face came over from the guard house and entered, having been sent for at the request of the Indians. He came into the room, trying not to show his pleasure at seeing his friends, nor his grief at his imprisonment and his evidently expected death; but these emotions passed over his face in quick succession, and then came the look of settled indifference that the Indian constantly tries to wear. His brother rose at once and went to Rain-in-the-Face, and, to the intense amazement of the few privileged spectators General Custer had allowed to enter, he kissed him.   An Indian kiss, to be sure; the lips were laid quietly on his cheek, with no sound or motion; but it is a solemn caress, and one never seen before, with one single exception, by the oldest Indian fighter here.   Several of the ranking Indians stepped solemnly to the prisoner and gave him the same dignified salute.   Then one of the old men of the tribe walked in front of him, and lifting his hand above his head and raising his eyes, said a few words in prayer to the Great Spirit for this unfortunate brother.   Rain-in-the-Face hung his head low on his breast, to hide the emotion that he thought would ill become a warrior as brave as he really is.

After a long speech by Iron Horn, delivered in the usual high monotonous key, the next in rank rose, and so on, till half a dozen had spoken.   Iron Horn thanked General Custer for his care of Rain-in-the-Face, asked permission to visit him again, begged him to write again to the Great Father and intercede for the life of their brother, and then, taking off the buckskin shirt he wore, he presented the highly ornamented garment to the General.   Then came such a singular request. It was the story of Damon and Pythias among uncivilized warriors.   Two shy young braves, sitting near the end of the circle among the untitled, asked through Iron Horn the privilege of sharing the captivity of Rain-in-the-Face.   Not many murderers or felons in the States find friends who in the hour of arrest or capture ask to share the prison with them.   Consent was given to this request, if the friends would be willing to be locked in the prison till the hour came for them to go home.

They rested in the guard house with their friend for a day and night, and then returned to the agency.   The imprisonment of Rain-in-the-Face continued for several months, till a circumstance occurred that gave him his liberty.

So far Mrs. Custer's narrative, written at the time.   The circumstance she speaks of introduces another story which will give an excellent idea of another phase of Custer's character, besides completing the record.   We are indebted for this story to the kindness of Mrs. Yates, widow of the brave captain whose party took the Indian. She entitles it the " Story of the Grain Thieves."

" It seems strange," says this lady, " that any one at all acquainted with the working and planning of Custer's mind, could accuse him of *rashness ;* there is the most wonderful denial of this imputation in every engagement which he entered during the war, in the planning of the Washita campaign, and last, but not least, to many minds, the following up and final arrest of the grain thieves at Fort Abraham Lincoln, a matter which some might deem of unimportance, but which should be considered of value in showing the patient energy and tenacity of purpose as exemplified in his character. It is of importance also, because it established him in the eyes of the lawless frontiersmen of Bismarck and its vicinity, as one whom it would be as well to respect, one who was quick to pursue and sure to overtake.

" During the spring of 1875, the grain from the several forage buildings at Fort Lincoln had been steadily disappearing. The river being still frozen, intercourse between the post and the town of Bismarck was fully established, and it became a difficult matter to trace the stolen grain to any particular parties, as well as a problem what to do with the parties in the event of finding it. Law and order had not resolved itself from the chaos of the newly-put-together town.

" The General was also hampered by being forbidden by order to make arrests outside of the military reservation, all exterior justice being meted out by the good mayor of Bismarck; who, ' slow to anger and plenteous in mercy,' the General feared might not prove as powerful a coadjutor as he could desire. With all these discouraging facts to dampen his ardor, he quietly went to work, early and late, gathering in his proofs in which he was greatly assisted by Lieutenant Carland, of the Sixth Infantry, formerly a lawyer. Ever watchful of the slightest opportunity, nothing escaped him. Believing with

Pope that 'the proper study of mankind is man,' he studied man as he found him in Bismarck.

"Once he arose in the night and himself inspected the grain on the landing to see that it was all right, questioning and examining the guard, and only retiring when fully satisfied that no robbery would be attempted that night. Months before the denouement, he knew where each of the dramatis personæ was, could have arrested any one of them, or even a half a dozen, if he had been rash; but, being patient, he waited until he possessed the required proofs to arrest every one who had been in the least connected with the disappearance of the grain, knowing well that in arresting only a part of the number, he gave the rest warning to escape.

"So when, one bright day, just before the breaking up of the river in the spring, he issued orders for the regiment to be in readiness to start at the call of the trumpet for Bismarck, not an officer of his command but was as astonished, and knew as little of what was expected of them, as did the citizens of Bismarck, when they saw the cavalry, fully armed and equipped, come riding into their little town.

"The Seventh Cavalry rode to the different places indicated by the General, and found the grain at every place pointed out by him, to the surprise and indignation of the honest citizens of Bismarck, who being in ignorance of the localities the thieves had chosen to secrete it, were naturally indignant at the slur cast upon their reputations. For a while loud talking ensued, and a riot of no mean pretensions was threatened. Finally, upon the General insisting, doors were thrown open to him, and the stolen grain in every instance was exposed to view, the soldiers turning the bags over, and showing the government brand. In the Mayor's own warehouse (he being also a prominent merchant at the time,) a number were discovered. You can imagine the good mayor's surprise at this last selection of a repository for these stolen goods.

"A number of arrests were made, the mayor now concurring

heartily with the military, and for temporary safe keeping the corn thieves were escorted by the cavalry back to Fort Abraham Lincoln and lodged in the guard house.

" Their trial, which took place at Fargo, Minnesota, occupied many months, and employed numbers of witnesses, the leading actors in the scene shortly afterwards finding their way into the penitentiary. There is one amusing occurrence connected with the above arrest, and following upon the order received by General Custer to arrest all those implicated in the robbery that could be found upon the military reservation of Fort Lincoln. Off this reservation, as before mentioned, such arrests devolved upon the mayor. The General, one day, became aware that two of the principal members of the gang were at that time in a shanty almost half a mile from the post. Not knowing the men, nor having any description of their appearance, his order to the officer of the day was merely, ' go to ——'s shanty, and arrest immediately two citizens who you will find there—put them in the guard house.' The officer of the day started off, and the General proceeded to make a call upon a certain family in the garrison. Seating himself near the window where he could command a view of the road in front of the officer's quarters, laughing and conversing meanwhile, his eye scarcely left the window.

"Presently, a wagon drove by, containing two inoffensive looking personages in citizen's attire ; there was nothing at all suspicious in their appearance, nor was it unusual for citizens to have business in, and drive through the post. Only, one of the men looked back anxiously over his shoulder. This act aroused the General's interest, but he allowed them to drive around— which they did slowly—until they were almost in front of the guard house; when he rose abruptly, excused himself to the lady, and stepping upon the porch, placed both hands to his mouth shouting ' *Guard, arrest those men !* '

" The wondering guard obeyed, the men were assisted to alight, having driven up to their destination themselves. Soon it became evident what had occasioned the anxious looks over their shoulders. In a lumbering wagon, drawn by four mules, stood the officer of the day, jabbing the mules with his sabre, and the while ejaculating in profound English.

" He had obeyed orders, had searched the shanty, but finding no one there, was about to return home without making the arrest, when he observed the men in the wagon. At first thinking they were honest hay cutters, he allowed them to make considerable headway from him. On second thought, he concluded to overtake them, but finding that at this rate they would soon be off the reservation, and no arrest could then be made, he seized the nearest vehicle, which was a heavy water wagon, ordering the soldiers to jump out. Clutching the reins with one hand and punching the wheelers with his sabre in the other, he came upon the scene just as the general had made the arrest in person."

The arrests were made after Rain-in-the-Face had been several months in the guard house, and amongst others there were two particularly hard cases, who had been caught driving wagons loaded with hay off the ground.

" The guard house," says Mrs. Custer, concluding her story, " was only a poorly built, wooden building, quite insecure, and these citizens had in one night cut a hole in the side of the rear wall, large enough to creep through. Two crept safely out, and Rain-in-the-Face, seeing the opening after they had gone, quickly made his escape. We found afterwards that he went at once to the hostile camp, and last spring he sent word by agency Indians that he had joined Sitting Bull and was awaiting his revenge for his imprisonment."

That he took it, all the world now knows, and they can see in his portrait taken from an excellent photograph, what sort of a man this desperado is. Truly he looks soft enough, and as innocent as a lamb, but for all that he is well known as one of the bravest men of his nation. The tribe were particularly proud of him for one thing, his extraordinary fortitude against

physical pain.   He was said to have hung for four hours in the
" Sun dance." *

* The Sun Dance, says Mrs. Yates, to whom we are already indebted, is a
test of nerve and endurance of the Indian ; in other words, it is the Military
Academy from which he graduates, a well-informed soldier. Here he is taught
to be wily, hardy, stoical and cruel. It is held in the middle of summer,
when the sun's rays are nearly vertical, and its heat therefore, the most
intense. One of its features is the exposure, upon platforms erected for the
purpose, of the nude forms of the Indian braves, to the direct and burning
rays of the sun. Lying on their backs, with eyes distended, their gaze is
fixed upon the solar king, until tears stream from their tortured and mal-
treated organs. Numerous tests are too horrible to mention, and would
require as much nerve to witness and describe, as to participate in them.
Visitors frequently faint away in the presence of such sickening details.

For these young Indian cadets to fail in the slightest detail, is certain
disgrace ; to *exceed* what is demanded by competent judges, calls forth
applause, admiration, and gifts. Many a chief goes back to the Sun Dance
for the beginning of his record. His bravery and endurance there is never
forgotten, and serves him in good stead ever after.

Not long since, an excellent engraving of a Sun Dance appeared in *Harper's Weekly.* In this picture, Indians could be seen undergoing the suspension test. This is done by cutting a gash under some of the sinews of the
back, immediately under the shoulder blades, passing thongs of buffalo
hide through the gashes, and by these thongs suspending the Indian to the
roof of a large tepee. Here he hangs until his own weight or motion causes
the thongs to cut through the sinews, when he falls to the ground, and has
successfully passed the trial. The summer before General Custer's expedition
to the Black Hills, a grand Sun Dance was held at Standing Rock, Dakota.
The tests were unusually severe ; the judges exacting. A Sioux, nick named
'Pete,' could not endure the suspension test, but fainted away, and upon
coming to, begged to be taken down. He was released, but henceforth was
irretrievably disgraced, compelled to dress as a squaw, and forever debarred
the privileges of a brave. The squaws held him in derision, and poor Pete's
lot was a gloomy one indeed. Pete accompanied the General on the Black
Hills expedition ; he bore his disgrace with equanimity, and had always an
amiable smile for everybody. The Indian scouts obliged Pete to cook and
do all their other menial labor.

At this same dance, Rain-in-the-Face so distinguished himself as to win
the popularity of several tribes. In the suspension test he was gashed so
deep, that he could not by his own weight cut through the sinews. He
hung in mid air for several hours, blood streaming from his wounds, and

The escape of Rain-in-the-Face to the hostiles was made in the spring of 1875 and during that summer these hostiles, clustered around the headwaters of the Yellowstone, began to send their war parties out near the settlements, while the agency Indians were perpetually slipping off to join them. Dodge's Black Hills expedition further contributed to unsettle the Indians, and when the miners moved in numbers into that region, it became evident that a general war with the Northern Sioux was impending. The short summer was the only salvation of the settlers, and when 1876 came, it was clear that the fight could no longer be averted.

Under these circumstances, the government resolved for the first time to make war on the hostiles.

going through the motion of dancing the while. He became faint from loss of blood, and the judges decided to cut him down. Rain-in-the-Face objected however to this, and so was allowed to swing in this manner for four hours—when the flesh at last gave way and let him down.

EIGHTH BOOK.—THE LAST CAMPAIGN.

CHAPTER I.

SITTING BULL.

WHILE the retreat of 1868 had pacified most of the Sioux, and especially the great chiefs Red Cloud and Spotted Tail, with their bands, there was a small portion of the Sioux nation which remained implacable in its enmity to the whites, and kept to its original habits of life, out in the wilderness. This portion was generally known by the title of " the hostiles," and the most powerful chief of the different bands was and is known by the title of Sitting Bull. To explain to the general reader the meaning of the words " nation," " tribe," and " band," a short sketch of Indian polity is here necessary.

The Indian tribes of the plains bear a strong likeness in their modes of government to the Arabs and Tartars. Abstractly it may be termed patriarchal, but actually it is nearly a pure republic. Every member of a band does just about what he pleases, and obeys his chief when it pleases him, subject always to the verdict of popular opinion and the physical ability of the chief to thrash him. While the dignity of chieftainship appears to be hereditary, it is subject to so many checks, and depends so much on personal ability to persuade one's followers to pursue a certain line of conduct, that it may be called a mere delusion, in the hands of any but a great warrior ; and prowess in war is the only sure road to real power among Indians. While the Indians, as a mass, are thus independent of all but persuasive influences, the patriarchal element so far prevails that

34

the family is the basis of the organization for war and peace.
The members of a family, in all its ramifications of brothers
and cousins, uncles and nephews, generally travel together,
hunt together, and fight together, agglomerating in time, with
their connections by marriage, into a " band " varying from two
to twenty or thirty lodges. These " bands " have a remoter connection, by blood ties, with other bands, and constitute together
a " tribe," which may number from two to thirty or forty
" bands." These tribes again have a still more remote blood
connection with other tribes, constituting a " nation," such as
the Sioux Nation, which comprises the Yankton, Brule, Teton,
Uncpapa, and several other tribes, each tribe in its turn embracing several bands.

The " hostiles," so called, are formed of bands differently
composed. The patriarchal ties noticeable in other bands are
replaced here by a mere alliance of convenience. Every Indian
who feels discontented at the agencies joins the " hostiles " and
attaches himself to the band of Sitting Bull or Crazy Horse,
the only two great chiefs who were, at the time we write of,
avowedly " hostile." Thus their bands, originally numbering
perhaps twenty lodges apiece, with a fighting force of a hundred
warriors to each band, were swelled by the arrival of discontented families to many more. The village of Crazy Horse, at
the close of the winter of 1875, was found to contain one hundred and five lodges, which, at the ordinary rate of five or six
warriors to a lodge or " tepee," furnished a force of about 550
warriors. Sitting Bull's band probably then numbered at least
150 lodges, he being a more famous chief than Crazy Horse.
During the summer time, the forces of both received constant
additions from the agency Indians, who came out for a summer's hunt, provided with plenty of breechloading and magazine
guns and ammunition. An inspection of the map near the close
of this part of our book will show the singular advantages which
the agencies offered for this. The position of the " hostiles "
was very well selected, near the head of the Yellowstone, in a

country surrounded by " bad-lands," which prevented the whites from near approach, except on great and protracted expeditions, like that led by Stanley. To form an idea of the " bad-lands," the eastern reader can use a familiar illustration. You have all no doubt seen a clay-field after a long and hot drought in summer, how it is seamed over with innumerable cracks, perfectly perpendicular, leaving miniature chasms between. Such, magnified by a hundred, are the "bad-lands" of the north-west. They are patches of clay soil, baked by the long and intense droughts of that climate into chasms four or five feet wide and perhaps twenty feet deep, absolutely impassable for wagons where they occur, quagmires in the early spring freshets, a labyrinth of ravines in the summer. These bad-lands surrounded the country of the hostiles in 1873, and surround them now.

So much for the natural advantages of Sitting Bull's position, considered in a defensive point of view, but a greater advantage accrues to him from the strategic lines of the country and the existence of the Indian agencies. A second look at the map will reveal how the agencies affect the strategic position.

Observe that the Missouri River, beginning in the north-west corner of the map, describes nearly a perfect circle around the country of the " hostiles," and remember that all the Indian agencies are on this river, and you will begin to realize what is meant by the "strategic advantages" of Sitting Bull. Beginning at the mouth of the Cheyenne River, there are Cheyenne Agency, Brulé Agency, Grand River Agency, Standing Rock Agency, Fort Berthold and Fort Peck and several other places, all full of friendly Indians, supported by Government, and ready to join the hostiles in the summer, bringing arms and ammunition with them. To give an idea of the supplies of the latter, let us take what went through in the spring of 1876 alone, for distribution to Indians. Our evidence is contained in the private letter of an officer on the spot. This officer has investigated the matter, and finds that the following shipments were made by river steamer to these agencies, and to Forts Benton, McLoud and Claggett, (also agencies) on the 21st May, 20th June, 6th and 30th July, 1876, while the war was actually raging. No less than 56 *cases of arms*, or 1120 *Winchester and Remington rifles*, and 413,000 *rounds of patent ammunition* went there on these steamers, besides large quantities of loose powder, lead, and primers. These shipments were all *for issue to Indians, through the Indian agents, or for sale through Indian traders.* The country to which they were sent contains only Indians, soldiers, and Indian traders or agents. These shipments moreover were as nothing to those of previous years, and especially those of the summer of 1875, when more than a million rounds of ammunition and several thousand stand of arms were sent through.

Now perhaps Sitting Bull's chief advantage can be seen, as first shown in the Yellowstone expedition of 1873. This expedition started from Fort Rice in the summer of 1873 and moved off at a leisurely pace, due west. Indian runners at the same time started off, up and down the Missouri, to carry the news. Many of them travelled luxuriously by the steamers the government was kind enough to supply, to carry stores to the agencies for the use of the Indians. By the time Stanley had reached the Little Missouri, (see map) every agency all along the line of the river was informed of his movements, and parties of warriors on their war ponies, with no burdens save arms, ammunition and food, were starting from the *circumference of the quarter circle*, to find Sitting Bull and have a little fun.

All those from the *upper agencies* had a shorter distance to travel than Stanley, and knew the country better. No wonder they arrived before him. The trail which Stanley struck on the Yellowstone was in all probability that of the real acknowledged "hostiles," the village of Sitting Bull, with a force of some 800 braves, but the reinforcements which afterwards swelled his numbers to 1500, in the fight near Pompey's Pillar must have come from the northern agencies, and Stanley says so in his report, specifying Fort Peck as "the centre of all the villainy of the Indian Department."

Thus, in carrying on war with the United States War Department, Sitting Bull had great and peculiar advantages from the nature of his position, and these advantages it was which had made him constantly triumphant. It may have seemed strange to many that Custer should have been able, alone, to have beaten the Indians of the Southern Plains, while the Sioux of the North had overcome all successive combinations against them, compelling the government to pacify them by giving them up all they asked, in the treaty of 1868.

The War Department had made a gallant struggle to hold this country, but Sitting Bull and the hostiles had beaten them. Look again on the map at the sites of old Fort Reno and old Fort Phil Kearny. The last is right at the edge of Sitting Bull's stronghold. It was the scene of the fearful massacre of 1868, when almost the whole garrison was annihilated. It was difficult to keep this fort supplied. Everything had to come by wagon train from Fort Fetterman on the south, while Sitting Bull drew all his supplies of ammunition from Fort Peck and a dozen other places, and lived on the buffalo by which he was surrounded. The white men could not starve him, but he could harass *them* constantly, and he did so. Finally the Department was compelled to abandon Fort Reno and Kearny, and gave up the country to Sitting Bull, by the treaty of 1868.

Five years later, in 1873, it was judged expedient to break that treaty and try a new line of operations, this time up the valley of the Yellowstone. This line possessed one and only one advantage : while the Yellowstone was navigable, supplies, and even an expedition, could be sent up by steamer, comparatively safe from the Indians. A fleet of light draught steamers with bullet-proof guards and a few Gatlings, may yet be found the true solution of the Sitting Bull difficulty ; as such boats can ascend the Big Horn River to within sight of the Indian stronghold. By land, as Stanley went, the Yellowstone route was as bad as the rest, except for provisions. It was very long, and did not stop the supplies of Sitting Bull. The only reason Stanley escaped serious disaster, was that he kept near the river and was able to use his artillery, while Sitting Bull was not as yet joined by any very formidable force of Agency Indians. In the war of 1876 all this was to be changed, and Sitting Bull was to find himself in a perfect position, occupying interior lines, able to strike at his enemies wherever he pleased and beat them in detail, and all the while able to draw his supplies and reinforcements from a number of concentrating lines, none of which his enemies were able to cut. Indians kept streaming in to his help from all the quarter circle of agencies, informing him of every step taken by his enemies, and bringing ammunition, guns, ponies, and men by hundreds.

Of Sitting Bull personally, not very much is known. It is many years since he attended a council, and he has been so long secluded from the whites that no portrait of him is extant. From the description of Agency Indians and others, he is said to be a heavily built Indian, with a large massive head, and (strange to say) *brown hair*, unlike most Indians. He is heavily marked with the small pox. The events of his life have been recorded by himself, and fell into the hands of the whites, by an accident, soon after the Phil Kearny massacre. A scout brought into one of the forts an old roster book, once belonging to the Thirteenth U. S. Infantry, which Sitting Bull had captured, and in this was found a series of over a hundred little Indian pictures, describing the various exploits of the artist. In the first he is shown as a young warrior, naked and unadorned, taking his first scalp by charging a Crow Indian mounted. From the mouth of the young warrior goes a line which joins him to his " totem " or symbol, a buffalo bull sitting upon its haunches, which identified the book as the diary of Sitting Bull. This totem is found in all the pictures. Almost every picture represents the killing of a man or woman or both, some Indians, some whites. A few represent Sitting Bull carrying off herds of horses. These pictures are in regular Indian style, such as a clever child, without teaching, might draw. There is no attempt at art, but there is no mistake as to what is meant. There are the men, the horses, the women, the Indian war bonnets, the white man's stovepipe hat, in the true spirit of caricature, the salient features seized and fixed. Fac-similes of many of these pictures were published in the *New York Herald*, and subsequently in *Harper's Weekly*, in the latter case accompanied by an article from Colonel Strother, better known as " Port Crayon." We have hardly judged them worth insertion here, however.

It was stated at one time that Sitting Bull, while hating the white Americans and disdaining to speak their language, was yet very fond of the French Canadians, that he talked French, and that he had been converted to Christianity by a French Jesuit, named Father De Smet. How true this may be is uncertain, but probably there is some foundation for it. The French Jesuits have always been noted for their wonderful success in winning the affections of the Indians, as well as for the transitory nature of their conversions, and it is very possible that Father De Smet may have not only baptized Sitting Bull at some time, but induced him and his braves to attend mass, as performed by himself in the wilderness. The benefits of the conversion seem however to have been only skin deep, as far as preventing cruelty in war is concerned.

One thing about Sitting Bull is certain : he is an Indian of unusual powers of mind, and a warrior whose talent amounts to genius, while his stubborn heroism in defence of the last of his race is undeniable. Cruel he may be ; that is from the instincts of his race : a general of the first natural order he must be, to have set the United States at defiance as he has for the last ten years. That he has been able to do this so long is owing to his skilful use of two advantages, a central position surrounded by " bad-lands," and the quarter circle of agencies from which he draws supplies and allies every campaign.

In the face of these advantages and of Sitting Bull's talents as a warrior, the government gave up the fight in 1868. In 1876, it was determined to try one more campaign against Sitting Bull. We shall see how it succeeded.

In the meantime, the people of America will not fail to remark that Sitting Bull's truest and most persistent allies are the Indian Department and the Indian traders, who supply him with Winchester rifles and patent ammunition, so that his men are better armed than the troops of the War Department. Better soldiers individually they always were, for every man is a perfect rider and good shot, while the regular cavalry is mainly composed of green recruits, so unreliable that even a chief like Custer did not dare to fight them mounted, but had to turn his men into mounted infantry. But the inferior troops have *discipline*, and had they as good or superior weapons, could beat the Indians, as they used to, before 1861. There is still an easy way to stop all these slaughters, which is to *stop the supplies of ammunition from going to the Indians*.

To accomplish this only one course can succeed. Congress in both branches *must be compelled by public opinion to abolish the Indian Department forever.* Every one admits the necessity of the step, but the corruption fund of this department is so great that public opinion has not yet succeeded in killing the abuse. Politicians of both parties are interested in the money, and nothing else holds the Indian Department together. The cost of the Indians to the government has risen in ten years from less than a million to twenty millions annually, and Indian agents and traders grow rich on the stealings of supplies used by Indians to kill soldiers, while the residue of the stealings goes into election funds. The events of the Indian war of 1876 have, however, opened the eyes of the people to much of this abuse. God grant that it may end in the final destruction of the " Indian Ring."

CHAPTER II.

CRAZY HORSE.

WAR having been once determined on against the Sioux, the only questions were, who should begin it, and where? It was finally resolved that three expeditions should start, one from the north, one from the south, and one from the east; and that the three should all strike for the country near the headwaters of the Yellowstone, where Forts Reno and Phil Kearny had formerly been established.

The three columns could not be, or at all events were not, despatched simultaneously. They were to start from two distinct departments, commanded by Generals Terry and Crook, whose headquarters were several hundred miles apart, and in the midst of different climates. Terry, whose northern column must start from Fort Lincoln, up near the borders of the British Territory, could not move as early as Crook, who was far to the south. The latter started his column on the 1st of March, 1876, from Fort Fetterman, and struck off to the north for the Powder River.

The column consisted of ten companies of the Second and Third Cavalry and two companies of infantry, with a strength of 700 men and 40 days supplies, on pack mules and in wagons. The whole was commanded by Colonel Reynolds, Third Cavalry, brevet Major-General, and was accompanied by Brigadier-General Crook, the department commander. This column started with fine weather in its favor, and every indication of opening spring. There were sixty wagons and 400 pack-mules in the train, making, with the cavalry horses, 1,500 animals for which forage had to be carried. Nothing was heard of this expedition till March 26, when the following telegram was received by General Sheridan from Crook:

FORT RENO, March 22.

We cut loose from the wagon train on the 17th inst., and scouted the Tongue and Rosebud Rivers until satisfied that there were no Indians upon them; then struck across the country toward Powder River. General Reynolds, with part of the command, was pushed forward on a trail leading to the village of Crazy Horse, near the mouth of Little Powder River. This he attacked and destroyed on the 17th inst., finding it a perfect magazine of ammunition, war material, and general supplies. Crazy Horse had with him the Northern Cheyennes and some of the Minneconjous, probably in all one-half of the Indians off the reservation. Every evidence was found to prove these Indians in copartnership with those at the Red Cloud and Spotted Tail Agencies,* and that the proceeds of their raids upon the settlements had been taken to those agencies, and supplies brought out in return. In this connection I would again urgently recommend the immediate transfer of the Indians of those agencies to the Missouri River. I am satisfied that if Sitting Bull is on this side of the Yellowstone, that he is camped at the mouth of Powder River. We experienced severe weather during our absence from the wagon train, snow falling every day but one, and the mercurial thermometer on several occasions failing to register.

GEORGE CROOK, Brigadier-General.

Such was the first brief intimation of the facts of the Powder River fight. After a while the history was amplified by the reports of the newspaper correspondents. From their accounts and the subsequent full report of Crook the whole story came out. After leaving Fort Fetterman nothing happened for some days. The expedition left Crazy Woman's Fork with ten companies of cavalry, on the night of March 7, with fifteen days' rations on pack mules. The infantry and wagon train were sent back to the rear. The command marched down Tongue River nearly to the Yellowstone, scouting the

---

* These agencies are to the south, not on the map in this work.

Rosebud and adjacent streams. No Indians were found in this entire region. The expedition then moved to the head of Otter Creek, where General Reynolds was sent forward with six companies, and by a rapid night march reached Powder River early on the morning of the 17th, where he surprised and attacked Crazy Horse's village of 105 lodges. He captured the village, and after an engagement lasting five hours entirely destroyed it.

So far the expedition very closely resembled that of Custer on the Washita. A trail in the snow had been found and followed, and the Indian village had been surprised. There the resemblance ended.

Custer's victory on the Washita had been complete and overwhelming, and he had brought away all his prisoners, besides destroying the most indispensable part of an Indian's property,—the horses—in the face of a superior force of overawed enemies. Reynolds had no such history. He found the village of the Indian chief all alone, and was free from other enemies. The contrast of his movements was great. It will be remembered how Custer, having found the enemy's village in the night, employed the time till morning in surrounding it. The correspondents with Reynolds tell a different story. From the account of the New York *Tribune* writer, (an officer of the expedition), which we shall in the main follow, the difference of leaders will be seen. This officer says:

At 4.20 A. M. we had marched thirty miles, and were, as near as we could tell, near the Powder River breaks. A halt was called here, and the column took shelter in a ravine. No fires were allowed to be kindled, nor even a match lighted. The cold was more intense than we had yet felt, and seemed to be at least 30° below zero. The command remained here till about 6 o'clock, doing their utmost to keep from freezing, the scouts meantime going out to reconnoitre. At this hour they returned, reporting a larger and fresher trail leading down to the river, which was about four miles distant. The column immediately started on this trail. The approach to the river seemed almost impractica-

ble.   Before reaching the final precipices which overlooked the
river-bed, the scouts discovered that a village of about 100 lodges
lay in the valley at the foot of the bluffs.   It was now 8 o'clock.
The sun shone brightly through the cold, frosty air.   The column halted, and Noyes's battalion, Second Cavalry, was ordered
up to the front.   It consisted of Company I, Second Cavalry,
Captain Noyes, and Company K, Second Cavalry, Captain Egan.
This battalion was ordered to descend to the valley, and while
Captain Egan charged the camp, Captain Noyes was to cut out
the herd of horses feeding close by and drive it up the river.   Captain Moore's battalion, consisting of Company F, Third Cavalry,
and Company E, Second Cavalry, was ordered to dismount and
proceed along the edge of the ridge to a position covering the
eastern side of the village, opposite that from which Captain Egan
was to charge.   Captain Mills's battalion was ordered to follow
Egan, dismounted, and support him in the engagement, which
might follow the charge.   These columns began the descent of the
mountain, through gorges which were almost perpendicular, and
it seemed almost impossible that horses could be taken through
them.   Nearly two hours were occupied in getting the horses of
the charging column down these rough sides of the mountain, and
even there, when a point was reached where the men could mount
their horses and proceed toward the village in the narrow valley
beneath, Moore's battalion had not been able to gain its position
on the eastern side, after clambering along the edges of the mountain.   A few Indians could be seen with the herd, driving them
to the edge of the river, but nothing indicated that they knew of
our approach.   Just at 9 o'clock Captain Egan turned the point
of the mountain nearest the river, and first in a walk and then in
a rapid trot started for the village.   The company went first in
column of twos, but when within 200 yards of the village the
command " Left front into line " was given, and with a yell they
rushed into the encampment.   Captain Noyes had in the mean time
wheeled to the right and started the herd up the river. . . . With
the yell of the charging column the Indians sprang up as if by
magic, and poured in a rapid fire from all sides.   Egan charged
through and through the village before Moore's and Mills' battalions got within supporting distance, and finding things getting
very hot, formed his line in some high willows on the south side
of the camp, from which point he poured in rapid volleys upon
the Indians.   Up to this time the Indians supposed that one company was all they had to contend with, but when the other bat-

talions appeared, rapidly advancing, deployed as skirmishers, and pouring in a galling fire of musketry, they broke on all sides and took refuge in the rocks along the side of the mountain. The camp, consisting of 110 lodges, with immense quantities of robes, fresh meat, and plunder of all kinds, with over 700 head of horses, was in our possession. The work of burning began immediately, and soon the whole encampment was in flames. While the work of demolition was going on under the direction of General Reynolds, the Indians poured in a well-directed fire from the sides of the mountain and from every available hiding-place. Not satisfied with this, they made a determined attack on the troops about noon, with a view to regaining possession of the camp. Captain Mills, who had charge of the skirmish line, perceived their movement, and asked for additional men. These were sent in promptly, and the attack was quickly and handsomely repulsed, the Indians retiring in disorder. After the work of destruction had been completed, the withdrawal of the troops began, and the whole command moved rapidly up the river, twenty miles, to the mouth of Lodgepole Creek, where it went into camp, after two days and one night of constant marching.

So far so good. It will be observed that the troops, instead of surrounding the Indians, had been surrounded by them, and finally fell back. Now mark the sequel.

After the fight was over, the troops marched rapidly up the river to the mouth of Lodgepole Creek. This point was reached at nightfall by all except Moore's battalion and Captain Egan's company. Company E. Second Cavalry, was the rear guard, and assisted Major Stanton and the scouts in bringing up the herd of horses. Many of these were shot on the road, and the remainder reached camp about 9 P. M. These troops had been in the saddle for 36 hours, with the exception of five hours during which they were fighting, and all, officers and men, were much exhausted. The horses had had no grazing, and began to show signs of complete exhaustion. Upon arriving at Lodgepole, it was found that General Crook and the other four companies and pack-train had not arrived, so that everybody was supperless and without a blanket. The night, therefore, was not a cheerful one, but not a murmur was heard. The wounded men lay upon the snow or leaned against a tree, and slept as best they could on so cold a night.

Owing to some misunderstanding, *our four dead men were left on the field to be mutilated by the Indians.* These men could have been removed easily, and that they were not, caused a great deal of dissatisfaction among the troops. Saturday at noon General Crook and the remainder of the command arrived. *In the meantime a portion of the herd of ponies had straggled into the ravines, and fallen into the hands of the Indians.*

This is very unlike the sequel to Custer's triumph, and shows forcibly the lack of an energetic leader and officers imbued with the same enthusiasm. The correspondent closes with the following paragraphs of unconscious severity.

It is hardly proper to close this sketch of the engagement without referring more particularly to those causes which prevented its complete success. First among these was the failure of Captain Moore's battalion to reach the position assigned it in the rear of the village, or a point covering the rear, before the charge was made by Captain Egan. This failure allowed the Indians to make good their escape to the rocky fastnesses of the mountains overlooking the valley, from which they subsequently poured in a galling fire upon our troops. Moore's battalion was a strong one in number, and needed only to be led to the front where it could be effective to do good service. When it was discovered that the battalion would not be at the place assigned it, and that its commander did not apparently intend to put it there, Major Stanton and Lieut. Sibley, *with five men, left it and went on, taking up the position which the battalion should have occupied,* and gave the flying savages the best enfilading fire they could. But they were too few to prevent the escape of the Indians. This was the first serious blunder. The next was that after the herd of ponies, numbering over 700, had been captured, driven twenty miles from the scene of action, and turned over to General Reynolds, commanding the troops, *he failed to place a guard around them, so that the greater portion of them strayed off during the night, and were picked up by the Indians.* Furthermore, there were large quantities of buffalo meat and venison in the village, which General Crook had directed, in case of capture, to be brought out for the use of the troops, who were on half rations of fresh meat. This was not done, and as a result, the soldiers have had no fresh meat except ponies since that time.

In short it became clear, when full news of the expedition leaked out, that the Powder River fight was an example of an opportunity thrown away, in which almost every one was to blame for only one thing—*want of energy*. Capt. Noyes actually allowed his men to unsaddle and *rest*, after he had first driven away the Indian herd, and while the fighting was going on, and for this he was afterwards court-martialed and reprimanded in general orders.

But the real trouble seems to have been simple enough—a *want of heart*, an *excessive caution* in every one, especially the leader. When Custer went after Indians, he himself was always in the advance, and looking out for his enemy. At the Washita, we have found him with the advanced scouts on all occasions, and watching his enemy *himself*. Here, on the other hand, we see neither Crook nor Reynolds out in front, the night wasted in idle waiting, and the battle commenced at 9 o'clock, with the result of everybody falling just a little short of his work.

The Powder River fight, which, under Custer, would probably have ended in the complete destruction of the band of Crazy Horse, ended in merely burning some of his property and exasperating him, while leaving him all his weapons and men, and almost all his horses. It was an ominous commencement for a campaign of disaster.

After that time, the curtain was hardly ever lifted till the commencement of the winter of 1876, and even then not in the form of a victory over hostile Indians, but the more questionable success of a movement of far less danger, that should have been made long ago. This movement was the surrounding and forcible disarmament of the Sioux at the principal agencies, taking from them their ponies, and compelling them to live peaceably; and the army is fain to be proud of this, lacking other subjects of congratulation.

Recognizing fully the difficulties which surround army operations against the Indians, we must still admit the worst to be the low character of the regular troops. In the infantry, this is marked by apparent inability to execute severe marches on foot, in the cavalry by an almost total incapacity to fight mounted against the Indians.   Infantry and cavalry advance well enough in the common skirmish line on foot, but there are so many recruits, so few veterans in the ranks, that the issue of a single combat between an Indian and a dragoon is, almost as a matter of course, the death of the dragoon.   Compelled as they are, by the inferiority of their men, to fight dismounted, too many of our cavalry officers have fallen into the pernicious habit which spoiled the Confederate cavalry during the civil war, which ruined all European cavalry from the invention of firearms till the days when Gustavus Adolphus once more introduced the charge sword-in-hand, and which again ruined them in the interval between his days and those of Frederick the Great. This habit is the *distrust of the sabre*, and the consequent timidity evinced by all concerned, when a hand-to-hand fight is necessary.   The Indians, with all their improved firearms, universally retain the lance with their other weapons.   The drilled soldier, possessing a sabre, uses it only as an orna-ment on dress parade, and leaves it in quarters when he goes out to fight—first, on the ground that its clattering may be heard by Indians, second, on the singular plea, put forth by Colonel Brackett, in his "History of the U. S. Cavalry," that "if the soldier gets near enough to an Indian to use his sabre, it is an even chance which goes under."   Can it be wondered at that Indians beat men who are so ignorant of the art of attack and defence, and who despise all the teachings of military history?   If it be true that the chances are now even, or in favor of the Indian, there is a simple remedy.   It is to teach the men how to use their sabres, till they trust to them.   When officers and men do that, the Indians will fear *them*, not *they* the Indians.

CHAPTER III.

CUSTER AND GRANT.

IT is now time to turn to that part of the campaign under
General Terry's orders. When Sheridan and Sherman
planned the destruction of Sitting Bull, it was ordered that Custer should be assigned to the command of the Dakota column.
It was organized at his post, was mainly composed of his regiment, and was repeatedly denominated in orders " Custer's
column." The reasons for giving him this post were perfectly
simple. *Custer had never yet met with a single disaster while
in command of an important expedition, and he had been
blessed with more complete success in his Indian expeditions
than any other officer in the regular army.* His only rival as
an Indian fighter was Crook, and Crook had gained his reputation by a pursuit and extermination of small scattered bands of
Apaches in Arizona, who were not blessed with a semi-circle of
Indian agencies in their rear to supply them with Winchester
rifles and patent ammunition. Besides this, Crook was getting
older, and having been made a brigadier, was not so likely to
work as Custer, who was still only a lieutenant-colonel, thanks
to the seniority rule. Brigadier General Terry, the department
commander, had never been in the field as an Indian fighter,
and felt quite content to leave the Indian laurels to Custer.

Terry was a brigadier who owed his sudden elevation to
his present rank to the capture of Fort Fisher. Having been
a volunteer only, and before that a lawyer, not a West Pointer,
Terry found himself in a peculiar position in the army. Had
he been a nervously energetic officer like Custer, the enmity

he would have excited among the old seniority officers, especially the graduates, would have been much greater. As it was, while they hated him passively, they had not the same opportunity to spite him, Terry being two steps higher than Custer. Only his great sweetness of temper and modesty preserved him from active enmity. Terry trusted Custer implicitly, and admired him greatly, and it was all settled that Custer should lead the Dakota column.

Then came a sudden interruption to all these plans, a chain of incidents which ended in a disaster to the nation and in the temporary triumph of Custer's enemies. The facts of this business are so important to the vindication of Custer's character from the attacks of these enemies, that the nation of which he was the pride will not deem wasted the space which brings them clearly to light.

While Custer was hard at work preparing for his part of the Sioux Expedition, eager for work and foreseeing a further triumph, he received a telegram from Mr. Helster Clymer, Chairman of a certain Congressional Committee, requiring his presence in Washington, to give testimony as to some alleged abuses in the War Department. At the time, Mr. Belknap, who had lately resigned the office of Secretary of War, was under investigation in regard to an alleged sale by him of a post-tradership * to a person called Marsh. The committee had stumbled on the evidence of this sale by accident, and the Secretary, overwhelmed with shame at the discovery of his appar-

---

* Post-traders now supply the place of the old sutlers, whose office was abolished a few years since. They have the exclusive privilege of trading at the post to which they are appointed, and where the garrison is large the privilege is exceedingly valuable, as much of the pay of soldiers and officers is generally spent in the post-trader's store, for little luxuries. The post-tradership given to Marsh was at Fort Sill, Indian Territory, where ten companies of cavalry were generally stationed, aggregating about 600 men and forty officers, including staff, etc. The pay of the garrison amounted to about $160,000 a year, and at the ordinary sutler's rates, it was pretty certain that at least $100,000 would be spent at the store, with a profit to the post-trader, at 100 per cent., of at least $50,000 per annum.

ent venality, had resigned his office under charges, and was at once impeached by the House of Representatives.

The defence of the delinquent secretary, so far as it appeared, was that his first wife had, unknown to him, sold her influence with him for the office, that his second wife, sister of the first, had continued the bargain with Marsh after the death of her sister, and that he, Belknap, was perfectly ignorant of the whole matter till shortly before the examination of Marsh, when the shame and misery, experienced by him at the exposure of the delinquencies of his two wives, was so great as to lead to his giving up the fight in advance. Although this is not the place to enter into the merits or demerits of the Belknap case, which has since been legally settled in his favor, it may be stated that this explanation was believed to be the truth by all those who were personally intimate with the ex-secretary's career. One of these was President Grant, on whose staff the Secretary had served as General Belknap, during the war, and who remained his firm friend in his trouble.

The Congressional committee was determined, however, to investigate every act of Belknap's career in regard to frontier posts, and began to call witnesses from all quarters, groping blindly after the facts. The vaguest hearsay evidence was snatched at, and at last some one suggested that General Custer knew something about corruption on the part of the ex-secretary ; he had been heard by some one to say that he had heard something on the subject, and so forth. On this vague information the sapient Chairman telegraphed a summons to Custer to come to Washington, and so started a train of circumstances which was to end in the untimely death of the best cavalry chief on the American continent. Custer was much disturbed. He telegraphed at once to Terry to know what he should do, stating that his own information was only hearsay, and devoid of value to the case, and asking whether an order was not necessary. He made these inquiries of Terry, knowing that his general had been bred a lawyer. At the same time, showing his scrupulous sense of justice, he asked whether he was not bound to go, and tell what little he knew and how he knew it. In the same telegram, showing his peculiarly sensitive honor, he asks for a court of inquiry on himself in regard to his own conduct towards a discontented officer of his regiment, concerning a transfer from one company to another, in which the officer complained that injustice had been done him. Terry's answer to this telegram was as follows :

HDQRS. DEPT. OF DAKOTA, ST. PAUL, MIN., March 16, 1876.

To Lieut. Col. Custer, Fort Lincoln, Dakota:

Despatch received. You need no order beyond the summons of the committee. I am sorry to have you go, for *I fear it will delay our movements.* I should suppose that if your testimony is not as to the facts themselves, and will only point out the witnesses from whom the committee can get the facts, your information might be communicated by letter or telegraph, and that being done, you might ask to be relieved from personal attention without exposing yourself to misconstruction. However, you must use your own judgment.

In regard to the other matter, I don't think that you need a court of inquiry. Your statement to me vindicated you in my eyes : a repetition to General Sheridan would doubtless vindicate you in his. A court could not be convened until after the summer campaign is over. *Your services are indispensable, and no thought of a transfer can be entertained.*

TERRY, Comd'g. Dept.

Custer took Terry's advice and telegraphed to Clymer as follows :

FORT LINCOLN, DAKOTA, March 16, 1876.

Hon. Heister Clymer :

While I hold myself in readiness to obey the summons of your committee, I telegraph to state that I am engaged upon an important expedition, intended to operate against the hostile Indians, and *I expect to take the field early in April.* My presence here is deemed very necessary. In view of this, would it not be satisfactory for you to forward to me such questions as may be necessary, allowing me to return my replies by mail.

GEO. A. CUSTER.

Clymer, proud of his power to see through a millstone much further than any one else, would not be denied, and made Custer come on, besides putting him through a cross-examination that lasted two days, and compelling him to tell not only all he *knew*, but all he *did not know*, into the bargain. After a month's torture of Custer, he finally found out that the latter had written him an honest letter, and that the committee might better have left him in Fort Lincoln.

To only one fact was Custer able to testify, of his own knowledge. This was that, on one occasion the contractor at Fort Lincoln had turned him over a large quantity of grain, *in sacks which had borne the Indian brand,* and which *he suspected had been stolen from the Indian Department,* as part of the gigantic system of fraud by which the Indian Ring played into the hands of army contractors. At the time this grain was issued to Custer he refused to receive it, and telegraphed to Department Headquarters on the subject, expressing his suspicions. In due time, his communication having been forwarded through regular channels, he received a *positive order to take the grain.* This order he stated to the committee, he *believed* to have come down from the Secretary of War. This evidence, while avowedly only on information and belief, was regarded by Clymer as implicating the Secretary in some fresh fraud, and on the face of things there was ample ground for Custer's honest suspicions of the whole business. It turned out afterwards, that Custer was mistaken as to the *origin* of the peremptory order. It really came from Terry alone, on the latter's responsibility. We shall see later how perfectly frank Custer was in the matter, and how ready publicly to retract his error.

Much has been said by strong political partisans as to this last public action of Custer. By those who were ardent supporters of the ex-secretary, and especially of his avowed friend, President Grant, the indirect and hearsay testimony which was all that Custer could give, was contrasted with the previous parade of its promised value made by the committee, and especially by the partisan newspapers on the side of the committee. Custer was called a "swift witness," a "retailer of gossip" and accused of intriguing for his summons in order to escape frontier duty. Much of this abuse might be now passed over on the score of partisan excitement, were it not that the writer of Custer's biography feels himself bound by a sense of duty to probe the truth to the very bottom.

As regards the Belknap case, it is certain that Custer's evidence was wholly immaterial. His only item of personal knowledge adverse to the secretary was founded on an honest mistake, which he was swift to acknowledge when it was pointed out to him. As a witness of the prosecution, he should never have been called.

Who called him ?

Helster Clymer and that ingenious committee which so studiously mismanaged the Belknap case, were the real parties to blame. Custer had telegraphed to Clymer, begging to be excused from attendance at Washington, as an important expedition was about to take the field, in which his presence was necessary. He earnestly begged to be left at his post, but his request was denied. Clymer was bound to have him in Washington for political effect, just as Johnson in old times had been determined to have Custer's name associated with his, in "swinging round the circle." In both cases the only party injured was the honest unsuspecting soldier. The more Clymer questioned him, the more ludicrous was his failure to extract anything but the truth. For this truth, Custer has been blamed by his enemies, when the real party to blame was the officious chairman who persisted in calling him. On Clymer's shoulders, moreover, rests the responsibility of *deferring Custer's departure after Sitting Bull a whole month*. Had he gone in April, before the Indians had gathered in force, Custer might be alive now.

One person in the United States, however, would not believe

in Custer's unwillingness to testify. Instead of this, he took Custer's presence and testimony in Washington as a personal affront to himself. This person was President Grant.

President Grant was once General Grant. As General Grant he was chiefly distinguished for one virtue, an indomitable resolution and obstinacy in following whatever plan he had resolved on, an iron determination to pursue it at whatever cost. This quality of determination in war had finally conducted him to success, because as a general his power was absolute. As the executive of a republic, it brought him hatred and ill-will, for the successful head of a republic must be an eloquent and persuasive man, who can win others to his side by flattery, and who knows how to yield outwardly, while gaining his ends by craft and subtlety.

Another virtue possessed by General Grant was that of faithfulness to his friends, and this virtue also tended to his success in war, while in peace it operated in exactly the opposite direction. Had it been accompanied by good judgment in the choice of friends, it might not have been so disastrous, but unluckily, Grant seems from the first to have fallen into the hands of very questionable friends, who would have fleeced him had he been a rich man, who were accused of fleecing the nation under his protection, he being a high officer.

The efforts of the Clymer committee and the House during the Belknap investigation had undoubtedly been directed towards the injury of Grant and his friends, who formed what was known under the general term of "the Administration;" and the animus of the whole attack was so evident, the persistency of the efforts to find something on which to hang more impeachments so untiring, that they had excited the bitterest indignation in Grant himself. His very virtues, pride, firmness, faithful friendship, conviction of honesty, tended to embitter his animosity against all connected with the attack on "his administration." He looked on them as mortal enemies, and never forgave them. Amongst these he now counted Custer. He never paused to inquire whether the latter was a

willing witness, whether his testimony was dragged out of him
or not ; he made up his mind that Custer had turned against
him in his period of trial, and he became bitterly and inexora-
bly incensed against him, personally.   Custer heard of this,
through private sources, and knew that the President's impression as to his own testimony was quite unfounded.   As
soon, therefore, as he was released from his attendance at the
committee, he called at the White House to pay his respects to
the President, hoping by a frank personal statement to disabuse
his mind of the mistake.   For the first time in his life, Custer
found himself treated with ignominy, compelled to wait in the
ante-room for hours, to see other persons getting audiences before him, while he himself was left perfectly unnoticed, although
his card was sent in from the first.   Three times he called at
the White House, and on neither occasion was he even noticed.
These visits were made at various times during his sojourn at
Washington, while he was daily expecting his release and return to Dakota.   He had left the fort, expecting to be gone
ten days at furthest : he had now been detained at Washington
for over a month, unable to go anywhere, uncertain of his
movements from day to day.   He was only able to take one
hurried trip to New York on one occasion, to have a little business talk with his publishers about his "War Memoirs," which
he had commenced during the past winter at Fort Lincoln.
This hurried visit was the occasion of the last glimpse of Custer caught by the writer of this biography, while in the edito-
rial rooms of the "Galaxy."   Custer looked worn and thin, and
somewhat worried, his hair cut short, a great change from the
debonair cavalier of the Waynesboro' fight.   His manner
conveyed the impression of a nervous man with his nerves all
on edge, in a state of constant repressed impatience.   He had
left his wife behind at Fort Lincoln, and knew that every day
brought the season of active operations nearer, while he was
away.   No wonder he looked worried.   At last he was released
from his attendance, May 1st, and went to the White House,

with a last, almost despairing effort to get an audience from Grant and to explain his action. Once more he was compelled to submit to the slight of being kept waiting in the ante-room among the President's lackeys. Time was going on: his detention by the official summons was over, and he knew that his duty imperatively called him back to Fort Lincoln, that very day. He sat down and wrote the following note, which he sent in.

To His Excellency the President :

To-day for the third time I have sought an interview with the President—not to solicit a favor, except to be granted a brief hearing—but to remove from his mind certain unjust impressions concerning myself, which I have reason to believe are entertained against me. I desire this opportunity simply as a matter of justice, and I regret that the President has declined to give me an opportunity to submit to him a brief statement, which justice to him, as well as to me, demanded.

Respectfully submitted.

G. A. CUSTER, Lt. Col. Seventh Cavalry,

Bvt. Maj. Genl. U. S. Army.

This letter was sent in to, and read by, the President. During the last visit, as we are credibly informed, General Ingalls, then acting quartermaster-general, found Custer in the ante-room, and went in to see the President. Ingalls was a good and just man, and a friend of both. He asked the President if he knew that Custer was outside, waiting. The President did—*he did not wish to see him.* Then, Ingalls urged, he should at least spare Custer the indignity of waiting outside, and send him a message to save his time—that so much was due to Custer's past services at least. Then the President sent out word that he refused to see Colonel Custer, and Custer sat down and wrote his quiet, manly letter, honest and proud, sad and dignified, like himself in every word. It was useless. *Grant refused to see him.*

Custer had no longer any pretext for staying in Washington. He had already been to call on the General of the Army, and found that Sherman was away in New York, but was expected back in the evening. He went off and secured his passage on the night train, calling on Inspector-General Marcy and Adjutant-General Townsend on the way. Adjutant-General Marcy had wished Custer, on the way back to Dakota, to perform some duty in Detroit which would delay him, but hearing from Custer of the urgency of his haste, on account of the lateness of the season, and of the necessity of his immediate presence at Fort Lincoln, gave him the following letter.

WAR DEPARTMENT, INSPECTOR-GENERAL'S OFFICE.

Washington, D. C. May 1st, 1876.

Lieut. Col. G. A. Custer, U. S. Army.

COLONEL :—Understanding that the general of the army desires you to proceed directly to your station, the service which I recommended you to perform in Detroit, Michigan, can be executed by another officer. And in the absence of the general you have my consent to omit stopping at Detroit for the purpose specified in the Adjutant-General's letter to you.

Very respectfully, your obedient servant,

R. B. MARCY, Inspector General.

Custer made a last call at Sherman's office. The General was not back from New York, and his length of stay was still uncertain. Custer took the train, and was soon whirling away toward Chicago. The next day, May 2d, General Sheridan was awakened from his slumbers by the following extraordinary telegram :

WASHINGTON, D. C., May 2d, 1876.

General P. H. Sheridan, Chicago, Illinois.

I am this moment advised that General Custer started last night for Saint Paul and Fort Abraham Lincoln. *He was not justified in leaving without seeing the President or myself.* Please intercept him at Chicago or Saint Paul, and order him to halt and await further orders. *Meanwhile, let the Expedition from Fort Lincoln proceed without him.*

(Signed)   W. T. SHERMAN, General.

It was the hand of Sherman, but the head of Grant. The grim implacable animosity of the President was aroused. Custer's testimony had made him the President's foe. Right or wrong, Grant was determined to punish him, and there was but one way to do it—deprive him of the command of the expedition, and so humiliate him. No one knew better than Grant that if Custer went in command of the Dakota column he was *certain to return victorious*, with fresh laurels. That pill was too bitter for the President to swallow. All that Sheridan could do, in the face of such a positive order, was to obey it. An officer was sent to the station, and Custer was stopped on the 4th of May by the following letter:

HEADQUARTERS MILITARY DIV. OF THE MISSOURI,
Chicago, Ill., May 4th, 1876.

Lieutenant-Col. G. A. Custer, Seventh U. S. Cavalry, Chicago, Ill.

SIR :—Agreeably to instructions contained in the enclosed copy of a telegraphic dispatch from the general of the army, of the 2d instant, the Lieutenant-General commanding the division directs you to remain in Chicago until the receipt of further orders from superior authority, to be furnished you through these headquarters.

Very respectfully your obedient servant,
R. C. DRUM, Assistant Adjutant-General.

There was nothing for it but to obey. Custer drove in haste to Sheridan's headquarters, and found him as friendly as ever. Sheridan knew no more of the cause of the order than did Custer himself, and told him so. He had no objection to Custer's telegraphing direct to Sherman for an explanation, and the astonished officer at once sent off the following dispatch :

CHICAGO, ILL.

General W. T. Sherman, Washington, D. C.

I have seen your despatch to General Sheridan directing me to await orders here, and am at a loss to understand that portion referring to my departure from Washington *without seeing you or the President,* as I called at the White House at ten o'clock A. M.

Monday, sent my card to the President, and, with the exception
of a few minutes' absence at the War Department, I remained at
the White House waiting an audience with the President until
three P. M., when he sent me word that he would not see me. I
called at your office about two P. M., but was informed by Colonel
McCook you had not returned from New York, but were expected
in the evening. I called at your hotel at four P. M. and about six
P. M., but was informed by the clerk that you had not returned
from New York. I then requested Colonel McCook to inform
you of the substance of the above dispatch, and also that I was to
leave at seven that evening to report to my command.

While at the War Department that day, I also reported the
fact of my proposed departure to the Adjutant-General and to the
Inspector-General of the army, and obtained from them written
and verbal authority to proceed to my command without visiting
Detroit, as previously ordered to do. At my last interview with
you, I informed you that I would leave Washington Monday night
to join my command, and you, in conversation replied that *" that
was the best thing I could do."* Besides, you frequently, during
my stay in Washington, called my attention to *the necessity for my
leaving as soon as possible.* I telegraph you direct, with the permission of the Lieutenant-General.

G. A. CUSTER, Brevet Major-General.

Later in the day he sent this further telegram :

CHICAGO, May 4, 1876. 2:30 P. M.

Gen. W. T. Sherman, Washington, D. C.

I desire to further call your attention to your statement to me,
in your office, that I should go in command of my regiment.

Also to your reply when I inquired if the President or other
parties had any charges to make against me. In leaving Washington, I had every reason to believe I was acting in strict accordance with your suggestions and wishes. I ask you as General of
the army to do me justice in this matter.

G. A. CUSTER.

No answer came to these despatches, and Custer well knew
the reason. It was not Sherman who was thus putting him to
torture, but some one behind Sherman who was able to command him. Grant was resolved to humiliate Custer, no matter

at what cost. He was stolidly determined to have his own way. As a last resort, Custer telegraphed a third time in the evening.

General W. T. Sherman, Washington, D. C.

After you read my despatch of to-day, I would be glad if my detention could be authorized at Fort Lincoln, where my family is, instead of at this point.

G. A. CUSTER, Bvt. Major General.

Not a word in answer to all this. Custer had committed no crime ; there were no charges against him. He had done nothing but obey orders all through, but it was necessary he should be punished, as the President could punish no one else. In this Grant showed great knowledge of human nature. No doubt he would have liked immediately to punish every officer who had testified against his "administration," but he had no means by which to do it. No one else of the witnesses was in command of an expedition, no one was a successful Indian fighter, no one else was a high-strung nervous cavalier, sensitive to a slight. Custer was the only man. It was so easy to punish him, by the simplest means : the reason assigned was so plausible. Grant knew that the torture lay in the *first* humiliation, the minor details were of little consequence. After all, the President, while a bitter foe, was not a cruel one. He had no objection to letting Custer see his family. So it appears by the following despatch :

CHICAGO, May 5th.

Brigadier General A. H. Terry, St. Paul, Minn.

The Lieutenant General directs me to transmit for your information and guidance the following telegram from the General of the Army :—

" Have received your dispatch of to-day, announcing General Custer's arrival. Have just come from the President, who orders that General Custer be allowed to rejoin his post, *to remain there on duty, but not to accompany the expedition supposed to be on the point of starting against the hostile Indians, under General Terry.*

(Signed,)   W. T. SHERMAN, General.

Please acknowledge receipt.

(Signed,)   R. C. DRUM, A. A.G.

> HDQRS. DEPT. OF DAKOTA,
> ST. PAUL, MAY 8th, 1876.

Official copy respectfully furnished for the information of Lieutenant-Colonel Custer.

GEO. RUGGLES, Ass. Adj. Genl.

It appears clearly from the next message that Sherman was not inimical to Custer, for he telegraphed to him kindly enough. Immediately following Sherman's telegram, will be found one from Custer, illustrating the frankness and completeness with which he always acknowledged his errors. It is the one we have before referred to, as connected with the matter of the grain frauds. Sheridan's telegram is as follows:

> WASHINGTON, D. C.

Gen. G. A. Custer, Chicago, Ill.

Before receipt of yours, had sent orders to General Sheridan to permit you to go to Abe Lincoln on duty, *but the President adheres to his conclusion that you are not to go on the expedition.*

W. T. SHERMAN, General.

The other telegram is as follows:

> SAINT PAUL, May 6th, 1876.

To Hon. Heister Clymer, Washington, D. C. :

General Terry, commanding the Department of Dakota, informs me that the report I forwarded from Fort Lincoln, regarding certain corn delivered at that post, for the use of the army, in Indian sacks, was received at his headquarters in the city, and after due investigation, was acted upon finally by *his* authority; and that it was *he* and *not the late Secretary of War,* who sent the order to Fort Lincoln, directing that, under certain instructions intended to protect the government, the corn in question should be received. The receipt of the order was reported to me, and at the same time I derived the impression that the order emanated from the War Department. *As I would not knowingly do injustice to any individual, I ask that this telegram may be appended to, and made part of my testimony before your committee.*

G. A. CUSTER.

Then Custer found himself, May 6, in St. Paul, and condemned by the President's order to remain behind and see his comrades go to war. How bitterly it must have recalled to him his equally unjust detention, eight years before, at Fort Leavenworth, and the disasters to the nation which had followed his punishment. That punishment led to the Phil Kearny massacre and Forsyth's disastrous siege on the island. It shows how free from vulgar ambition and how pure was Custer's patriotism, that he, the proud soldier, publicly insulted and humiliated without the pretence of a fault on his part, should have written such a letter as this, which follows. The last words we commend to the nation that loves him. We also commend Terry's letter of transmittal.

HEADQUARTERS DEPARTMENT OF DAKOTA,
SAINT PAUL, MINN., May 6th, 1876.

Adjutant General, Division of Missouri, Chicago.

I forward the following :—

To HIS EXCELLENCY THE PRESIDENT, through Military Channels.

I have seen your order, transmitted through the general of the army, directing that I be not permitted to accompany the expedition about to move against hostile Indians. As my entire regiment forms a part of the proposed expedition, and as I am the senior officer of the regiment on duty in this Department, I respectfully but most earnestly request that while not allowed to go in command of the expedition, I may be permitted to serve with my regiment in the field.

I appeal to you as a soldier to spare me the humiliation of seeing my regiment march to meet the enemy and I not to share its dangers.

(Signed)   G. A. CUSTER,
Bvt. Maj. Genl. U. S. Army.

In forwarding the above, I wish to say expressly, that I have no desire whatever to question the orders of the President, or of my military superiors. Whether Lieut. Col. Custer shall be permitted to accompany my column or not, I shall go in command of it.

I do not know the reasons upon which the orders already given rest ; but if those reasons do not forbid it, *Lieut. Col. Custer's services would be very valuable with his command.*

(Signed)   TERRY,
                                          Commanding Department.

It will be seen that Terry is cautious as to expressing an opinion, being restrained from speaking out by official reticence. He could not say to his superior officer, whether he thought it or not;—" Look here; this is a scandalous shame. Custer has done nothing wrong, he has only obeyed the law and told the truth ; and the President is taking a mean and cowardly advantage of his power to punish Custer indirectly, because he dare not do it directly." The old adroitness of the lawyer appears in all of Terry's conduct. He makes no enemies ; even the old West Pointers, over whose heads Fort Fisher had jumped him, could not find it in their hearts to hate him.

But the opposition papers were not so mealy-mouthed. All over the land they teemed with double-leaded articles on " Grant's tyranny " and " Custer's degradation," and took the quarrel up, not because they cared for Custer, but because they could make political capital out of it. All the foul vultures of politics flocked to see the battle, expecting a feast at its conclusion. The " administration " papers were thus in a manner forced into the fight, and into an attitude of antagonism to Custer, which has pursued him beyond his grave. This was unfortunate enough, and it is to be hoped that it will go no further. I have written in this chapter a plain statement of facts, and introduced copies of the original documents, on purpose to show that Custer's action in the whole of this matter was entirely unpolitical, and in the earnest hope that it may prevent his memory from being made the subject of a partisan fight. No man was ever more thoroughly an honest soldier and less of a politician than Custer, and no man has suffered more from the efforts of those vampires of life, the politicians, to make use of him in their quarrels.

Two men were to blame for all the trouble : meddling, officious Heister Clymer, who insisted on making Custer come to Washington ; obstinate, implacable Grant—the man, not the President—who would not listen to a word, and who was actually *willing to imperil the whole fate of the Sioux campaign and to permit hundreds of lives to be lost, to gain his revenge on Custer.* The question has nothing to do with one party or the other, but the responsibility of all that follows rests personally on these two men—the busy-body and the implacable tyrant. One was willing to imperil a nation to serve his faction, the other was ready to forget his office, to prostitute his position, to sacrifice a hecatomb of innocent lives, to gratify his private revenge. From the consequences of that act he cannot escape.

Grant was satisfied with his first disgrace of Custer, or dared not face the criticism which would have greeted the announcement of the fact that the President of the United States was willing to imperil the success of an important expedition to gratify his private revenge. That was going a step too far : so Grant yielded to Custer's petition so far as to let him go as a subordinate, in the expedition which *Grant well knew in his heart that Custer alone was fit to command.*

The papers said this openly, both opposition and independents, whereupon the administration papers felt themselves compelled to print alleged utterances of General Sherman to the effect that there were " plenty of officers in the army just as capable as Custer." Here again the officious meddling of Custer's injudicious friends only embittered his single real enemy, Grant, and compelled Sherman, as an official person, to appear hostile to Custer. Possibly the general of the army did *say* there were plenty of officers fit to take Custer's place, but he *knew* well enough that there was not one, for it was now May 7th,

36

and the operations of every other officer had so far been marked by want of energy all through, especially in the *fiasco* of the Powder River fight. The fact was, and Sherman, Grant, and Sheridan knew it, none better, that no one could replace Custer's peculiar qualities. " *Custer*," said Sheridan at Fort Leavenworth, seven years before, " *You are the only man that never failed me.*"

Write those words in gold on his monument. None could wish a prouder epitaph.

NOTE. Since this chapter was printed and stereotyped, the author has received information from the publishers of the *Galaxy*, that tends further to disprove the accusation that Custer was willing to go to Washington before the committee. In conversation with members of the firm, while on his way to Washington, Custer distinctly stated that he knew nothing of his own knowledge, as to the Belknap or other cases, that could be of the slightest value to the committee. He displayed the greatest anxiety to be back at his post, and the peremptory summons of the committee was a great disappointment to him. As he expressed it, he had " begged of the committee to allow him to remain at Fort Lincoln, where he was so busy *preparing the expedition of which he had been promised the command.*"

Mrs. Custer, who of all persons, is most capable of judging of her husband's wishes, has also most positively assured the author that it was with the greatest unwillingness that Custer departed from Fort Lincoln, and with the fear before his eyes that it would end in disaster to the expedition.

CHAPTER IV.

THE GREAT EXPEDITION.

THE slight and partial success of the Powder River fight was productive of one very serious result, as it turned out. General Crook virtually agreed, and the authorities agreed with him, as to the substantial truth of the following statement, made by a writer present with the expedition. He said : Instead of 15,000 or 20,000 hostile Indians in this country, the expedition has demonstrated that there are probably not 2,000 all told.

The Tribune correspondent in his report also said :

It does not seem probable that there are half as many hostile Indians in this northern country as the War Department has supposed. For nearly two weeks this command has been marching through the best part of the whole unceded Sioux lands, and it has not seen 1,000 Indians in all. I doubt if there are 3,000 hostile people south of the Missouri and east of the Big Horn Mountains. Other military expeditions will soon follow this one, and in the end all these tribes will be glad to take agency rations, poor and insufficient as they generally are, for the rest of their days.

These sentiments were echoed by others, and formed the basis of the calculation on which the expeditions to come were composed. The strength of the columns was as follows, Crook had ten companies of the Third Cavalry, five of the Second Cavalry, with six companies from the Fourth and Ninth Infantry, an aggregate strength of 1,300 men. His route was north from Fort Fetterman. (See map.)

Gibbon, whose route was due east from Fort Ellis, Montana, had four companies of the Second Cavalry and two companies of the Seventh Infantry, a total force of some four hundred men, including train, etc.

The Terry column moving west from Fort Lincoln consisted of the whole of the Seventh Cavalry—twelve companies—under Custer, and three companies of the Sixth and Seventeenth Infantry, with four Gatling guns and a detachment of Indian scouts. Official returns show that this force comprised twenty-eight officers and seven hundred and forty-seven men of the Seventh Cavalry, eight officers and one hundred and thirty-five men of the Sixth and Seventeenth Infantry, two officers and thirty-two men in charge of the Gatling battery, and forty-five enlisted Indian scouts. The wagon train contained one hundred and fourteen six-mule teams, thirty-seven two-horse teams, and seventy other vehicles, ambulances, etc., with eighty-five packmules, and employed one hundred and seventy-nine civilian drivers.

Thus there was a total force of twenty-seven hundred armed men seeking for the Sioux, divided into three columns, respectively of the strength of four hundred, one thousand and one thousand three hundred. These three columns were to start from the circumference of a circle with a radius of some three hundred miles, to concentrate somewhere in the country where Reynolds had struck Crazy Horse and his band.

Crook did not leave Fort Fetterman till May 29th. His column reached old Fort Reno, June 3d. In this vicinity the expedition rested, while a party of scouts were detached to the encampments of the Crows and Shoshones, tribes of Indians inimical to the Sioux, to obtain their assistance as scouts and light troops. On the 7th of June the column was on the head of the Tongue River, near old Fort Phil Kearny, where, on the 8th a war party of Sioux came down and tried to stampede the American horses, bringing on a skirmish which resulted in the repulse of the Indians. On the 14th the column was joined by a number of Crows, Shoshonés and Nez Percés whom the scouts had brought back, and on the 16th the whole party started to find the bands of Sitting Bull and Crazy Horse, reported to be on the Rosebud River, to the north. The Crows who came in reported that they had seen Gibbon's camp *on the other side of the Sioux*, on the Tongue River, and that the United States forces had already been attacked by Sitting Bull's people, who had taken some horses from them.

Thus it will be seen that up to the 16th June, the United States programme was carried out as fairly as could be expected, and that two of the converging columns had already arrived within striking distance of Sitting Bull and his friends. It was now that its faults were to be glaringly exposed. The regular force near the enemy amounted to 1700 men, whereof 400 were separated from the other 1300 by a rough mountainous country of some hundred miles, and between the two lay Sitting Bull and his braves, in a compact body.

On the 16th, Crook advanced his force early in the morning. Each man carried four days' rations, the infantry were mounted on mules, and the train was left behind them. The destination of the column was Sitting Bull's village, on the Rosebud River, sixty miles north. By the evening of the 16th, the column had marched forty miles, and went into camp for the night. The *Tribune* correspondent says very justly, " This was the first mistake." Crook should have marched all night and attacked at daybreak, but just as in the case of the Powder River fight, *the time was wasted*. The mistake is claimed by the correspondent to be the fault of the Indian allies, who had been out hunting buffalo that day, and who gorged themselves with meat at night and refused to advance. A poor excuse is better than none.

The next morning Sitting Bull turned the tables on Crook by attacking him, and the story told by the correspondent is instructive. It shows what a tissue of blunders and cross purposes a battle may become under the command of the oldest of generals, in Indian warfare, when all are not animated by the same spirit.

The Crows and other scouts had been sent forward to find the Sioux village, and the correspondent proceeds:

"June 17th, having marched seven miles, *being in camp unsaddled,* successive shots were distinctly heard, and the advance of the Sioux confirmed by our scouts pouring over the hills. Our present position, *being surrounded by bluffs,* was an untenable one, and one well chosen by the Sioux for their attack. The advance was sounded, and the line of battle then formed, was "Noyes' battalion" right, "Mills'" right centre, "Chambers'" centre, "Indian allies" left centre, Royall (with "Henry's battalion," and one company of Mills) left. Mills' and Noyes' battalion were pushed forward, charging the enemy in gallant style. The rest of the line did not advance. Mills and Noyes were ordered to march on the village, which order fortunately for them was revoked. Royall's right was separated from the main command by about a quarter of a mile. He occupied a very important and dangerous position; one which if held by the enemy would have rendered Crook's line on the bluff untenable unless he had advanced. Having occupied this place under a heavy fire from the commencement of the fight (8 A. M.,) until 2 P. M., Captain Nickerson of General Crook's staff brought, attended with great personal danger (as the Indians seemed to divine his mission), orders for Colonel Royall to retire or connect his line with General Crook's. This was effected, instead of by a forward movement, by a sort of *left about wheel, or retreat.* The Indians seized this favorable opportunity by advancing and occupying the place vacated by ourselves and pouring upon us a galling fire from three different directions, charging upon our lines and trying to capture our led horses, our men being dismounted as skirmishers. Royall, by maintaining successive lines of retreat, aided by the great gallantry of his men and officers, succeeded, *with loss,* in joining Crook's command.

This loss was diminished by the charge made by our allies and two infantry companies from Crook's left upon the advancing Sioux. This charge should have been made when we first commenced our retreat movement. It was in what may be called "Death Hollow" during the retreat, while superintending the movements of his battalion, that Colonel Henry was severely wounded in the face, the ball entering near the left temple, and coming out the right side of the face.

" The order now was for all the troops to advance upon the village, supposed to be some six miles off. This order was twice given and twice changed, the latter owing to ammunition becoming short, and upon the representation of the guide, who had lived with the Sioux, that it would be impossible to pass through a difficult canon and secure the village without immense loss to our troops. These reasons, besides caring for his wounded, decided General Crook to go into camp on the battle-field of the day, which he did.

" *The next two succeeding days, without further molestation, we returned to our permanent camp.*"

It will be seen that the correspondent puts the very best face on the battle that could be put there, but none the less it is impossible to hide the fact that Crook was taken by surprise. "Being in camp unsaddled" is the commencement of the fight, while on a march to "surprise" an active foe. In the course of the battle, Crook's left is *driven in with serious loss*, and only saved from annihilation by the charges of the Indian allies and the infantry. The Herald correspondent puts on a still better face, by claiming a substantial victory, but even he cannot hide the fact of real defeat. He says :

The object of the scout which was *so unsuccessful and yet not without an encouraging result*, was to discover and destroy the village of the Sioux, which the guides, white, half-breed and Indian, agreed in declaring to be on the Yellowstone River, between the mouths of the Rosebud and the Tongue. It proved to be nearer the base of the expedition than was believed, and *General Crook's ignorance of its proximity*, due to the negligence and inactivity of the Crow allies, who were entrusted with the work of scouting, is the cause of failure of the movement. The Sioux were certainly repulsed in their bold onset, and lost many of their bravest warriors, but when they fled, could not be pursued without great danger in the rough country through which their way lay. Had his scouts proved faithful, *so that he could have been prepared to occupy the commanding positions with infantry in advance of the main column,* he would have had warning of the concentration of the enemy to impede his course, and could have driven him back into the village and ended the campaign by destroying it. It will be seen that the blame of the miscarriage of the scout belongs to the Crows, whose instinct, vigilance, and knowledge of their own country was relied upon to render every move of the force intelligent. On the contrary, their undisciplined frenzy and failure to discover the lodgment of the enemy in time to frustrate their meditated attack precipitated a battle which began with a stupendous advantage on his side and in a spot of his own choice naturally suitable to the success of their method of warfare. The Sioux's strength was masked, except when, *emboldened by the disastrous withdrawal of the left wing of the cavalry*, they made a dash from both ends of a deep hollow which lay in its way and exposed it to a murderous fire, and suddenly swarmed on the front, left and rear. Then it was that the timely fire of the infantry upon their main body, the charge of the Snakes into the hollow and a rapid pursuit of them for three miles, dismayed them utterly and they fell back and disappeared. *Had it not been for their occupation, unperceived by the General, of positions from which they could pour an enfilading fire upon both flanks of the body of cavalry on the left,* they would not have stood in the face of the troops a moment after their first charge.

The last sentence, " had it not been " etc., is decidedly good. It shows that Crook was outgeneraled by Sitting Bull, and that the latter had troops not accustomed to the direct charge, and that is all. The Indians fought in their own way, and did all they wanted. They drove Crook back to his camp.

Meanwhile what were Terry and Gibbon doing? The reports show the following state of things :

Generals Terry and Gibbon communicated with each other, June 1st, near the junction of the Tongue and Yellowstone Rivers, and learned that a heavy force of Indians had concentrated on the opposite bank of the Yellowstone, but about eighteen miles distant. For fourteen days the Indian pickets had confronted Gibbon's videttes.

General Gibbon reported to General Terry that the cavalry had thoroughly scouted the Yellowstone as far as the mouth of the Big Horn, and no Indians had crossed it. It was now certain that they were not prepared for them, and on the Powder, Tongue, Rosebud, Little Horn, or Big Horn rivers General Terry at once commenced feeling for them.

Major Reno, of the Seventh Cavalry, with six companies of that regiment, was sent up Powder River 150 miles to the mouth of Little Powder to look for the Indians, and, if possible, to communicate with General Crook. He reached the mouth of the Little Powder in five days, but saw no Indians and could hear nothing of Crook. As he returned, he found on the Rosebud a very large Indian trail, about nine days old, and followed it a short distance, when he turned about up Tongue River, and reported to General Terry what he had seen. It was now known no Indians were on Tongue River or Powder River, and the net had narrowed down to Rosebud, Little Horn and Big Horn Rivers.

General Terry, who had been waiting with Custer and the steamer *Far West*, at the mouth of Tongue River, for Reno's report, as soon as he heard it, ordered Custer to march up the south bank to a point opposite General Gibbon, who was encamped on the north bank of the Yellowstone. Terry, on board the steamer *Far West*, pushed up the Yellowstone, keeping abreast of General Custer's column.

General Gibbon was found in camp, quietly awaiting developments. A consultation was had with Generals Gibbon and Custer, and then General Terry definitely fixed upon the plan of action. It was believed the Indians were on the head of the Rosebud or over on the Little Horn, a divide of ridge only fifteen miles wide separating the two streams. It was announced by General Terry that General Custer's column would strike the blow.

In order to understand the position of affairs, it will now be necessary to lay before the reader an outline sketch of the lines of the campaign so far, and show the position of the contending parties at this time. (See map.) This sketch indicates with sufficient accuracy for the reader the progress of the campaign. It shows the routes of the three columns up to the juncture when Custer was sent after the Indians, and the lines of march. It will be seen that after Gibbon's and Terry's junction the two were about a hundred miles from Crook, and that the Sioux were between them. Crook, after his defeat, fell back to the head of the Tongue River. The Powder, Tongue, Rosebud, and Big Horn Rivers all run north into the Yellowstone, and

Sitting Bull was between the head-waters of the Rosebud and Big Horn, the main tributary of the latter being known as the Little Big Horn. Thus stood matters when Terry sent off the following despatch to Sheridan, from his camp at the mouth of the Rosebud River. He writes:

No Indians have been met with as yet, but traces of large and recent camp have been discovered twenty or thirty miles up the Rosebud. Gibbon's column will move this morning on the north side of the Yellowstone, for the mouth of the Big Horn, where it will be ferried across by the supply steamer, and whence it will proceed to the mouth of the Little Horn, and so on. Custer will go up the Rosebud to-morrow with his whole regiment, and thence to the head-waters of the Little Horn, thence down the Little Horn.

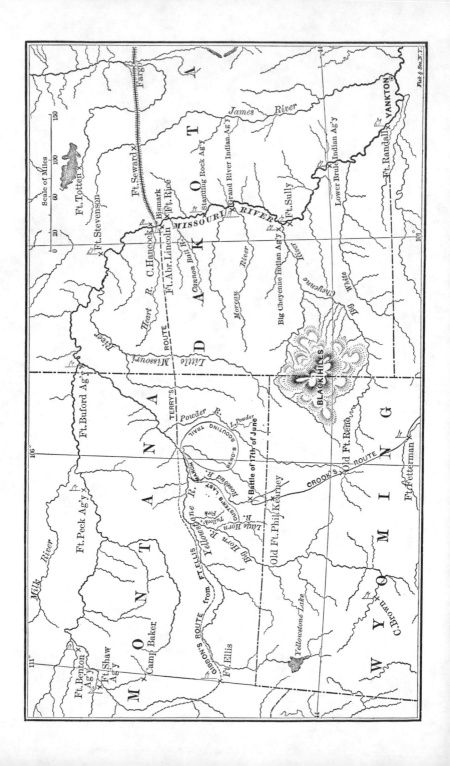

CHAPTER V.

THE LAST BATTLE.

BEFORE entering on the consideration of Custer's last march and battle, it is necessary to correct a mistaken impression set afloat by those same insincere friends and real enemies who had already done their best to embroil and embitter the close of his life. This impression is, that Custer, during the whole of the last campaign, was suffering from depression of spirits, that he felt his disgrace keenly, that he was slighted by General Terry, and that these stings induced him to act rashly. The facts are exactly the reverse.

General Terry, from the very commencement of the expedition, trusted Custer implicitly, and the very best feeling existed between them. No one was more modest than Terry, nor more willing to defer to the experience of Custer; and inasmuch as the route followed by the Terry column was the very same as that followed three years before by the Stanley expedition, General Terry was only too glad to avail himself of Custer's help to pilot the column, just as Stanley had in his time. It became Custer's regular duty to ride ahead of the main body with a battalion of the Seventh Cavalry, and to mark out the day's march for the wagons by leaving a broad trail. An officer present during the whole compaign, whose name we at present withhold, says:

As he seemed to me first, so he was to the last, the incarnation of energy. How often I watched him in our march to the Powder River, like the thoroughbred he rode, champing the bit and chafing to be off, longing for action. Our last day's march before reaching Powder River was through the worst and roughest country that I have ever seen a train taken over in campaign.

Early in the day the guides and scouts were baffled by the labyrinth of ravines and confusion of bad-lands. Custer took the lead and took us through. I heard General Terry express his satisfaction that evening in these words : " *No one but General Custer could have brought us through. He is the best guide I ever saw.*" Notwithstanding his manifestation of a little restiveness during this march, I was glad to know that he was steadily revealing his fine qualities to General Terry, and winning his way to the position which drew from his commanding officer the *carte blanche* under which he marched up the Rosebud on the 22d June. It will not do for any one to say that he disobeyed orders on that occasion. He did as every one capable of comprehending him and his orders knew that he would do, and by those orders I am willing that he shall be judged, not by documents or explanations outside of them.

The reader will now very naturally ask to see these orders and find what they were. Fortunately they exist, and are as follows :

Lieut. Col. Custer, Seventh Cavalry :

COLONEL :—The Brigadier-General Commanding directs that as soon as your regiment can be made ready for the march you proceed up the Rosebud in pursuit of the Indians whose trail was discovered by Major Reno a few days since. It is, of course, impossible to give any definite instructions in regard to this movement, and, were it not impossible to do so, the Department Commander places too much confidence in your zeal, energy and ability to wish to impose upon you precise orders which might hamper your action when nearly in contact with the enemy. He will, however, indicate to you his own views of what your action should be, and he desires that you should conform to them unless you shall see sufficient reason for departing from them. He thinks that you should proceed up the Rosebud until you ascertain definitely the direction in which the trail above spoken of leads. Should it be found, as it appears to be almost certain that it will be found, to turn toward the Little Big Horn, he thinks that you should still proceed southward, perhaps, as far as the head-waters of the Tongue, and then turn toward the Little Big Horn, feeling constantly, however, to your left so as to preclude the possibility of the escape of the Indians to the south or south-east by passing around your left flank. The column of Col. Gibbon is now in motion for the mouth of the Big Horn. As soon as it reaches that point it will cross the Yellowstone and move up at least as far as the parks of the Big and Little Big Horn. Of course its future movements must be controlled by circumstances as they arise ; but it is hoped that the Indians, if upon the Little Big Horn, may be so nearly inclosed by two columns that their escape will be impossible. The Department Commander desires that on your way up the Rosebud you should thoroughly examine the upper part of Tulloch's Creek, and that you should endeavor to send a scout through to Col. Gibbon's column with information of the result of your examination. The lower part of this creek will be examined by a detachment from Col. Gibbon's command. The supply steamer will be pushed up the Big Horn as far as the forks of the river are found to be navigable for that space, and the Department Commander, who will accompany the column of Col. Gibbon, desires you to report to him there not later than the expiration of the time for which your troops are rationed, unless in the meantime you receive further orders.

Respectfully, etc.,

E. W. SMITH, Captain 18th Infantry.

Acting Assistant Adjutant-General.

These orders are quite clear and explicit on one subject. Custer was sent out to find the Indians by following their trail up the Rosebud, and Gibbon was to hunt them from another direction, first up the Yellowstone, then up the Big Horn River. This would bring the two columns together on the Big Horn somewhere to the south of the place where the battle finally occurred, if both moved at the same rate, for their trails would then be each round two sides of a rectangle, from corner to corner. The first corner was the junction of the Rosebud and Yellowstone, the opposite one Sitting Bull's village on the Big Horn. Nothing, however, was said in the order about rates of marching, and Custer was left entirely to his own discretion as to what he should do if he struck the enemy first. The only limit placed to his time in the order is the period for which his troops are rationed. That period was fifteen days. The only expression of opinion on future movements is found in the sentence "*it is hoped that the Indians, if upon the Little Big Horn, may be so nearly enclosed by the two columns that escape may be impossible.*" The only fear of Terry seems to be that the Indians will escape. On Custer's way up the Rosebud, he is directed to examine "the upper part of Tulloch's Creek." This creek runs into the Big Horn near its mouth. Its "upper part," was some ten miles to the right of Custer's actual trail, which followed that of the Indian village previously found by Reno. Custer was to "endeavor to send through a scout to Colonel Gibbon's column." If he found that the trail turned, (as it did) to the right, Terry "*thinks you should still proceed southward*" to the head waters of the Tongue before turning after the Indians. All these instructions, it will be noticed, are entirely advisory and permissory, *not peremptory*. Terry expresses his conviction of the impossibility of giving any precise orders "which might hamper your action when nearly in contact with the enemy," and only desires Custer to conform to his views "unless you shall see sufficient reason for departing from them." It is quite clear on the face of these orders that Custer cannot be held legally or morally responsible for any departure from Terry's advice. The whole matter is left entirely in his discretion, the general placing "too much confidence in your zeal, energy and ability" to give any orders, beyond one to report in fifteen days. On his discretion solely he must be judged. In following him through the course of this his last march, we shall embody so much of the official report of his second in command, Major Reno, made at the close of the operations, as covers the period to Custer's death, illustrating it by the evidence of other persons, taken since that time. This report is valuable on account of its presumed reliability as to dates, times and places. It was first published in the *Army and Navy Journal* of New York City, the official Army paper, and is addressed according to military etiquette, to the chief of Terry's staff for the time being. It commences as follows:

HEADQUARTERS, SEVENTH CAVALRY,
CAMP ON YELLOWSTONE RIVER, July 5, 1876.

Captain E. W. Smith, A. D. C. and A. A. A. G. :

The command of the Regiment having devolved upon me, as the senior surviving officer from the battle of June 25th and 26th, between the Seventh Cavalry and Sitting Bull's band of hostile Sioux, on the Little Big Horn River, I have the honor to submit the following report of its operations from the time of leaving the main column until the command was united in the vicinity of the Indian village.

The regiment left the camp at the mouth of Rosebud River, after passing in review before the Department Commander, under command of Brevet Major-General G. A. Custer, lieutenant-colonel, on the afternoon of the 22d of June, and marched up the Rosebud twelve miles, and encamped. 23d. Marched up the Rosebud, passing many old Indian camps, and following a very large lodge pole trail, but not fresh, making thirty-three miles. 24th. The march was continued up the Rosebud, the trail and signs freshening with every mile until we had made twenty-eight miles, and we then encamped and waited for information from the scouts. At 9.25. P. M., Custer called the officers together, and informed us that, beyond a doubt, the village was in the valley of the Little Big Horn, and that to reach it, it was necessary to cross the divide between Rosebud and Little Big Horn, and it would be impossible to do so, in the daytime, without discovering our march to the Indians ; that we would prepare to move at 11 P. M. This was done, the line of march turning from the Rosebud to the right, up one of its branches, which headed near the summit of the divide.

About 2 A. M. of the 25th, the scouts told him that he could not cross the divide before daylight. We then made coffee and rested for three hours, at the expiration of which time the march was resumed, the divide crossed, and about 8 A. M. the command was in the valley of one of the branches of the Little Big Horn. By this time Indians had been seen, and it was certain that we could not surprise them, and it was determined to move at once to the attack.

Previous to this no division of the regiment had been made since the order was issued, on the Yellowstone, annulling wing

37

and battalion organizations. General Custer informed me he would assign commands on the march. I was ordered by Lieutenant W. W. Cook, adjutant, to assume command of Companies M, A and G ; Captain Benteen, of Companies H, D and K ; Custer retaining C, E, F, I and L, under his immediate command, and Company B, Captain McDougall, in rear of the pack train. I assumed command of the companies assigned to me, and without any definite orders moved forward with the rest of the column, and well to its left. I saw Benteen moving further to the left, and, as they passed, he told me he had orders to move well to the left, and sweep everything before him ; I did not see him again until about 2.30 P. M. The command moved down the creek towards the Little Big Horn valley. Custer, with five companies on the right bank ; myself and three companies on the left bank ; and Benteen farther to the left, and out of sight. . . .

Here we must pause awhile. Major Reno, Brevet-colonel Benteen and President Grant have made the pause necessary, by official accusations of Custer's action up to this point. Major Reno, near the close of his report, accuses Custer in these words:

I think (after the great number of Indians there were in the village) that the following reasons obtained for the misfortune ; his rapid marching for two days and one night before the fight, attacking in the daytime at 12 M., and when they were on the *qui vive*, instead of early in the morning, and lastly, his unfortunate division of the regiment into three commands.

General Terry, in a subsequent despatch to Sheridan, *quoting Benteen*, accuses Custer of the same fault, and states that Custer had told him that his marches " would be at the rate of thirty miles a day."

Custer, according to Reno's report, left Terry at noon 22d June, and struck Sitting Bull on the morning of June 25th, having made one night march only. On the face of Reno's report, the night march was only from 11 P. M. to 2 A. M., or three hours. Then came a rest of three hours, with feed for man and horse, the march resumed at 5 A. M. the Indians seen at 8 A. M., finally struck at 12.30. This gives a period of three whole days in all, at 30 miles a day, making 90 miles. The actual distance, measured on the best accessible map, makes the length of Custer's trail just 90 miles; and we can afford to allow 10 more for windings. According to Reno's report, the distance marched to the evening of the 24th June was 73 miles (12+33+28) leaving only 27 miles for the distance covered during the following night and day march. In Terry's despatch of self-justification, above referred to, he says, "I learned from *Captain Benteen*, that on the 22d the cavalry marched 12 miles; on the 23d, 25 miles; from 5 A. M. till 8 P. M. of the 24th, 45 miles, and then after night 10 miles further, resting but without unsaddling, 23 miles to the battle-field." This account adds just 15 miles to the actual distance. It also subtracts 8 miles from Reno's report of the march of the 23d June, and puts on 17 miles to Reno's account of the march of the 24th. Where Reno says 33, Terry, *quoting Benteen*, says 25; where Reno says 28, Terry, *quoting Benteen*, says 45.

President Grant, who hated Custer, as he had reason to, having injured him, distorts the facts still more in his published interview with a Herald correspondent, months after. We give this part of the interview entire, question and answer.

CORRESPONDENT—Was not Custer's massacre a disgraceful defeat of our troops?

The PRESIDENT—(with an expression of manifest and keenly felt regret)—I regard Custer's massacre as a sacrifice of troops, brought on by Custer himself, that was wholly unnecessary—wholly unnecessary.

CORRESPONDENT—How so, Mr. President?

The PRESIDENT—He was not to have made the attack before effecting a junction with Terry and Gibbon. He was notified to meet them on the 26th, but instead of marching slowly, as his orders required, in order to effect the junction on the 26th, he enters upon a forced march of *eighty-three miles in twenty-four hours*, and thus had to meet the Indians alone on the 25th.

Thus Reno, who, whatever his faults, is apparently an honorable man, who labors to tell the truth, makes the whole march of the 24th and 25th June only 55 miles (28 + 27) agreeing with the map; Terry, *quoting Benteen*, makes it 78 miles (45 + 10 + 23); Grant, the President, in his eagerness to bury a dead man out of sight, makes it 83 miles.

On the face of Reno's report, and compared with the actual distance, judging Custer as we have a right to, solely on his "zeal, energy and ability," not on supposed orders, which Terry's written instructions prove he never received, it appears that so far he had done everything that a cool and wary Indian fighter could have done. At all events the Indians *had not escaped*. Let us see now what followed, still quoting Reno. His report proceeds thus:

As we approached a deserted village, in which was standing one *tepee*, about 11 A. M., Custer motioned me to cross to him, which I did, and moved nearer to his column, until about 12.30 A. M., when Lieutenant Cook, adjutant, came to me and said the village was only two miles ahead and running away. To "move forward at as rapid gait as I thought prudent and to charge afterwards, and the whole outfit would support me;" I think those were his exact words. I at once took a fast trot, and moved down about two miles, when I came to a ford of the river. I crossed immediately, and halted about ten minutes or less, to gather the battalion, sending word to Custer that I had everything in front of me, and that they were strong.

I deployed, and with the Ree scouts on my left, charged down the valley, driving the Indians with great ease for about 2½ miles. I however, soon saw that I was being drawn into some trap, as they certainly would fight harder, and especially as we were nearing their village, which was still standing; besides, I could not see Custer,* or any other support, and at the same time the very earth seemed to grow Indians, and they were running towards me in swarms, and from all directions. I saw I must defend myself, and give up the attack mounted. This I did, taking possession of a point of woods, and which furnished, near its edge, a shelter

---

* This fact, of not seeing Custer, evidently frightened Reno excessively, and his story shows how unfit he was to take part in any operation requiring combined efforts. Had he gone on, *as he was ordered,* he would have found Custer supporting him, in the most effective manner possible, by attacking the enemy in rear.

for the horses; dismounted, and fought them on foot, making headway through the wood. I soon found myself in the near vicinity of the village, saw that I was fighting odds of at least five to one, and that my only hope was to get out of the wood, where I would soon have been surrounded, and gain some high ground. I accomplished this by mounting and charging the Indians between me and the bluffs, on the opposite side of the river. In this charge, First Lieutenant Donald McIntosh, Second Lieutenant Ben H. Hodgson, Seventh Cavalry, and A. A. Surg. J. M. De Wolf, were killed. I succeeded in reaching the top of the bluff, with a loss of three officers and twenty-nine enlisted men killed, and seven men wounded. Almost at the same time I reached the top, mounted men were seen to be coming towards us, and it proved to be Colonel Benteen's battalion, companies H. D. and K; we joined forces, and in a short time the pack train came up. As senior, my command was then companies A, B, D, G, H, K and M, about 380 men, and the following officers: Captains Benteen, Weir, French and McDougall; First Lieutenants Godfrey, Mathey, and Gibson; Second Lieutenants Edgerly, Wallace, Varnum, and Hare; A. A. Surg. Porter. First Lieutenant De Rudio was in the dismounted fight in the woods, but having some trouble with his horse, did not join the command in the charge out, and hiding himself in the woods, joined the command after nightfall of the 26th.

Still hearing nothing of Custer, and with this reinforcement, I moved down the river in the direction of the village, keeping on the bluffs. We had heard firing in that direction, and knew it could only be Custer. I moved to the summit of the highest bluff, but seeing and hearing nothing, sent Captain Weir with his company to open communication with the other command. He soon sent back word, by Lieutenant Hare, that he could go no farther, and that the Indians were getting around him; at this time he was keeping up a heavy fire from his skirmish line. I at once turned everything back to the first position I had taken on the bluff, and which seemed to me the best. I dismounted the men, had the horses and mules of the pack train driven together in a depression, put the men on the crests of the hills making the depression, and had hardly done so, when I was furiously attacked; this was about 6 P. M.; we held our ground with the loss of eighteen enlisted men killed and forty-six wounded until the attack ceased, about 9 P. M.

A perusal of the first part of this account will show that whatever the length of the previous marches, the horses in Reno's column were not so fagged out but what they could take " a fast trot " for two miles to the ford, and then drive the Indians two and a half miles further. This makes nearly five miles at a fast pace in column or in ranks, with packed saddles, and exhausted horses could not have done that.

The next point to be considered is that of dividing the regiment into three commands. Here Custer is again blamed by Reno at the close of his report, as well as in a letter which the author lately received from him, totally unsolicited, and in which he tries to justify his conduct. In the report he calls it " *his unfortunate division of the regiment into three commands* ; " in the letter he says " The division of the regiment into three separate and *independent* commands he was responsible for, and must always be held so."

It will be here observed by those who have read this history through, that Custer's invariable method of attack on an enemy was the same which he adopted on the Big Horn, an attack on front and flank at all events, both flanks and front if possible, from all sides at once if he had time to execute it. In every battle in the civil war when he was in an independent position, he always worked his command by fractions, so as to attack an enemy on several points at once, and always succeeded, because he was always heartily seconded by men who adored him. He counted much on the moral effect to be produced on an enemy by combined attacks and a cross-fire, and always found his calculations correct. In fact only one thing *could* vitiate them. This was, cowardice or disobedience in the leader of any of the fractions which were to work simultaneously ; and this misfortune Custer had never hitherto suffered. His subordinates were used to be put into tight places, where everything at first seemed hopeless, trusting implicitly to their leader's combinations to get them out.

Next, were these commands *independent ?* We can hardly

see that, any more than regimental commanders are independent in a brigade. No general can do anything if his colonels will not support him, no colonel can fight a cavalry regiment under Upton's tactics if his battalion commanders slight, disobey, or even misunderstand his orders. Custer was a peculiar man. He fought in a peculiar way, and needed to have men under him used to his rapid energetic style, and *who understood him*. Did Reno understand him, and was he used to him? The official record says not. He had never served under Custer in the field, nor seen an Indian fight since the civil war.

Let us see whether he supported Custer. He says he "charged down the valley, driving the Indians with great ease for about 2½ miles." Then he suddenly stops. Why? He says he "saw he was being drawn into some trap." An officer present with the expedition, who examined the ground, but whose name we prefer to withhold for the present, writes as follows:

He [Reno] marched until he came to the village, dismounted, and occupied a timber bottom, which completely sheltered him and his horses. Girard (the interpreter) says, corroborated by Herndon, a scout, not many Indians in sight at this time, *and firing at* 500 *and* 600 yards. So long was the range that Charley Reynolds, another scout, said, "*No use firing at this range; we will have a better chance by and by.*" An officer present says that Reno mounted and dismounted, and then mounted again in hot haste, and made what figures in his report as a "charge." He is the only person I have heard call it by that name. The surgeon present says there was only one man wounded before Reno abandoned the timber, and his loss begun when he was making the charge, *men and horses shot from behind*. Think of the charge they must have made, across the Little Horn, and were checked in their flight by Benteen running into them. I say running into them, because it was mere accident. But where was Custer? He moved down to the lower end of the village from three to four miles. How long did Reno engage the Sioux village? Not over thirty minutes. What is the conclusion? That Reno was in and out of the fight before Custer was engaged. If further proof is wanting, it is found in the fact that Reno says in his report he heard Custer's firing from the top of the hill to which he had retreated.

Besides the letter from which this extract is taken, the author has received a letter from another officer present with Major Reno, in response to one asking several detailed and specific questions as to the fight in the bottom, the subsequent halt on the hill, and the possibility of coöperation with Custer on the part of Reno and Benteen. This letter is especially valuable, because written with Major Reno's sanction and knowledge, and representing his side of the question as fully as could be desired. In the expression of opinion on probabilities this officer coincides with Reno, but his *facts* corroborate those stated by the other officer, whose opinions are exactly opposite. The facts furnished by Major Reno's friend are as follows :

" At the time Reno ceased his forward movement, no man had been killed or wounded, but the cloud of dust denoted an immense number of Indians a short way off, and several times that number between us and that cloud, which was over the village, *advancing in their peculiar manner and passing to our left and rear*. . . The command was *dismounted*, the horses placed in a wood, and the men deployed on foot across the plain. The number of Indians continued to increase and to surround us. Colonel Reno ordered us to *prepare to mount*, which of course took every one to the wood. We were *mounted as though to charge, and in an instant afterward dismounted*, and I supposed we were to fight it out there, when a fire opened from the rear through the brush . . . *We were ordered to mount*. I was by the side of Colonel Reno, going out of the wood, and asked if we were to *charge through*. He said *yes*, and the command moved, Colonel Reno leading. I was here separated from the command for a time, and on turning towards it, saw it moving towards the ford that led to the hill. The *column was fighting at close range* from all sides. I rejoined with difficulty, and followed close along the rear to the ford, and here the confusion began. Previously the men had kept *in column*, using their pistols. When the ford was reached, it was each man for himself. In passing up the hill, *beyond the river*, horses and men were joined together, and some of the hindmost suffered necessarily.

So far, as to the facts of the fight in the bottom, Reno's friend even exceeds the testimony of Reno's harshest critics as to his incapacity and utter demoralization during the attack of the Indians. We have italicized the places of most importance, as they tell the real story. "Advancing in their peculiar manner," —what does this mean in plain English? That the Indians were all at full speed, crouching over the necks of their fleet little ponies, flogging away with their short whips, and all the time yelling out their "*Hi!—yip—yip—yip—yip—hi yah!!!*" firing random bullets in the air. These sights and sounds seem to have deprived Reno of all presence of mind. This he shows clearly by his repeated changes of policy, mounting and dismounting four times in as many minutes, and finally charging out *in column*, firing pistols, said column speedily becoming a huddled mass of frightened fugitives.

As to the halt on the hill, this officer differs materially with Reno and Benteen, in point of time. He admits hearing a few shots down the stream, but no heavy firing, and states that it was an hour before Benteen arrived, and half an hour more before the packs came up, whereas Benteen and Reno both agree that they came together, almost immediately after Reno's action. In this matter it is pretty clear that the recollection of Major Reno's friend must deceive him, as he places Weir's advance almost immediately after the junction, and it is clear from Reno's report that Weir must have started out after five o'clock, for it was only fifteen minutes from his return to the beginning of the siege on the hill (at 6 P. M.) on Reno's showing. This officer, like Benteen, thinks that Custer had been destroyed by the time Benteen arrived on the hill, whereas Kill Eagle's evidence, subsequently mentioned, shows that this was not the case till sunset. He makes one curious assertion in giving his estimate of the Indian warriors, which he places at 3,500. It is this: *in a village, standing, squaws, old men, and boys, are as effective as the ordinary recruit.*" Endorsing such opinions, is it any wonder Reno's battalion was beaten, when they are ready to succumb to squaws, old men, and boys?

Now let us return to Reno's report, and try it by the test

of time and place. He says that Adjutant Cook told him to attack at 12.30, that he advanced altogether 4½ miles, crossed a river, halted ten minutes, had his fight, and came back, meeting Benteen. When did he meet Benteen? Look back to the report. He there says of Benteen, "I did not see him again till about 2.30 P. M." That gives two hours for his advance of 4½ miles, fording the river twice, driving the enemy 2½ miles and the dismounted fight. Our period of thirty minutes for the fight in the bottom seems to tally with Reno's report. It is clear that it was a short fight, and Reno confesses his over caution in the words "*I saw that I was being drawn into some trap.*"

The next question is, how long did Reno remain on the hill with his seven companies, in safety and unassailed. Here again his report helps us. He met Benteen at 2.30 P. M. : he was "*furiously attacked ; this was about* 6 P. M." The time is thus complete. Three hours and a half of waiting on the hill, listening to Custer's volleys, and not a step taken to renew the attack. Another piece of evidence is found in the narrative of Herndon, the scout, who was with Reno. When the major "charged" out, Herndon's horse fell and threw him, then ran away, leaving him in the bush, where he was joined by thirteen soldiers, three of them wounded and left behind. His story was published in all the papers, but I quote from the *Army and Navy Journal* of July 15, 1876, as a semi-official paper, and the one chosen by Reno for publication of his report. Statements in that paper on army subjects are apt to be more reliable than elsewhere, as, being the only professional paper in the country, all army officers watch its columns and correct every mistake. Herndon says of the "charge" which he saw from the timber, " Little resistance was offered, and it was a complete rout to the ford. I did not see the men at the ford, and do not know what took place, further than a good many were killed when the command left the timber." Herndon and his thirteen comrades remained in the timber unmolested for nearly *three hours*, after Reno's flight, hearing firing down the river about two miles, while nearly all the Indians in their front left, and went down the valley. Then the little party got out and went to Reno, meeting only a roving group of five Indians, whom they beat off, then crossed the river to Reno. In fifteen minutes after, the siege on the hill commenced.*

What should Reno have done? His only real safety was to hug the timber and defend himself, surrounded or not. Custer had done so on the Yellowstone in 1873, ninety against three hundred; Robbins had done even better in defending his wagons in 1867, forty against six hundred. In both these cases there was no apparent hope of succor coming, and yet Robbins and Custer found the reward of their tenacity, help coming when it was least expected, and victory following. On Reno's own statement, he had one hundred and forty-five men, who in a circle, lining the edge of the wood, could have held it for hours. The Indians were fighting mounted, and could never have stormed the wood, and help was coming. Custer had promised to come. If Reno could get no further he could at least defend himself, die in his tracks if need be, like a soldier. Instead of this, he tried to escape by running away from an enemy who had the advantage in speed, and who could ride alongside of the demoralized cavalry, pouring in perfect streams of bullets from their Winchester rifles. By his inexperience in Indian warfare, Major Reno thus gave himself up, helpless, to the favorite style of fighting of his enemies, wherein their superior horsemanship and superior arms had a full chance to assert themselves. Looking for personal security, he took the course least adapted to secure it.

---

* "Lieutenant de Rudio, mentioned in Reno's report, was also left behind, and remained in the wood, together with Mr. Girard, (the interpreter) Private O'Neill, and a half breed scout. All these four got off, some that night, some next night. De Rudio's account shows a general careless haphazard state of things among the Indians, entirely opposed to any deliberate trap or generalship.

The major indeed seems, from his hesitating movements in the fight, mounting and dismounting, to have been quite overwhelmed from the first by the novelty of his position, cowed by the fierce yells and rapid charge of the Indians, and finally to have completely lost his head. For all this we wish it distinctly understood that we do not deem Reno so blamable, as for subsequent events. It was his first Indian fight, and many a man has done badly in his first fight, who has afterwards succeeded. We should not have occasion to dissect his conduct in the affair, were it not for that unjust sentence in his official report in which he throws the blame of a disaster, brought on by his own incapacity, on the shoulders of his dead chief. The facts shown by himself in the same report, illustrated by eye-witnesses, pass a different verdict on his actions.

But now, where was Benteen all the time of this fight? His own statement, published in the New York *Herald,* gives his movements. It seems that when he was sent out on the left bank of the stream with orders to sweep everything, he found no Indians, and that he recrossed the stream, and rejoined the main trail. He says, "the whole time occupied in this march was about an hour and a half," to the main trail, about three miles from the point where Reno came back over the ford. From Major Reno's statement in the same paper, in reply to a letter of General Rosser, we learn that the division into battalions which sent Benteen off to the left was made at *half past ten* A. M. *An hour and a half* brings us to *noon* and Benteen within three miles of the battle field. At 12.30 Reno was ordered by Cook, the adjutant, to attack, and trotted off. At this time Benteen says :

About three miles from the point where Reno crossed the ford I met a sergeant bringing orders to the commanding officer of the rear guard, Captain McDougall, Company B, to hurry up the pack trains. A mile further I was met by my trumpeter, bringing a written order from Lieutenant Cook, the adjutant of the regiment, to this effect : " Benteen, come on ; big village ; be quick ;

bring packs." And a postscript saying, "Bring packs." A mile or a mile and a half further on, I first came in sight of the valley and Little Big Horn. About twelve or fifteen dismounted men were fighting on the plain with Indians, charging and recharging them. This body [the Indians] numbered about 900 at this time. Colonel Reno's mounted party were retiring across the river to the bluffs. I did not recognize till later what part of the command this was, but was clear that they had been beaten. I then marched my command in line to their succor. On reaching the bluff I reported to Colonel Reno, and first learned that the command had been separated, and that Custer was not in that part of the field, and no one of Reno's command was able to inform me of the whereabouts of General Custer.

Reno's report states that he met Benteen at 2.30 P. M. It seems thus, *that it took Benteen two hours and a half to cover a distance of three miles.* What was he doing all this time? One incident, furnished us by an officer who was present, shows.

With Custer on this campaign was his brother, Boston Custer, who was the civilian forage master of the column. It seems that Boston Custer came to the rear during this period, went to the pack train, in rear of Benteen, got a fresh horse, and passed Benteen on his way back, speaking to some of the officers. Benteen was then watering his horses. Where did he water? He could only have done it at one place, *where he crossed the river*, that is, three miles above the ford where he met Reno. Boston Custer had time to get back to the general and be killed in the fight. Benteen kept on at a slow pace. Did he obey the order "*Benteen, come on; big village; be quick; bring packs?*" What did this order direct from Custer mean? what could it mean, but that Custer wanted every man in his fight? He had sent in Reno, and he needed Benteen's battalion and the company guarding the packs with himself. That this was his intention is proved by Reno, in his letter to Rosser, by these words:

Trumpeter Martin, of Company H, and who the last time of any living person heard and saw General Custer, and who brought the last order his Adjutant, Colonel Cook, ever penciled, says *he left the general at the summit of the highest bluff on that side, and which overlooked the village and my first battle-field, and as he turned, General Custer raised his hat and gave a yell, saying they were asleep in their tepees and surprised, and to charge.* Cook's order, [Custer's order, through his adjutant] sent to Benteen, and which I afterwards saw and read, said, " Big village ; big thing ; * bring up the packs."

Thus Benteen and Reno both unite in ascribing the same plan to Custer, that of charging with all his force from two points. Both admit by their testimony that they disobeyed orders. Reno was ordered to " charge : " he obeyed by opening a hesitating skirmish and then running away. Benteen was ordered to " come on ; be quick." He obeyed by advancing three miles in two hours, and joining Reno in a three hours' halt. The order to " come on " was from Custer, not Reno. Benteen made, on his own statement, no effort to obey it. He might have known where Custer was. Reno lets that much out. Benteen *could have questioned Trumpeter Martin, who brought the order.* No, he stopped, and let his chief perish.

Looking at all the testimony impartially from this distance of time, the conduct of Benteen is far worse than that of Reno. The major did his best in his fight, and it was nothing but want of experience in command and in Indian warfare that caused his defeat. Benteen's case is different. He was an old Indian-fighter, a man of remarkable personal courage, as he proved in the subsequent battle, had often fought under Custer, and knew his business perfectly. That he should have, as his own testimony confesses, deliberately disobeyed the *peremptory order of Custer* to " come on," argues either a desire to sacrifice Custer, or an ignorance of which his past career renders him incapable.

* There is a great difference between the words " big thing " and " be quick," and I am inclined to believe that the expression " big thing " is an afterthought of Major Reno's, as tending to confirm the notion which he inculcates all through his report and evidence, that Custer ran into a trap and was full of rash eagerness. Benteen got the order and he says it was " be quick," and that " bring packs " was repeated.

Custer told him to " come on " and he " reported to Colonel Ren ." Well then, it may be said, what did Benteen, afterwards? The rest of his testimony shows what he did. He says:

While the command was awaiting the arrival of the pack mules, a company was sent forward in the direction supposed to have been taken by Custer. After proceeding about a mile, they were attacked and driven back. During this time I heard no heavy firing, and there was nothing to indicate that a heavy fight was going on, and I believe that at this time Custer's immediate command had been annihilated.

The rest of the story you must get from Colonel Reno, as he took command and knows more than any one else.

It is curious in Benteen's evidence how his only estimate of time comes in *before* the battle. Afterwards, there is not a word about time. Who would think that this brief paragraph covered from 2. 30 to 6 P. M. If the one company was sent forward, why was it not supported by the whole outfit? Why was Custer left alone with his battalion, while the other battalions were out of danger?

The answer to the questions is given by Reno and Benteen, in their evidence, almost unassisted by others. The reasons were, *Reno's incapacity and Benteen's disobedience.*

We have now examined Reno and Benteen : it is time to go to Custer. Where was Custer during all this time, from 12.30 to 6 P. M.? Let Reno, Terry, and *the trail* answer; assisted by Trumpeter Martin, the last white man who saw Custer alive; Curly, the Upsaroka scout, the last living being of his column; and Kill Eagle, an Indian chief who was in Sitting Bull's camp, who has since come into Standing Rock agency to surrender, and has given evidence.

Reno, in his letter says that Custer, after leaving him, " moved rapidly down the river to the ford, at which he attempted to cross." Curly, the Crow scout, calls it about four miles, and such the trail shows it, on account of the winding of the ravines. Reno's advance was about 2½ miles in a diagonal line. Consequently his skirmish line at the edge of the woods was not over two miles from the ford which Custer tried to cross. The Indian village was 3½ miles long, and Custer struck it about the middle. When did he strike it? We get this from the examination of Kill Eagle, published in the New York *Herald* of October 6th, '76. The deposition was taken by Captain Johnston, First Infantry, acting Indian agent. We extract all that concerns the fight.

The troops struck our trail on the tributary, followed it down, swam their horses over the Greasy Grass Creek and struck the camp at the upper end, where there was a clump of timber. On the southwest end of the camp they dismounted and tied their horses in the timber and opened the fight. When the firing commenced the Indians rushed to the scene of action. I and my men were lower down, about the middle of the camp. The Indians drove the soldiers back out of the timber, and they crossed the Greasy Grass Creek below the mouth of the tributary, taking their position on the high hills, bare without any grass. There they were reinforced by the soldiers who had not crossed the creek (Colonel Benteen and Captain McDougall). Before retreating across the creek the soldiers (Colonel Reno) got into the camp and set fire to some of the lodges. On retreating across the creek to take position on the hill, they left their dead behind them. Another party appeared on top of a long hill moving toward the south.

After quitting the party on the knolls, word came that soldiers were on the left across the creek, and there was great excitement in the camp, the Indian warriors rushing to the left to meet the troops. The Indians crossed the creek and then the firing commenced. It was very fast at times, then slower until it died away. (He describes the firing as follows :—He claps the palms of his hands together very fast for several minutes, stopping suddenly, which denotes the sound of the firing when they (Custer) first began. After a few seconds elapses he repeats the same as above and continues, but all the time lessens the quickness of the patting and sound until it gradually dies out.) The United States troops were all killed on the east side, none crossed the stream.

I got the following information from Sitting Bull himself :—

After crossing the creek with his warriors, he met the troops (Custer) about 600 yards east of the river. He drove the soldiers back up the hill. He then made a circuit to the right around the hill and drove off and captured most of the horses. The troops made a stand at the lower end of the hill, and there they were all killed. In going around the hill the Cheyenne Indians killed a warrior, thinking he was a scout who left this agency ; but he was not, he was a hostile.

Q. How long did the fight last on the right?

A. It was about noon when they [Reno] struck the camp, and it *only lasted a few minutes.* The fight at the lower end (*under Custer*) *was not finished till near sunset.*

Q. Did all the warriors leave the right and go to the left ?

A. They did ; the *whole thing left.*

Q. When Reno was driven across the creek where was Sitting Bull ?

A. I don't know.

Q. What were the families doing when the fighting was going on on the hill ?

A. The women fled to the lower end of the camp and left everything.

Q. What did they do when they heard the firing on the left by Custer ?

A. The upper end of the camp was at this time all deserted, and at the lower end of the camp they took down and packed the lodges ready for flight.

Q. I have heard that after the Custer fight, the Indians went back to the other end and attacked there again. How is it ?

A. That is correct ; the Indian soldiers went back and attacked the troops (Reno) on the hill again.

Q. Did you hear the firing ?

A. Yes, I heard the firing while moving away.

It must be explained that Kill Eagle took the opportunity of the confusion, to steal away from Sitting Bull's camp. His evidence shows that there was no design or trap on the part of the Indians, that they were really surprised, that Custer's attack was a second surprise, and that they were in the wildest confusion : this too, when Reno's hesitating assault had convinced them that there was nothing to be feared from him.

38

Now for Custer's fight. The trail shows that he came down to the ford, and was there driven back, leaving dead men and horses. The rest of the description is thus given by an officer of the general staff who examined the ground, and refers to the map which we annex.

From this point he was driven back to make successive stands on the higher ground. His line of retreat stretches from the river to the spot indicated on the map as that where he fell. On the line of retreat, Calhoun's company seems to have been thrown across it to check the Indians. At a distance of about three-quarters of a mile from the river, the whole of Calhoun's company lay dead, in an irregular line, Calhoun and Crittenden in place in the rear. About a mile beyond this, on the ridge parallel to the stream, still following the line of retreat indicated on the map, Keogh's company was slaughtered in position, his right resting on the hill where Custer fell, and which seems to have been held by Yates' company. On the most prominent point of this ridge, Custer made his last desperate stand. Here, with Captain Yates, Colonel Cook, Captain Custer, Lieutenant Riley, and others, and thirty-two men of Yates' command, he went down, fighting heroically to the last, against the tremendous odds which assailed them on all sides. It is believed by some that, finding the situation a desperate one, they killed their horses for a barricade. From the point where Custer fell, the line of retreat again doubles back toward the river through a ravine, and along this line in the ravine, twenty-three bodies of Smith's company were found. Where this line terminates near the river, are found the dead men and horses of Captain Custer's company commingled with Smith's, and the situation of the dead indicates that some desperate attempt was made to make a stand near the river, or to gain the woods.

There we have the short and simple history of the fight which was going on within two miles of Benteen and Reno, for three long weary hours. It is dry and simple in its words, but what a wealth of heroism that simple story reveals. This little band was made of Custer's men, under Custer's best officers, Custer's little knot of chosen friends. All we can do is to fill out its details. *On this line, Calhoun's company was thrown across to*

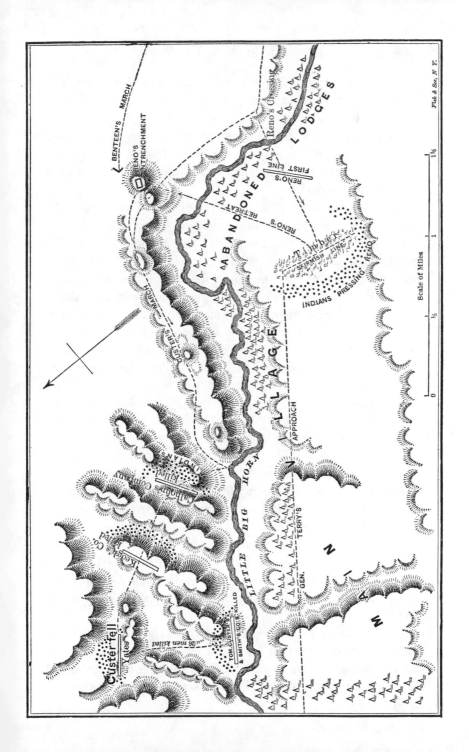

Fisk & Son, N.Y.

Scale of Miles

BENTEN'S MARCH

RENO'S INTRENCHMENT

Reno's Crossing

ABANDONED LODGES

RENO'S FIRST LINE

RENO'S RETREAT

SKIRMISH LINE

RENO'S BATTLE

INDIANS PRESSING RENO

CUSTER'S MARCH

VILLAGE

LITTLE BIG HORN

INDIANS

Calhoun's Company killed

Keogh's Co. killed

TOM CUSTER'S & SMITH'S MEN KILLED

28 men killed

Custer fell
Yates

APPROACH

GEN. TERRY'S

N

A

M

check the Indians. The men lay dead in an irregular line, Calhoun and Crittenden in place in rear. This is the order of the tactics, the officers watching and moving along their line, within a few feet. There they fell, every man in his place. They were ordered to stay and be killed, to save the day, and they obeyed orders. Who then was Calhoun, that he was the first ordered to die?

Lieutenant James Calhoun of the Seventh Cavalry was the husband of Custer's only sister; he was Custer's dearest of all friends on earth; he was the bravest and gentlest of men, with the face and form of an Apollo, bright fair hair and dark eyes, a man whom a lady who knew him well describes as the "handsomest man I ever saw." He was a gentleman's son, with all the education of a gentleman, and the most refined literary taste, who yet had not hesitated to enlist as a private soldier in the regular army, and had actually worked his way up, refined and sensitive as he was, in the midst of all the discomforts, hardships and degradations which surrounded the life of a private soldier at the close of the war, to a well-earned commission. He married Maggie E. Custer in Monroe, Michigan, March 7th, 1872, and acted as Custer's post-adjutant during the time the regiment was divided. He was remarkably quiet and reserved in demeanor, but hid beneath his calm dignity of outward seeming the most lofty aspirations. Too young to have gained distinction in the civil war, he hoped yet to gain it by unwavering fidelity to his duty. Duty was his one watchword, and by it he hoped to attain success. Such was the bright brave youth whom Custer told to stay behind and be killed, that so the day might be saved. Did Calhoun murmur—did he question the order? Why did Custer leave him there to die?

Not a murmur came from the one, and the other showed by this his first sacrifice that he placed the country above all his earthly loves. "The country needs; I give her a man who will do his duty to the death: I give them my first brother. I leave my best loved sister a widow, that so the day may be saved. Farewell."

Well did Calhoun redeem that trust. Every man in his place, no faltering, no going back, Calhoun's company kept on firing till the last cartridge was gone, and one by one dropped dead in his tracks under the fire of the swarms of Indians that kept dashing to and fro before them, firing volley after volley. Down they went, one after another, cheered up by this grand figure of DUTY, young Calhoun encouraging them to the last. With him young Crittenden of the Twelfth Infantry, a mere boy, only appointed the previous fall, and temporarily with the cavalry in his first and last battle, as cool as his chief, cheered and steadied by the calm princely dignity of courage that inspired that glorious stand. So they stood till the last man was down, and Crittenden was killed, and then came the friendly bullet that sent the soul of James Calhoun to an eternity of glory. Let no man say such a life was thrown away. The spectacle of so much courage must have nerved the whole command to the heroic resistance it made. Calhoun's men would never have died where they did, *in line*, had Calhoun not been there to cheer them. They would have been found in scattered groups, fleeing or huddled together, not fallen in their ranks, every man in his place, to the very last. Calhoun, with his forty men, had done on an open field, what Reno, with a hundred and forty, could not do defending a wood. He had died like a hero, and America will remember him, while she remembers heroes.

Let us go on with the tale. *About a mile beyond, Keogh's company was slaughtered in position, his right resting on the hill where Custer fell.* Custer had chosen the best ground to be found, and was determined to retreat no farther. By this time he must have realized that Reno had been beaten, but he trusted at least to Benteen to come and help him. The Indians were all around him, but a vigorous attack by Benteen on their rear would beat them, could Custer only hold them long enough.

Keogh was an older soldier than any there. He had been

an officer in the Papal service in the days when Garibaldi made
war upon the Holy Father, and he had served on the staffs of
Buford and Stoneman during the war. The sight of Calhoun's
men, dying as they did, had nerved Keogh's men to the same
pitch of sublime heroism. Every man realized that it was his
last fight, and was resolved to die game. Down they went,
slaughtered in position, man after man dropping in his place,
the survivors contracting their line to close the gaps. We read
of such things in history, and call them exaggerations. The
silent witness of those dead bodies of heroes in that mountain
pass cannot lie. It tells plainer than words how they died, the
Indians all round them, first pressing them from the river, then
curling round Calhoun, now round Keogh, till the last stand on
the hill by Custer, with three companies.

How that fight went, Curly the Upsaroka scout, tells us, he
the only man who escaped alive, and who got away to the
steamer *Far West* lying at the mouth of the river. His testimony was taken by the officers of Terry's staff, through an
interpreter. It is plain and prosaic in its simplicity, but it tells
the tale.

He says he went down with two other Crows and went into action with Custer. The General, he says, kept down the river on
the north bank four miles, after Reno had crossed to the south
side above. He thought Reno would drive down the valley, so
that they could attack the village on two sides, he believing Reno
would take it at the upper end, while he (Custer) would go in at
the lower end. Custer had to go farther down the river and farther away from Reno than he wished on account of the steep bank
along the north side ; but at last he found a ford and dashed for
it. The Indians met him and poured in a heavy fire from across
the narrow river. Custer dismounted to fight on foot, but could
not get his skirmishers over the stream. Meantime hundreds of
Indians, on foot and on ponies, poured over the river, which was
only about three feet deep, and filled the ravine on each side of
Custer's men. Custer then fell back to some high ground behind
him and seized the ravines in his immediate vicinity. The Indians completely surrounded Custer and poured in a terrible fire

on all sides. They charged Custer on foot in vast numbers, but were again and again driven back. The fight began about 2 o'clock, and lasted, Curly says, almost until the sun went down over the hills. The men fought desperately, and, after the ammunition in their belts was exhausted, went to their saddlebags, got more and continued the fight. He also says the big chief, (Custer) lived until nearly all his men had been killed or wounded, and went about encouraging his soldiers to fight on. Curly says when he saw Custer was hopelessly surrounded, he watched his opportunity, got a Sioux blanket, put it on, and worked up a ravine, and when the Sioux charged he got among them, and they did not know him from one of their own men. There were some mounted Sioux, and seeing one fall, Curly ran to him, mounted his pony, and galloped down as if going towards the white men, but went up a ravine and got away.

When questioned closely by one of the officers,* he mentioned one little fact about his escape that is pregnant with light on Custer's fate. When he saw that the party with the General was to be overwhelmed, he went to the General and begged him to let him show him a way to escape. General Custer dropped his head on his breast in thought for a moment, in a way he had of doing. There was a lull in the fight after a charge, the encircling Indians gathering for a fresh attack. In that moment, Custer looked at Curly, waved him away and rode back to the little group of men, to die with them. How many thoughts must have crossed that noble soul in that brief moment. There was no hope of victory if he stayed, nothing but certain death. With the scout he was nearly certain to escape. His horse was a thoroughbred and his way sure. He might have balanced the value of a leader's life against those of his men, and sought his safety. Why did he go back to certain death?

Because he felt that such a death as that which that little band of heroes was about to die, was worth the lives of all the general officers in the world. Thanks to the story of the Crow

* This officer told the story personally to Mrs. Custer afterwards.

scout, we know that he had the chance to live alone, and that he deliberately accepted death with his men as the worthier. He weighed, in that brief moment of reflection, all the consequences to America of the lesson of life and the lesson of heroic death, and he chose death. The Indian hovered round the fight, still watching: in the confusion he was not noticed, or taken for a Sioux. He had washed off his Upsaroka paint, and let down his hair like a Sioux. Let us see what he saw.

Curly did not leave Custer until the battle was nearly over, and he describes it as desperate in the extreme. He is quite sure the Indians had more killed than Custer had white men with him.

There was the little group of men on the hill, the Indians hovering round them like hounds baying a lion, dashing up close and receding, the bullets flying like swarms of bees, the men in the little group dropping one by one. At last the charm of Custer's charmed life was broken.

He got a shot in the left side and sat down, with his pistol in his hand. Another shot struck Custer and he fell over. The last officer killed was a man who rode a white horse (believed to be Lieut. Cook, Adjutant of the Seventh, as Lieuts. Cook and Calhoun were the only officers who rode white horses, and Lieut. Calhoun was found dead on the skirmish line, near the ford, and probably fell early in the action).

At last they were all gone, every officer of the group. Custer fallen and Cook killed, the remaining men broke. Then the scout fled too.

He says as he rode off he saw, when nearly a mile from the battle-field, a dozen or more soldiers in a ravine, fighting with Sioux all around them. He thinks all were killed, as they were outnumbered five to one, and apparently dismounted. These were no doubt part of the thirty-five missing men reported in the official despatches of General Terry. Curly says he saw one cavalry soldier who had got away. He was well mounted, but shot through both hips, and Curly thinks he died of his wounds, starved to death in the bad lands, or more likely his trail was followed, and he killed by the Sioux.

Thirty-two men of Yates' company fell with their chief and the other officers on the hill, the rest of them, with Captain Custer's and Captain Smith's men, tried to cut their way to the river and all fell in the ravine, as marked on the map. Then, says Kill Eagle, the Indian wounded came streaming back into Sitting Bull's camp, saying: " *We have killed them all : put up your lodges where they are.*"

From the account of some Indians who went across the line into British America, to trade with the Manitoba Indians, we gain more particulars of the last fight than Curly could see. The scout was so utterly broken down with fear and agony of mind when he reached the steamer, that he could not for a long time give a connected account, but his exultant enemies have filled the gap with their boasts. From these it appears that when only a few of the officers were left alive, the Indians made a hand to hand charge, in which Custer fought like a tiger with his sabre when his last shot was gone, that he killed or wounded three Indians with the sabre, and that as he ran the last man through, *Rain-in-the-Face kept his oath and shot Custer.*

While this account disagrees with that of Curly, I am inclined to believe it, for several reasons. Curly was some way off, the confusion was great, and the two brothers Custer were dressed alike and resembled each other closely in figure. I am inclined to believe that it was Colonel Tom Custer whom Curly saw fall as he described it. On the other hand, several Indians who were in the fight have told the same story about the sabre, and have given Big Rain or Rain-in-the-Face, as the man who shot the General. We know Custer to have been a man of great strength and activity, one who had used the sabre freely in the civil war; and in his last struggle such a man would have been as able to kill three Indians, as was Shaw the famous English guardsman at Waterloo, who was seen to kill *nine* French cuirassiers with his sword before he was shot. A last reason that is convincing is this. It is well known that the Indians did not mutilate Custer's body, it being the only one in that group entirely spared.   The only reason for such a respect could have been a reverence for his valor.   It is also well known that the Indians regard the striking of a living enemy *with a hand weapon* as the highest proof of valor possible, placing a very different estimate on shooting an enemy.   All the reports of the Indians who reached the British Possessions were unanimous in saying that they dreaded the sabre more than any thing, and this is easily understood when their superstition as to hand weapons is considered.   It seems certain that they would never have reverenced Custer's body as they did, had he not struck down their best men in that grim hand-to-hand fight, wherein, among all the brave and strong, he was the bravest and best swordsman of all, the other officers having had but little teaching in the use of the sabre.   Be that as it may, it is known that he must have died under circumstances of peculiar heroism to win such respect, and that he was only killed by the bravest Indian of the whole northwest, a man whose unflinching fortitude had enabled him to hang in the air *for four hours* in the Sun Dance.

So fell Custer, the brave cavalier, the Christian soldier, surrounded by foes, but dying in harness amid the men he loved. Who fell with him?

There by his side lay his brother Tom, brave Colonel Custer, a double of the General, who had enlisted as a private soldier at sixteen, was an officer at nineteen, who wore what no other officer in the army could boast of, two medals, each for a flag taken from an enemy in battle.   Brave and gentle, courteous and tender, a model officer of cavalry, God be with gallant Tom Custer till the last day.   He died like all the Custers, with his face to the sky and his feet to the foe.

Not far off, close together, lay two more of the same family, poor young Boston Custer and little Autie Reed, Custer's nephew, son of that good gentle Christian woman, who had saved Custer himself from a reckless career, whose prayers had

AUTIE REED.

BOSTON CUSTER.

CAPT. CALHOUN.

COL. TOM CUSTER.

helped to make him the Christian knight he became. Brave boys, nearly boys both, no sworn soldier of the state could die more nobly than they, who would not abandon a brother and kinsman. They could do little for him, but they could die with him. Autie was fresh from school a few weeks before, and wild to see the Plains with " Uncle Autie." To take him along it was necessary to give him some official employment, and Custer, knowing that the rough hard life would make a man of the boy, had him and another schoolmate appointed herders, to help drive the great herd of cattle with the column. Rough as the lot was, the lad never complained. He was seeing wild life, which was all he wanted, and had obtained leave to go on this scout with the General. Boston Custer's official position was that of forage master to the Seventh Cavalry, which he had held some time. He had been for years of a consumptive tendency, and his only chance for life was the open air existence of the plains. How far better for him the wild heroic death he died, under the blue sky, fighting like a true Custer, to the slow lingering failing end of a consumptive, which was his certain portion had he lived.

So closed the lives of the three Custers and their young nephew, fallen on that stricken field. It is time to turn to the comrades that fell with them.

There is something remarkable in the power which Custer apparently possessed of attracting to his side and intimate companionship the noblest and best of the men with whom the army brought him in contact; and the facts of his death bring out this power in a conspicuous manner. It is clear that when he made the division of the regiment into battalions in the morning, Custer knew that heavy work was coming, and intended to take the heaviest work into his own hands, as he always did. Into his own battalion he seems to have gathered all of his own familiar friends, including his three brothers, as knowing he could depend on them to the death. His confidence was well repaid, and we may say to-day, without fear of contradiction, that Custer and Custer's friends were the flower of the Seventh Cavalry. The battalion that fell with Custer held them nearly all.

There was the Adjutant, Brevet-Colonel Wm. W. Cook, the last officer left living, and whose final fall broke the hearts of his men and ended the battle. Cook was a model of manly beauty, in a very different style from that of Calhoun. Fully as tall (both were over six feet) and as powerfully framed, Cook was the image of a typical English Life Guardsman, with his highbred aristocratic features and long wavy black moustache and whiskers. Like Keogh, he was a foreigner, having been born in Canada, whence he entered the American service in the Twenty-fourth New York Cavalry, rising to its colonelcy. The reader has seen his name frequently during Custer's life on the plains. One proud sentence will be his best epitaph. In choosing an officer to command the sharp-shooters of the Seventh Cavalry in the Washita campaign the question was not, says Custer, " to choose a good one, but among many good to choose *the best.*" He chose Cook. Let it be written : " Custer said he was his best officer."

By his side was gallant Yates, captain and brevet colonel, tender and true, a man like Calhoun, of old family and gentle blood, who had not hesitated to enter the ranks as a soldier in the war, had enlisted as a boy of sixteen and worked his way up to a captaincy in the Regular Army. Yates was a true, sterling fellow, a soldier to the backbone, with the crack company of the Seventh. They used to call his troop the " band-box troop," so neat were they always, with an affectation of military dandyism. It was a tradition in that company that every man who died from it, " died with his boots on," the homely western phrase that tells such a story of unflinching courage. There fell brave old Yates, game to the last, with every man of the little " band-box troop " in his place, round their leader, who fell with a smile on his lips. He and they had done their duty, and died like men. God will help the widow and fatherless.

The last company commander of all fell near Yates, Lieutenant and Brevet Captain Algernon E. Smith, one more member of that little circle of refined quiet gentlemen who had shared Custer's friendship at Fort Lincoln. Captain Smith was one of the bravest and most modest of men. One little incident will illustrate his character better than a volume of description. During the civil war, while a captain of volunteers, Captain Smith was detailed on the staff of General Terry, at that desperate storming of Fort Fisher which gave Terry his star in the Regular Army. During the storming, a regiment faltered under the tremendous fire, having lost two color-bearers and all its field officers. Smith seized the colors, led on the regiment, sprang on the parapet, and was among the first in the works, where he fell severely wounded, his left shoulder smashed by a musket ball. For this he was brevetted major of volunteers. The wound healed, but in such a manner that he could never after lift his left arm above the shoulder. He was appointed to the Seventh Cavalry in 1867 and served in every campaign, in familiar intercourse with his brother officers; yet very few in the regiment even knew he had served in the civil war, and none of the ladies would have known that he had been wounded, but for an accidental remark by his wife in 1875, from which it came out that he could not put on his uniform without assistance, on account of his crippled left arm. Algernon Smith died as he had lived, a simple, modest soldier, in front of his men; while behind him lay the twenty-three bodies of the poor disheartened remnant that tried to cut their way out, when all was over and their beloved officer killed.

And now we come to the last of all, the youngest of that little band, Lieutenant William Van W. Reily. His portrait lies before me as these words are written, and it is hard to keep the cold composure of the impartial chronicler as I think of his peculiarly touching history. His father, a gallant officer of the U. S. navy, went down in his ship in the Indian Ocean, and not a soul came back to tell the tale, before Reily was born. That father sailed away from a bride of a few months never to return, and his boy left the mother who idolized him, to meet a similar fate, amid foes as pitiless as the ocean waves. Willie Reily fell next to Custer, and his fair young body was found lying at the feet of his commander. A good, noble-looking face he had, with a certain wistful musing expression, prophetic of his early fate. He had been ill for some time before the expedition started, and the surgeon wished to order him on some post duty, but he refused to stay, and was eager to share the fate of his regiment whatever it might be. He had his dearest wish; he died like his brave father, at his post doing his duty. Let no man say such an end was sad: it was heroic. We must all die some time, but not all like him. To him and all such, America says, " God bless our brave dead."

I have told the facts of Custer's last battle as closely as the means at hand will permit the truth to be ascertained. Beginning my task with a strong impression, produced by the official reports, that Custer had been rash and imprudent, and that the conduct of Reno and Benteen had been that of prudent and brave soldiers, a careful examination of all the accessible evidence has left me no other course than to tell the whole story, to vindicate the reputation of a noble man from unjust aspersions. I leave the facts to the world to judge whether I am not right in these conclusions :—

1. *Had Reno fought as Custer fought, and had Benteen obeyed Custer's orders, the battle of the Little Horn might have proved Custer's last and greatest Indian victory.*

It may be objected to this conclusion that the numbers of the Indians were too great to admit it : but a careful examination of the conflicting statements leads to the belief that these numbers have been exaggerated by Reno in his report, to cover

CUSTER'S LAST FIGHT.

his own conduct. He estimates the Indians at 3,500 "at the least," and the popular impression has since increased this estimate any where up to ten thousand. Herndon, the scout, a much cooler person, puts them at only 2,000 or 2,500 ; and Benteen thinks they were only 900. One means of approximate computation is unwittingly offered by Reno. Near the close of his report, he mentions the whole village as defiling away before his eyes, and says, " the length of the column was fully equal to that of a large division of the cavalry corps of the Army of the Potomac, as I have seen it on the march." The divisions of the Cavalry Corps, at their strongest, were about 4,000 men ; and they had *no women and children with them*. Making the very smallest allowance for led horses, pack horses, squaws and children, it is clear that at least one-half of the column must be taken away to leave the true number of warriors. This would give us 2,000, and if we allow 500 for the losses in fighting Reno and Custer, we come to Herndon's estimate. These numbers were four to one of Custer's, but he had fought such odds before, at the Washita, and come out triumphant. The obstinacy of his attack shows that he expected to conquer. He could have run like Reno had he wished, and Reno says in the report he thought Custer had done so. It is clear, in the light of Custer's previous character, that he held on to the last, expecting to be supported, as he had a right to expect. It was only when he clearly saw he had been betrayed, that he resolved to die game, as it was then too late to retreat.

2. *Had not President Grant, moved by private revenge, displaced Custer from command of the Fort Lincoln column, Custer would be alive to-day and the Indian war settled.*

The Dakota column would have been confided to the best Indian-fighter of the army ; Reno and Benteen would never have dreamed of disobeying their chief, had they not known he was out of favor at court ; Custer and Gibbon would have coöperated, as men both familiar with Indian warfare; and cross-purposes would have been avoided.

The action of a court of inquiry, which will be able to call forth the testimony of officers whose names the author withholds from the public at present, will settle whether these conclusions are correct or not. Many witnesses have been deterred from speaking by fear of those superiors whom their evidence will impeach; and these witnesses will be able to swear in public to what they have hitherto only dared to say and write in private. The nation demands such a court, to vindicate the name of a dead hero from the pitiless malignity, which first slew him and then pursued him beyond the grave.

NINTH BOOK.—SOLDIER AND MAN.

CHAPTER I.

CUSTER, THE SOLDIER.

THE popular idea of Custer as a soldier is that of a brave, reckless, dashing trooper, always ready to charge any odds, without knowing or caring what was the strength of his enemy, and trusting to luck to get out of his scrapes. In the public mind, he has always been associated, even by his admirers, with Murat and Prince Rupert, as a type of mere impetuosity.

A great deal of this impression among civilians has been the effect, partly of the frequency of his dashing personal exploits, but very largely also to a combination of the sneers of professional soldiers envious of his fame, and of the anxiety of the war correspondents to write home a " picturesque " letter. During the civil war, the so-called war correspondents seldom knew much of military life, and had rarely been soldiers before that war. As a consequence, they wrote home a great many ridiculous stories about Custer, the product of camp gossip. He was accused of putting his hair up in papers, of wearing stays, using curling tongs, etc., and the ingenious correspondent of one New York paper set the seal on the whole by a stilted account of the runaway of Don Juan and Custer at the last parade. He thus became, to a large part of the public, a perfectly ideal personage, as unlike the real Custer as Tom Moore's poetry was unlike the real quiet, domestic Tom Moore.

The real Custer was as far from being the reckless harum-scarum cavalier of public fancy as possible. He was a remarkably quiet, thoughtful man, when any work was on hand, one who never became flurried and excited in the hottest battle, and who, on a campaign, was a model of wary watchfulness, a man who was *never surprised during his whole career*, and who was equal to any emergency of whatever kind.

Three times during Custer's service as a brigade commander, did he find himself surrounded by enemies and compelled to cut his way through; and on none of those three occasions could the slightest blame attach to *him* for the dilemma. The first time was at Brandy Station; and there the fault was that of Meade or Pleasonton, who had divided their cavalry forces, so that when the separate units came together, the enemy was between them. The second time was at Buckland's Mills, where the disaster was due entirely to Kilpatrick's headlong rashness, after he had been warned of his danger by the wary Custer. The third time was at Trevillian Station, in 1864. There his danger was due to the accidental direction of a force of the enemy, driven in by Custer's friends from another direction. It was, in fact, Brandy Station reversed.

As a division commander, having no one else to trouble him, being responsible for his own actions, he was never in the slightest difficulty, and this is true of his whole after career. Put Custer in chief command, and he never made a mistake: put him under any one else, except Sheridan—as perfect a soldier as himself—and he was always suffering for the blunders, mistakes, or faint-heartedness of others, either his superiors or coadjutors.

The consequence was, to both Custer and Sheridan, the envy and detraction of all those who could not understand their peculiar quality of *instant and correct decision under fire,* as to the right thing to do. This faculty is given to very few indeed. In the Army of the Potomac, Custer and Sheridan were its only possessors, in the highest degree, the degree possessed by such men as Napoleon, Cromwell, Gustavus Adolphus,

Cæsar and Hannibal. It made them both supreme as "battle commanders," whatever their merits as strategists. Their detractors, who could not understand this faculty, tried to belittle it, by setting down Sheridan as a "mere trooper," Custer as a reckless rider and fighter, a harum-scarum light dragoon.

In Custer's case, the prejudices of those who did not know him, invariably preceded his entrance on any new command, as invariably to be replaced by a feeling akin to adoration, from all who served under him, if they possessed any nobility and generosity of character. To dislike him was the infallible result either of want of personal knowledge, which was innocent, or of some meanness of character, with which Custer's impulsive generosity clashed. Of his first appearance in the Third Cavalry Division, General (then colonel) A. B. Nettleton, commander of the " Fighting Second Ohio," thus speaks :

I had never seen General Custer, prior to his promotion to the command of our division, but he was well known to us by repute. Some of us were at first disposed to regard him as an adventurer, a disposition which a sight of his peculiar dress and long locks tended to confirm. One engagement with the enemy under Custer's leadership dissipated all these impressions, and gave our new commander his proper place. Once under fire, we found that a master hand was at the helm, that beneath the golden curls and broad-brimmed hat was a cool brain and a level head.

One thing that characterized Custer was this : having measured as accurately as possible the strength and *morale* of his enemy, and having made his own disposition of troops carefully and personally, he went into every fight with complete confidence in the ability of his division to do the work marked out for it. Custer's conduct in battle was characteristic. He never ordered his men to go where he would not lead, and he never led where he did not expect his men to follow. He probably shared with the private soldier the danger of the skirmish line oftener than any officer of his rank, not from wantonness of courage, but with a well-defined purpose on each occasion. He knew that the moral effect of his personal presence at a critical moment, was equal to a reinforcement of troops, when a reinforcement could not be found.

A large part of Custer's success was due to the fact that he was a good pursuer. Unlike many equally brave and skilful officers, he was rarely content to hold a position or drive his enemy : he always gathered the fruit, as well as shook the tree of battle. He regarded his real work as only beginning, when the enemy was broken and flying.

Although his special forte was the command of cavalry in the field, he was not deficient in camp. He was a good disciplinarian, without being a martinet; particularly thorough in maintaining an effective picket line or outpost service, on which depends the safety of an army in quarters. By unexpected visits to the outposts by day and night, he personally tested the faithfulness and alertness of officers and men on picket duty. On more than one occasion, I have known him take the trouble to write a letter of commendation to the commander of the regiment on the picket line, praising the manner in which the duty was performed. There was nothing of the military scold in his nature. By timely praise, oftener than by harsh criticism, he stimulated his subordinates to fidelity, watchfulness, and gallantry.

General Nettleton is quite competent to give an opinion of Custer, for he served under him with the most distinguished gallantry; and his regiment, the Second Ohio Cavalry, won this official praise from their division commander, in a letter to Governor Brough of Ohio : "I assure your excellency that in my entire division of twelve regiments, from various States, there is not one on which I rely more implicitly than on the gallant Second. I have known it repeatedly to hold its place against terrible odds, when almost any other regiment would have felt warranted in retiring."

Of Nettleton himself he says: "I regard him as one of the most valuable officers in the service, and do not know his superior in the army, as regards *the qualities needed in a good cavalry commander.*"

We quote these words to show that in Nettleton a perfectly competent critic is found, as well as one possessing personal knowledge of Custer. His testimony is merely the echo of that of every officer of capacity who ever served under that general.

Some may think that in all this too much is claimed for our hero; but this verdict can only be given by those who have not examined the evidence on which the estimate is founded. As an army commander like Sheridan, as a corps commander, there are no means of estimating his powers, for he never had an opportunity of exhibiting them. As a cavalry officer, pure and simple, the most carping criticism can find no flaw in Custer's career, from the day he led the Michigan Brigade into the battle of Gettysburg, to that in which he fell, fighting like a lion bayed by the hunters, deserted by his supporting detachments. He was, in fact, as nearly perfect as a cavalry commander can be.

Viewed from the standpoint of Seydlitz and the Great Frederick, and that at present prevailing in Europe, the actions of Custer are faultless, as far as he himself is concerned. The only wrong feature pervading them is one which was the fault of the system in which American cavalry has always been trained, and which even Custer could not remedy entirely, though he did his utmost towards checking it. This was, the undue dependence of the men and officers on their firearms, and their reluctance to use the sabre. This fault Custer constantly strove against, and during his valley campaigns succeeded in forcing his men by personal example into charging with the sabre, with invariable success whenever it was employed. We must, however, for the truth's sake, undeceive the civilian reader who imagines that the sabre was the exclusive weapon used in any of the so-called "sabre charges," either of Custer's or any other cavalry command, during the war. A rattling irregular fusillade of pistol and carbine shots almost invariably accompanied the charge, and, as a rule, the men were very poor swordsmen, solely from want of fencing practice.

Since the war, the case has been still worse, the use of the sabre having been practically abolished; and the diminished power of Custer, reduced as he was from a general to a field officer, added to the fact that he found the sense of his brother officers generally against him on this point, prevented his giving the queen of cavalry weapons that attention which it deserves.

But as a cavalry leader, Custer displayed more genius and natural talent than any officer in the American army; genius, moreover, of a kind that would have raised him to eminence in any service. Had Custer, with the same natural talent, served in the Franco-Prussian war as an officer of uhlans, there is little or no doubt that he would have risen to higher command than he attained in our own service. The well known personal supervision of Von Moltke, which has made the Prussian army what it is, by promotions for merit alone, would never have passed by Custer, with his wonderful faculty of seizing the moment and its fleeting opportunity.

The best cavalry leader America has ever produced, is the only truthful verdict that experience can pass on him : a great cavalry leader for any time or country, history will finally pronounce him ; worthy to stand beside Hannibal's "thunderbolt" Mago ; Saladin, the leader of those "hurricanes of horse" that swept the Crusaders from Palestine ; Cromwell, Seydlitz or Zieten ; a perfect general of horse.

CHAPTER II.

CUSTER, THE INDIAN-FIGHTER.

IF we devote a separate chapter to the consideration of Custer as an Indian campaigner, it is not because we deem that any different grade of talent is required for fighting Indians other than that which obtains in a contest with a civilized foe, but rather as a concession to the popular idea that such is the case. This idea is partly due to the natural propensity of " old Indian-fighters" to magnify their own office, but also to the equally common tendency of mankind in general to ignore talent and special genius as a possible factor of success in any pursuit, making experience and age the only tests of competency. A comparison of results obtained in both kinds of warfare, will give strong reason to believe that Indian-fighting, the same as Arab-fighting in Algeria, is by no means as difficult to master as the art of fighting a properly equipped, civilized foe. Many an officer who has attained considerable success as an Indian-fighter, has turned out but a poor general in campaign against a regular enemy, whereas generals of remarkable talent in civilized warfare—real generals, not mere " scientific soldiers," so miscalled—have never failed to give a good account of a barbarian foe, be it Indian, Arab, African, or Tartar.

The natural tendency above referred to, has however produced in the American army a very exaggerated estimate of the necessity of long experience in Indian fighting to produce a perfect officer, and a fashion of depreciating every officer, no matter what his talent elsewhere, if his Indian experience be *brief*. When Custer first went on the plains, he found this feeling in full force, and was constantly confronted with the express or implied statement that Indian-fighting was so totally different from other warfare that his previous experience was valueless, and that he would have to sit humbly and learn at the feet of this or that officer, because the latter was " an old Indian-fighter."

Very early in his Indian career, however, Custer seems to have discovered that few army officers were able to supply him with much valuable information on the Indian subject; and his keen perception showed him at the same time who *could* do it. He saw that the officers, especially the oldest of them, were too slow for him, just as they had been during the war, and he also saw that the rough and ready scouts, who lived in the same style as the Indians, would be his best masters. From them he seems from the first to have taken lessons, readily and humbly enough, as he tells us in his recorded experiences on the plains. His first master was Comstock, the scout who rode with him in his first campaign against Pawnee Killer; and Pawnee Killer himself, with Romeo and California Joe, gave him excellent lessons. When we consider that Custer made his first appearance on the plains the beginning of April, 1867, perfectly "green," as the old Indian-fighters thought, that the whole of his experience was limited to the months of April, May, June and a few days of July in that year, that from that time till September, 1868, he was under arrest and suspended from field service, it will appear that he must have used his time well to have called forth from his superior officers the request that met him in Monroe in 1868. His Indian-fighting experience was then limited to *less than four months ;* there was a whole army to choose from ; the officers of the Seventh Cavalry had all been out on the plains a whole year ; General Sully, an Indian-fighter then possessing a high reputation, was in com-mand ; yet, such was the confidence in Custer's ability, pro-duced by his record of three months and a half, that Sherman, Sheridan, *Sully, and all the officers of the regiment, old and new*, joined in a request to have Custer back for the command of the field expedition.

He came, and what was the result ? In six months he had pacified the whole of the southwestern tribes, first by a battle, then by diplomacy, exhibiting throughout the campaign a combination of boldness and dexterity, of tact and shrewdness, that was crowned with complete success, and that stamped him as the best Indian-fighter in the service. Measured by his *deeds* and comparing them with those of any Indian-fighter in the service, no matter what his reputation, this claim is by no means extravagant. The exploits of those officers who fought Indians before the civil war, were not attended with the same difficulties which surrounded Custer and the Indian-fighters of the present day. In those days the troops were better armed than the Indians; now the Indians are better armed than the troops ; then there was no Indian Department to feed the Indians and supply them with patent ammunition ; now this business has become recognized as the regular employ-ment of an Indian agent. In the old times the army was left alone to manage the Indians, to fight them if necessary, and Indian wars were easily settled on the plains; now the army officer has to fight the Indians first and the Indian Department afterwards. All these things made Custer's task a much harder one than those of the officers who engaged in an occasional Indian skirmish before the civil war. With the services of any recent Indian campaigner, no matter who or what he may be, Custer's record need fear no comparison. The *results* of his campaign of 1868-9, when he was in full and unrestricted command, were superior to those gained by any other officer in the service, since 1866, and nothing but prejudice can gainsay the undoubted facts.

What was it then, that gave Custer his remarkable success as an Indian-fighter, after such a brief experience, and what were the qualities which, so early in his career, gained him the implicit confidence—not of Sheridan, which was his already—

but of Sherman, who had only met him a few times, of Sully, who had not seen him at all in service? It was his remarkable tact, shrewdness, and quickness to learn, the ardor with which he applied himself to the study of the Indian character, and the safety which had accompanied his most apparently audacious operations against the enemy, in his three months' service. Besides this, when under arrest and suspension, Custer had not been idle. He had made up his mind to master the problem of Indian character, and he devoted his enforced leisure to the task. Where another man would have been brooding, Custer was working, and he devoted his winter of disgrace at Fort Leavenworth—to what, think you?—to learning the Indian sign language, which passed current among all the tribes, and serves as a medium of communication between Indians speaking every variety of language. This he studied to such good purpose, then and after, that he was able to converse, without an interpreter, with Indians of any tribe, as far as the sign language carries any of them.

That old Indian-fighters in those days appreciated his knowledge of Indian character is evinced by the words of General Sturgis, himself an old *ante-bellum* Indian-fighter of considerable reputation, which words we have quoted elsewhere.* Custer, quick to learn Indian tactics, was equally quick to learn the habits and natures, peaceful and warlike, of the Indians themselves. An amusing anecdote, whose authenticity is vouched for, will show the tact and shrewdness with which he played on every point in Indian character.

While in camp on the Black Hills expedition, in 1873, being then in the zenith of his reputation as an Indian-fighter, Custer retained a great many of his Indian scouts near headquarters, under command of Bloody Knife. One day, as Custer was writing in his tent, one of these Indian scouts came in, a good deal the worse for liquor, and began with some maundering complaint of something that had offended him. Custer

* Page 475.

looked up, saw the man was drunk, and ordered him out of the tent. Like all Indians in liquor, this one was insolent, and squaring himself before the general, became louder in his complaints and boasts of his own importance.

Without another word, Custer sprang up, with the peculiar catlike agility he possessed, and quick as lightning struck the Indian two blows, in regular professional style, sending him to grass, with an ugly lump under the eye, and a nose badly punished. The Indian was knocked half out of the tent door, and as Custer made a step towards him, as if to renew the assault, the red man picked himself up with surprising humility, and ran like a deer to the scouts' quarters, howling all the way.

Custer returned to his writing as if nothing had happened. Very few men possessed the physique to have punished a powerful Indian so quickly, but Custer's knuckles were very bony, and from a lad he had been the strongest of his playmates. So far he had done nothing but what any powerful man of quick decision would have done. It is the sequel of the story which shows his tact.

In a few minutes after, there was a great commotion in the Indian quarters, and the voices of the warriors could be heard, all together, in the high monotonous scream of the excited Indian, trying to lash himself and fellows to fury. It brought out the guard in some alarm, and the other soldiers began to tumble out of their tents to see the fun. Custer, of course, heard the disturbance and knew the cause, but he continued tranquilly writing, as if deafness had suddenly afflicted him. The noise increased, and he could hear the stern tones of the officer of the day in the wrangle, but even that dreaded official's authority did not appear to cow the Indians, for their fierce chattering grew shriller every moment. He heard in the hubbub the English words " Guard house! Guard house! Big chief— Guard house!" and a smile gathered over his face as he went on writing.

Presently a sudden hush came on the tumult. He heard

steps approaching, and a knock on the tent door, followed by the entrance of the officer of the day, who wore a countenance of some anxiety.

It appeared from the officer's report that the Indians were insisting that the same measure of justice should be meted to Custer as to other offenders. They had been accustomed to see every man found fighting in camp put in the guard house. The big chief had hurt their comrade badly, therefore the big chief ought to go to the guard house. While we cannot help smiling at the idea, it must be admitted that the rude sense of justice of the Indians was perfectly correct. The officer of the day further stated that he had pacified them by coming to see the big chief, but that they were very firm in their demands.

It may be imagined by some that there was no great difficulty in this case, but the contrary is the fact. If Custer had allowed the first Indian to be drunk and insolent, he would have lost control over his capricious allies, who would have despised him. If he now refused them *justice* they all would leave him, probably to join the hostiles. Custer's decision was instantly taken, though not in words.

As soon as the officer had concluded his report, the General walked out of the tent, and found his Indian allies in a group, quite silent now, watching the tent.

" Tell the chief to come here," said Custer to the officer of the day. In a few moments Bloody Knife approached, in a very lordly manner. As he left his comrades, he waved them back, with the grand air of a " big Injun" full of his own importance.

Custer approached the chief several steps to meet him, took off his hat, and swept a low and ceremonious salute. Then shaking Bloody Knife's hand cordially, he and the Indian mutually ejaculated " How ! how !"

Still retaining the chief's hand, he led him into his own tent, and seated him in his own chair, an honor that gratified Bloody Knife still more.

Then the general took up an Indian pipe, filled it, lighted it, took a few whiffs, and handed it to the chief, the two sitting opposite to each other in solemn silence all the while. By this time the Indian was swelling with importance, and evidently imagined that the white chief was about to apologize and offer presents to pay for the wrong he had done. He behaved however, with the strictest decorum, as an Indian generally does at a council.

After several mutual whiffs, Custer gravely asked what had procured him the honor of this visit.

Thus exhorted, Bloody Knife, in broken English, uttered his complaint with ceremonious gravity.

"Big chief hurt Injun heap bad—near kill um—cut face open—Injun much heap mad—say big chief must go guard-house."

And the chief grunted and relapsed into silence, smoking vigorously.

"Is your man badly hurt?" asked Custer, after the usual pause of ceremony.

"Much heap bad—face all blood—may be die—Injuns put um in bed—tink he die—say big chief must go guard-house."

And he grunted a second time, feeling that he had made a point, then ceremoniously handed the pipe to Custer. The fact probably was, he was waiting to be bribed.

After a minute's pause, Custer spoke very gravely.

"Listen. I am the big chief here. All these soldiers are under me, and all their chiefs too. You see that?"

The chief bowed gravely, and grunted.

"You are the chief of the scouts. All the Indians are under you, because you are a great warrior. You see?"

A more decided grunt of approbation and gratified vanity.

"Whenever any of my soldiers has a complaint, he goes to his chief, and his chief comes to me. You see?"

A sort of doubtful grunt. The Indian began to see that something else was coming.

"No one ever enters this tent but chiefs and great warriors. *Them* I am always glad to see. *You* I am glad to see. *You* are a chief, and a great warrior. You see ?"

The grunt this time was one of unmixed satisfaction.

"When a man comes into my tent without first going to his chief," pursued Custer slowly, watching his auditor closely, " he dishonors his chief—you see ?—makes a squaw of his chief —you see ?—throws dirt in his chief's face—you see ?—says ' You are no chief—you are a squaw—a dog.'—Do you see ? "

In his turn, Custer resumed the puffing of his pipe, which he had interrupted to speak.

For fully a minute there was a dead silence.

Then the chief rose, and Custer laid aside the pipe and followed suit. Not being a smoker, he was only too glad to do it.

The chief shook his hand ceremoniously.

" *How !* How !" said he. Then suddenly dropping his dignity, he shot out of the tent toward the Indian quarters, and a moment later, Custer heard his voice raised in a perfect frenzy of rage, yelling out an impassioned appeal to his followers to avenge him on the man who had made a squaw of so great a chief as Bloody Knife, the Arickaree.

A few moments later, all the Indians rushed to the quarters, where the poor sufferer was in bed, nursed by his friends, pulled him out, and commenced lashing him with their heavy buffalo whips, the chief being the heaviest in his blows. The innate sense of the necessity of subordination in military society was aroused. Even the wild savage could see the force of Custer's lucid argument, though delivered in a strange language, and with some words only half understood.*

Custer had no more trouble with his Indian scouts, and he showed the same knowledge of Indian character throughout his career. The story of Rain-in-the-Face partly illustrates it,

* A partial version of this anecdote first appeared in the Chicago *Inter Ocean,* and subsequent investigation by the author has resulted in the above facts. Poor Bloody Knife fell with Custer at the Little Horn.

but there are enough anecdotes of the kind to fill a book much larger than this, which cannot now be told. In the southwest and northwest alike, when the outside world deemed that Custer was merely stagnating in ordinary army style, he was carrying on his study of Indian character, and acquiring ascendency and reputation among the tribes. In his visits to New York, he took occasion to learn a good many feats of conjuring, sleight-of-hand, etc., which he used in various adroit ways to increase this ascendency ; so that, at the time of his death, he had the reputation among the Indians of being a great magician or " medicine man," which increased the awe with which they regarded him. That, and his super-human courage, which Indians of all men are the first to respect, procured him the last honor which they could pay to his mortal remains. They dared to kill him from afar with bullets—that was merely the crooking of a finger—but something in that dead body struck even Rain-in-the-Face with a sense of awe, and the bravest Sioux of the northwest did not dare to lift his hand to strike dead Custer.

Will any be found to take his place and do as well as he has done? It is hard to say. So far, the American army has produced but one Custer, and it is doubtful whether the peculiar combination of qualities which made him what he was, will ever be duplicated. If one be found to lead men to success as he has done, he must be looked for among the younger officers of the army, the men whose careers are yet to culminate, who show symptoms of life amid the too general stagnation of frontier service. Two at least of this class, the hope of the army of the future, have developed talents of the same nature as those of Custer, and which may in time equal them in degree. To them the country looks to give it a successor to Custer the Indian-fighter, in quickness of resolution, impetuosity of attack, sagacity of plan. One of them, since the greater part of these pages were written, has gained the only success of a disastrous campaign, by meeting Sitting Bull on open ground and aided by artillery, repulsing his attack with severe loss; the other, by his now nearly forgotten raid over the Mexican border, showed the possession of just such boldness and enterprise as were conspicuous in Custer; and to Miles and Mackenzie the army looks to give them another successful Indian-fighter, a man not afraid of the Indians, but fighting as if he expected a *victory*.

But, as we have before this insisted on, the greatest reform necessary in the present regular cavalry, to make it uniformly effective against Indians, is in the instruction of the rank and file, and especially in the cultivation of that neglected weapon, the sabre, to raise the morale of the force. As it is, it takes more than ordinary bravery and conduct in any officer to achieve success with the half-trained recruits that form the main body of the frontier army; and the disuse of the sabre has turned the once brave American dragoon into a timid skirmisher, who shrinks from the shock of the levelled lance, and seeks safety in infantry tactics.

CHAPTER III.

CUSTER, THE MAN.

IF the readers of this book have not by this time formed some idea of the character of Custer as a man, the labors of the author have been spent in vain, and it would be useless to write further. Still, inasmuch as the beautiful family and social life of our hero has not been fully treated of elsewhere, we have judged it best to say here a few words on the subject, to complete the picture.

Of General Custer's personal appearance at various times of his life the portraits and illustrations of this book will give a good idea. They were, most of them, made by an artist who knew Custer well when he was a young officer, and whose war experience has enabled him to give truthful pictures. The face and figure of our hero varied much at different times of his life, his face as a cadet being smooth and beardless, and by no means as handsome as it afterwards became. In the portrait on wood, with the broad hat and open collar, we have Custer at Appomattox, haggard and gaunt after his tremendous labors: in the steel portrait which heads the book, we have him in later life, with the strong impress of mature thought, and an earnestness of expression that tells of his single-minded nobility of purpose. It gives very truly his habitual expression during the long periods of deep musing into which he was wont to fall, when he would sit for hours totally silent.

In society, apart from these occasional moody intervals, he was exceedingly light-hearted, with a boyish tendency to frolic and playfulness that seemed common to all the Custer boys. In

Fort Lincoln, where he was thrown almost alone during the winter into a very small circle of intimate friends, he and his brothers, Tom and Boston, were the life of the place, while the refining influence of the society of the few ladies that clustered round Mrs. Custer made the circle extremely delightful. No man valued more highly than Custer the influence of women to ameliorate men, and no man had more reason. The little group of ladies, Mrs. Custer, Mrs. Calhoun, Mrs. Yates, Mrs. Smith, and the one or two young ladies from Monroe who were always visiting Mrs. Custer, made the home circle at the fort a perfect haven of rest to the officers fortunate enough to possess Custer's friendship.

The general was always very fond of children. One of his Eastern friends, whom he frequently visited, tells how he would often leave a circle of fashionable people, with whom he was very shy and reserved, to sit in a corner with two children, who begged him for Indian stories. Although very reticent to others about his deeds, he always unbent to these children, and so won their hearts that to-day they always protest that General Custer was the kindest and nicest gentleman that ever visited their father's house. I set a high value on this fact. Children, especially girls, are unerring readers of character, and there must have been something singularly pure and frank in Custer's character to have attracted the love of these children.

Another point in Custer was his perfect nobility of forgiveness. We have seen how his court-martial in 1867 was caused by an officer, brave and capable enough, but who hated him. Only a year later, this same officer, then out of the service, applied to Custer for a position as trader or sutler in an expedition commanded by him, expressing his sorrow for the past. *Custer at once gave him the place,* which was in his gift. Yet his critics have called him " a good friend and a bitter enemy." Never was a falser saying. The man seemed incapable of private malice. Even under the unjust persecution of Grant he was cheerful, and always said to those who spoke bitterly of the

President, " Never mind: it will all come right at last. The President is mistaken ; but it will all come right at last, if I do my duty." *He was never known to return an injury.*

In his devotion to duty and honesty, to fair dealing and justice, he was almost fanatical. There indeed he was stern, and his indignation at the robbery and rapacity of the Indian ring and the post traders' ring was frequent and outspoken. It caused all his subsequent trouble. He saw the poor agency Indians robbed while the agents grew rich, and his anger, which could not find vent through official channels, was heard in the press, and given to the world in his " Life on the Plains." Can we blame him for that ?

Custer knew, as every officer in the army knows, that the Indian Department is a perfect mine of wealth to the men of politics, and that, were it not for the supplies of arms furnished to the Indians by that department, there would be no Indian wars. He and his men were finally shot to death with bullets loaded into Winchester metallic ammunition at New Haven and Bridgeport, Connecticut, and furnished to the Indians by the Indian Bureau. He knew that in every fight he had with Indians, they confronted him with weapons sold them by traders under the protection of the agencies. He knew that every attempt by honest men in Congress to abolish this grand corruption mine had been defeated by the vote of a purchased majority. He knew that the reason for this vote was the enormous amount of power given by the use of such a huge corruption fund for political purposes. He knew that the very arms sold to hostile Indians were made a means of cheating them, so that a single Winchester rifle, worth thirty dollars, sold for two hundred buffalo robes at Fort Peck. He saw all these soulless cheats around him bartering away the lives of the frontier settlers by the hundred for their gain, and he groaned in spirit, and spoke out again and again, in fiery anger against such monstrous wrongs. Can we blame him ?

His one fault, to the sense of cool selfish men of the world, was his outspoken frankness, his anger at wrong, his want of concealment. Make the most of that, and it is a noble fault. It brought him his death.

Truth and sincerity, honor and bravery, tenderness and sympathy, unassuming piety and temperance, were the mainspring of Custer, the man. As a soldier there is no spot on his armor, as a man no taint on his honor.

We have followed him through all his life, and passed in review boy, cadet, lieutenant, captain, general, and Indianfighter, without finding one deed to bring shame on soldier or man. People of the land he loved, my task is ended. Would it had been committed to worthier hands. Four simple lines, written by an unknown poet, form his best epitaph.

> Who early thus upon the field of glory
> Like thee doth fall and die, needs for his fame
> Naught but the simple telling of his story,
> The naming of his name.

TENTH BOOK.

PERSONAL RECOLLECTIONS

OF

GENERAL CUSTER.

BY

LAWRENCE BARRETT,

THE GREAT TRAGEDIAN.

CONTRIBUTED AT THE JOINT REQUEST OF MRS. CUSTER,
THE AUTHOR, AND THE PUBLISHERS.

GEORGE ARMSTRONG CUSTER was of that great industrial class from which so many of our original men are springing. With no marked advantages of education, no influence to push forward his fortunes, or wealth to command situation, he yet passed through such a career, was so rapid in growth and development, that he was ripe in honors when the bullet of the Indian warrior pierced his heart. Advancement so swift, a career so brilliant that his deeds have become household words in the land, indicate the possession of more than ordinary qualities in the subject of this memoir. Leaving, at barely his majority, the military academy where his original address and marked demeanor had placed him, without the usual influence which people's our national training schools, he was thrust at once into a command at the outbreak of the war. Having barely reached a man's estate, unused to the world, unacquainted with men, untrained in active warfare, he was suddenly to be called upon for the exhibition of the qualities which lead and govern armies. The sword of the cadet was to be unsheathed by youthful hands amidst the din of a civil strife, unexampled in history for the fierceness of its character and for the importance of its results. Out of this trial our hero was to emerge covered with the glory of a veteran, decorated, after five years of service, at the age of twenty-six, with the stars of a Major-General, and renowned from one end of the country to the other —throughout the world indeed—as an original and brilliant fighter, a bold and dashing soldier, a successful commander. The greater part of his career, so sadly terminated, was passed where the fight raged hottest, where death and carnage reigned supreme ; and finally, at the age of thirty-seven, an age when the careers of most men are beginning, he was snatched away, covered with glory, the mourned darling of a nation. We must look into the records of heroic ages for a parallel to this career, through which our biographer has so lovingly followed him. The incidents of that extraordinary military history can be followed and proven in the annals of the war. Dates and official records will amply note and verify the conspicuous part borne by General Custer. His place among the heroes of our country will be gratefully allowed so long as patriotism endures ; his chivalrous deeds will be immortalized by bard, and perpetuated by historian. The chapter of great warriors will hereafter be incomplete, which does not record the exploits of Custer and his gallant riders, from Bull Run to the Appomattox.

It is the misfortune of men in high public station that the brilliancy of their professional careers obscures the private character of the individual. They are seen through a misty veil and by their position shut out from the close observation of their fellows. It was my happiness to have known intimately, and to have enjoyed for many years the society of General Custer, and it may, therefore, be allowed me to record my impression of him as divested of the pomp of war, and mingling in the pursuits of social life. Abler hands may collect and en-gross the various incidents of this heroic life, compiling a suitable biography for his countrymen's instruction, and these reminiscences should be accepted simply as a tribute of affection to a dearly beloved friend. No one had followed General Custer's military career with more enthusiasm than the writer. The successive battles in which he bore so conspicuous and gallant a part were studied with ardor by his then unknown friend, who was thus prepared, should the moment ever arrive, to meet with interest and embrace with affection the hero whose deeds had already won ardent admiration. The stirring incidents of the war had developed two men whose exploits had made them objects of the writer's sincere attachment. Both young, their rapidity of promotion alike extraordinary and acquired by absolute merit, it was my happiness to claim their friendship and at last bring them together. In the war they had fought side by side, each unacquainted with the other, except in their achievements. At my fireside they came together in friendly meeting and cemented in private the attachment which sympathy of character always creates. One now lies ill among the Berkshire hills, his youthful form scarred with wounds received in his country's service; the other, dead at thirty-seven, sleeps where no stone may mark his resting-place, beneath the blood-stained sod of the cold and cheerless plains.

In the fall of 1866, while fulfilling an engagement at St. Louis, I met the General for the first time, and under such peculiar circumstances that they may bear narration. The play was over, the curtain fallen, and while still preparing to return to my hotel after my night's entertainment, a knock was heard at my dressing-room door. Obedient to the answering summons, entered a tall, fair haired, blue eyed, smiling gentleman, clad in military undress. Apologizing for the intrusion, he gave his name as General Custer. No such introduction was necessary. By those well known features I recognized at once the young cavalry leader. He had been sent to bring me to the hotel where he was temporarily resid-

ing, while en route to his command at Fort Leavenworth. I
was to go with him to meet Mrs. Custer and other members of
his party. Excuses were set aside. He pleaded "orders"
which must be obeyed, and refusal was impossible. A happy
hour in his society was passed ; and thus began an acquaintance,
ripening within the next ten years into the most genuine friendship, in which I learned to esteem the qualities of the man as
sincerely as I had admired the achievements of the soldier.

At that early time General Custer had not outgrown the
habits of the camp. He still wore the long hair which is so
familiar in his early pictures, his face was bronzed and sun-
burned by out-door exposure, his bearing a mixture of the
student and the soldier. No pen portrait of General Custer
would be complete which did not give the simple, boyish side
of his character, seemingly more marked from the daring, ad-
venturous spirit which the war had made us familiar with.
His voice was earnest, soft, tender and appealing, with a quickness of the utterance which became at times choked by the
rapid flow of ideas, and a nervous hesitancy of speech, betray-
ing intensity of thought. There was a searching expression of
the eye, which riveted the speaker, as if each word was being
measured mercilessly by the listener. Peculiarly nervous, he yet
seemed able to control himself at will. His fund of humor was
betrayed by a chuckle of a laugh, such as those who have ever
known Artemus Ward will remember—a laugh which became
infectious and seemed to gurgle up from the depths of the full
and joyous heart of the sunny, affectionate Custer.

In the years which passed on, following our first meeting,
duty separated, vacations reunited us. Custer's appointment
to duty in Kentucky afforded me several weeks of his society,
during which we were rarely apart. At that time he ran over
his remembrances of the war to me, speaking of himself with
modesty, of others with enthusiasm, until it became a delight
to listen. Thus I had the description of the winter campaign
against the Indians on the Washita before it was in print, told

in his graphic, fervent style, and acted over until it seemed as if I were a participant in the strife. At this time he began those sketches in the *Galaxy* which were at once received with favor. Again separated, we were next to meet during the tour of the Grand Duke Alexis, in whose suite he had been placed by the government. Here his truly American characteristics gained him a friend, whose quick eye discerned the depths of that genuine nature and valued it. The friendship which arose between the Russian Grand Duke and General Custer, from their association on this tour, was very honorable to both. The polished courtier discerned in the young Democrat those sterling qualities of manhood which maintained their individuality in the midst of ceremonies and flatteries, and the correspondence which passed between them upon the return of the Grand Duke to Russia was highly gratifying to Custer. Enjoying his vacation as keenly as a school-boy, General Custer was always apparently "awaiting orders," and when they came, his whole manner changed: he seemed to put on the soldier with the uniform. He often said that his duties on the plains were the happiest events of his life—not that he loved war for war's sake, but that he loved to feel that he was on "duty." The freedom of the plains, the constant companionship of his idolized wife—now sitting in the shadow of her last and greatest bereavement—his horses and his gun his regiment and its beloved officers, amply replaced the allurements of civil life.

It was impossible for Custer to appear otherwise than himself. He had none of that affectation of manner or bearing which arises from egotism or timidity. Reticent among strangers, even to a fault, his enemies, if he had any, must have recognized his perfect integrity of character. Indeed, this reticence often caused him to be misunderstood, and he himself frequently complained that he could not be "all things to all men." It was only in the companionship of his intimates and close friends that the real joyousness of his nature shone forth. Then he was all confidence, his eye would brighten, his face light up and

his whole heart seemed to expand. He had something of the
Frenchman in his gayety, much of the German in a certain tenacity of purpose. Utterly fearless of danger, he seemed in private to become as gentle as a woman.

[Some have thought that Custer's courage was of the bull-
dog kind; that he knew no danger and feared none. Nothing
can be further from the truth. He said to the writer that,
the first few battles he was in, he was almost overcome with
fear: he also intimates this very clearly in his "War Memoirs."
His courage was purely a triumph of mind over physical
fear. Toward the close of the war he became convinced that
he would not be killed. The truth doubtless is that he was
fully conscious that he possessed the ability to rise in his profession, and he had determined to do so at all hazards. He
chose the post of danger at the head of his column, simply because he was aware that it was the place to obtain success.
He knew that thus, and thus only, he could inspire his men with
confidence, and make of each a hero. All this was the result of
a deliberate plan. He had counted the cost of success and was
fully prepared to pay it. He wanted honor and distinction
among his fellow men, or death on the field. He put this spirit
into his division by his example, and they were invincible.]*

In the society of ladies, with whom his deeds had made him
a favorite, he manifested none of the gallantries which arise
from vanity.

When ordered to Fort Lincoln, General Custer was lost to
me for several months, but our correspondence was constant.
He was eager that I should visit him, and it was only by a pres-
sure of professional duties at the time, that I was denied the
pleasure of being his companion upon the first expedition to
the Black Hills. The succeeding fall he made his vacation with
me, and for two happy weeks we were constantly together.
This was in Chicago. If an engagement to dinner took him
away, he would hasten at its conclusion to my dressing-room at

* Remarks by another intimate friend of General Custer.

the theatre; and thence, arm-in-arm, we would return home together. Thus I have seen him in the midst of social temptations, sufficient to overcome ordinary men, maintain the strict sobriety of his habits. He never touched wine, nor used tobacco in any form, and I never heard a profane word from his lips. His obstinate valor as a soldier made him courteous and forgiving to a defeated enemy and he became a Democrat in his opinions, regarding the manner in which the south should be treated after the close of the rebellion. This made him unpopular at headquarters, and perhaps influenced his promotion and hindered his career. He loved his profession and was jealous of its fame, tenacious of the honor of his cloth, and intolerant of the abuses which the army suffered by that pernicious system wherein politics were the means by which many unworthy men entered the service. He had that love of military display which distinguishes the Frenchman, and his uniform was the badge of his glory. A fondness for theatrical representations he shared in common with the members of his profession, and a more enthusiastic auditor I never saw.

The last winter of Custer's life now approaches. He had obtained leave of absence for two months, intending to spend his time in New York; and, that he might leave behind him a record of his career, and also that he might eke out his slender income, his sketches in the *Galaxy* were resumed. It was during this vacation, extended to five months in all, that the happiest hours of my association with him were passed. Being myself for the winter in New York, we made all our engagements mutual, going into company together, meeting at my own fireside always on Sundays; and each evening during the run of " Julius Cæsar" the place of honor in my dressing-room at Booth's was filled by my dear friend. Those were indeed happy hours. I recall especially one passed at the Century Club, where he was the recipient of great attentions. How bright and joyous he was, and how eager that his friend should know and enjoy the friendship of those whom he himself esteemed. Surrounded by the followers of literature, science, and art, and their cultured patrons, the young soldier, whose whole life and education were of the camp, attracted the attention and won the respect of all who met him. With that rare facility given but to few, he drew from the artist and the historian the best fruits of their labors, and as warmly listened as he could warmly speak. His love for art was no affected dilettanteism. Appreciating the glories of nature with an enthusiast's soul, he learned to trace her likeness in the works of her copyists. The studio of Bierstadt was a happy resting-place for him. Here, while the great painter labored, the young soldier would lovingly follow the master hand, identifying the exactness of the picture by his own knowledge of the scenery or groupings so vividly reproduced. It has been said that " military experience so exhausts the body, by daily, and for the most part useless exercises, that it renders it difficult to cultivate one's mind," but this was not true of General Custer. Not having received in his youth the advantages of a college education, he betrayed the keenest desire for knowledge and cultivation.

[General Custer was a great reader, and his taste ran almost entirely in the line of the best literature. His pleasure seemed to be, to constantly add to his stock of information. He spent a large share of his time during the winter seasons in reading such works as "Napier's Peninsular War," "Napoleon's Campaigns," and works of this class which would perfect him in his profession. Often he would spend a whole day and a large part of the night over a few pages of these works: having a large map before him, he was determined to fully understand each movement and campaign made by these great masters of the art of war. Perfection in his chosen profession seemed to be the main-spring of all his actions. He was ready to make any and all sacrifices which would contribute to this end. He seemed thoroughly to have adopted the motto that "nothing is done while anything remains to be accomplished." His powers of mental work were fully equal to his physical endurance ; six hours of sleep seemed to be all he required, and his great mental activity rendered it almost impossible for him to be idle an hour.]

A distinguished gentleman whose Friday evenings at his home on Fifth Avenue were regarded as happy privileges for the best minds of the metropolis, extended to the General hospitality and advantages which were eagerly accepted and as earnestly enjoyed. Here, where the flame of thought was of the loftiest character, Custer would sit, an attentive and admiring listener, drinking from the rich fountain of instruction. After an evening thus passed, and upon emerging into the silent avenue, the impressions of the recent conversation still upon us, excited by the interchange of friendly converse, he would take my arm, and against my entreaty become my escort home, alleging as a reason his want of exercise, although I knew that in his loving care he feared some danger might befall his friend, and thus went far out of his way to see me safely housed. Such acts as these, trivial though they seem in narration, are those which make that fearful day in June so terrible to me, making it seem impossible that I am never again to clasp that hand so true and tried, never again to look into that face so dearly loved.

The winter passed only too quickly. His original leave of two months had been granted by his immediate superior, General Terry, his friend as well as commander, and his extended leave came from General Sheridan, no less friendly. But another extension, earned by him surely through his months of labor at Fort Lincoln, was refused as soon as asked, and he was at once ordered to rejoin his regiment by General Belknap, then Secretary of War. For some unexplained reason, General Custer believed the secretary to be his enemy, and dreaded the final appeal for that extension of leave which his affairs so much demanded. When refusal came, although it disappointed him, it did not the less find him prepared for obedience to orders. His literary work for the *Galaxy* had been undertaken, as has been stated, to eke out his income and more generously support the expenses of his family, and he had formed another plan by which he hoped to still more liberally provide for the future of all those dependent upon him. The agent of the Literary Bureau, Mr. Redpath, of Boston, having made him a liberal offer to deliver a number of lectures during the next winter, he was, at the moment the Secretary's orders came, perfecting his plans to that end. After the summer's campaign he was again to visit New York, his lecture in the meantime to be written, and we were to " rehearse " his appearance before the public passed judgment upon him. This project was left incomplete as to details, but he looked forward to its accomplishment as a happy means of increasing his income and meeting face to face his admirers, the public.

Custer went one March day upon his journey. No forebodings of evil embittered the parting : we were to meet again. He had not yet fallen under the public accusation which was afterwards hurled upon him. Although he left so many pleasant associations and gave up so many personal enjoyments, he was going to his duty, and that sufficed. A winter trip across the Dakota plains had no terrors for him, nor for her who never left his side while it was her privilege to remain there. After many hardships they at last reached Fort Lincoln, and then began his preparations for the fatal expedition. Loving friends, unacquainted with the details of warfare, and jealous only of his reputation, will always, perhaps unjustly, believe that had all gone forward as it began, under his own personal control, the disaster and annihilation which followed would never have occurred. No reflection upon the capacity of General Custer's superiors is here intended, but it may be justly claimed that the complications which followed as the result of the appearance before the investigating committee at Washington, arose, in a great measure, from the disorders of a change of command almost in the enemy's front; that suspicion on the one side, and crippled powers, laboring under ungenerous and undeserved imputations, upon the other, created a confusion which could not but be detrimental. The belief will always prevail among the friends of General Custer that familiarity with the Indian mode of warfare, a certain subtlety in his preparations for attack or resistance, and the "dash" which has never been denied him, well fitted him to organize and conduct such a campaign. He who had so often challenged the bravest of the red warriors and wrung from them the title of the "Big Yellow Chief," was fully able not only to lead his own "gallant Seventh," but also to organize the campaign and overlook the plan. This was denied him. At the supreme moment of his fortunes he was summoned to Washington.

The appearance of General Custer before the Investigating Committee at Washington and the effect of his testimony upon the public mind are already familiar to the reader. The fact came upon his most intimate friends unannounced, and the unfavorable comments of the party press upon his evidence and his character caused the greatest surprise to those who knew him best. The most reserved and reticent of men had suddenly become politically conspicuous, and calumny was busy with that hitherto spotless name. The political temper of the time had undoubtedly, much to do with the effect produced by his testimony. The strife of party, and the bitterness with which men of opposite opinions assailed each other; the influence upon the approaching election of the investigation then going forward; the reputation for truth and candor never denied to General Custer; combined to make the attacks upon him unusually severe. He had never obtruded his political sentiments, but they were known to his friends and were never disowned. He could not have sought the unenviable position in which he found himself; he had endeavored by every honorable means to escape from it, but in vain. The effect upon his nature of the abuse suddenly heaped upon him, may be measured by the desire he had always evinced to escape public observation, except in the line of his duty; and this was, undoubtedly, one of the saddest eras of his life. The esteem of his countrymen, earned by years of hard service and dearly prized, seemed in an instant to be taken from him. His report upon the evils of the post-trading system had been forwarded to the head of his department long before; his acquaintance with those evils was known to many; not to have answered frankly the questions of the committee would have exposed him to self-contempt. How easily could he have trimmed his sail to the popular breeze, and floated into the smooth waters of political favor. The promotion which his valor had earned; which was due to his merit; which had been bestowed upon his inferiors; lay within his grasp; but the sacrifice was one from which his proud soul revolted. The perfect integrity of his character should never be sullied, to purchase that preferment which had been denied to his public services, and which was in every way due him. He could honestly exclaim, "It is better to be right than to hold the most exalted rank." That he was wounded none who knew him can doubt. In the midst of those exposures which tarnished the reputation of so many brother officers, he had happily escaped. At his post upon the distant frontier, occupied with the duties which he loved, surrounded by a small band who regarded their young commander with veneration, he might well feel happy in his escape from that political whirlpool which engulphed so many of his friends, and which swallowed up reputations gained in hard-fought fields. Now, against his will, called peremptorily from the organization of his command, he found himself helplessly drawn into the current, publicly condemned for speaking that which he knew to be true, commented upon by enemies in the coarsest terms, the target of political rancor. The depth of his humiliation was reached, when, upon leaving the capital, he waited for hours at the door of the President, and was, at last turned away with studied contempt. The effect of these slights upon his proud and sensitive heart may be imagined. Upheld as he was by the conscience which whispered that he had done his duty, he must still have suffered much in concealing his sorrow from the world; though he scorned to complain, as he would have scorned to bend before the calumny of his enemies. Our last meeting, which took place at the close of his first visit to Washington, was yet full of happiness. Rallied upon his political relations, he sunnily threw aside his chagrin, and seemed indifferent to all but the approaching separation, anxious only that our plan for the next winter should not fail. No premonition of danger clouded our parting. The thought that he was going into action, into certain peril, did not make me fearful. He was so associated with success, had escaped from so many dangers, his long future career was so hopeful, that he seemed invincible. He predicted a severe campaign, but was not doubtful of the result. His plans were well laid, his command efficient; and he joyfully obeyed the summons to return to his duty, happy to escape from the scene where truth was repaid with calumny.

The delay in Chicago; the deprivation of command which overtook him there by order of the President; all these anxious days passed while awaiting the orders of his superiors, were undeserved cruelties. The influences which at length ended his suspense, and gave him a subordinate place in the expedition planned by himself, have been explained elsewhere. The disgrace of being supplanted by an inferior in rank or an envious rival was averted, and thus much of the bitterness of his position softened. If he could have chosen his successor, he could not have been better pleased than with the appointment of General Terry. Under him he declared he would go with the command, if obliged to serve as a common soldier. By the tender consideration and courtesy of that gallant officer Custer was permitted to recover that confidence in himself of which his unmerited trials must have well nigh robbed him. With the delicacy of a gentleman, the appreciation of a kindred soul, Terry restored him to the command which was his due, in fact, if not in appearance, and brought to his aid the advice and experience of the young cavalier whose counsel would be

41

invaluable, whose valor and foresight would be a support, and to whose sword the service would so soon be indebted for its defence. Those who knew General Custer best, can well understand how he valued such a privilege. To have been left behind would have been worse than death, when his gallant Seventh and so many of his old comrades were in the field. As he rode out of Fort Lincoln for the last time, he was as full of glee as a child; his duty lay before him, his glory, of which no enemy could rob him. That the wishes of the nation, which followed that gallant band and looked hopefully forward to its movements as a final solution of the Indian question, dwelt with the greatest confidence upon the frontier experience of General Custer, will scarcely be denied. In every campaign he had been victorious, and the wiles and stratagems of the foe were familiar to him. Calumny and envy must be silent before the intrepid heroism of that immortal band as they rode into the "jaws of death," where perished not only the noble Custer and his adoring followers, but also the hope of a nation, the shield of a devoted family.

Glancing back over these pages, how poor and unworthy seems the picture I would paint. Compared with the image engraved upon the heart, this transcript is cold and artificial. When the smoke of the battle has passed away, when envy and cowardice have been consigned to their merited oblivion, some truer likeness shall be made of him who was the bravest of the brave. His career may be thus briefly given : He was born in obscurity; he rose to eminence : denied social advantages in his youth, his untiring industry supplied them; the obstacles to his advancement became the stepping-stones to his fortunes ; free to choose for good or evil, he chose rightly ; truth was his striking characteristic ; he was fitted to command, for he had learned to obey; his acts found their severest critic in his own breast ; he was a good son, a good brother, a good and affectionate husband, a Christian soldier, a steadfast friend. Entering the army, a cadet in early youth, he became a general while still on the threshold of manhood ; with ability undenied, with valor proved on many a hard fought field, he acquired the affection of the nation ; and he died in action at the age of thirty-seven ; died as he would have wished to die ; no lingering disease preying upon that iron frame.   At the head of his command, the messenger of death awaited him ; from the field of battle where he had so often " directed the storm," his gallant spirit took its flight.   Cut off from aid ; abandoned in the midst of incredible odds ; waving aloft the sabre which had won him victory so often ; the pride and glory of his comrades, the noble Custer fell : bequeathing to the nation his sword ; to his comrades an example ; to his friends a memory ; and to his beloved one a Hero's name.

INDEX.